Group Psychotherapy and Addiction

انوستاه ولله.

Group Psychotherapy and Addiction

Edited by

BILL READING RMN, MA, DIPSOCSCI, DIPDYPPSYCH
East Kent Community Alcohol Service

and

MARTIN WEEGMANN BA(HONS), DIPCLINPSYCH, MINSTGA
Ealing Substance Misuse Service

W
WHURR PUBLISHERS
LONDON AND PHILADELPHIA

© 2004 Whurr Publishers Ltd
First published 2004
by Whurr Publishers Ltd
19b Compton Terrace
London N1 2UN England and
325 Chestnut Street, Philadelphia PA 19106 USA

British Library Cataloguing in Publication Data

A catalogue record for this book
is available from the British Library.

ISBN 1 86156 448 1

Typeset by Adrian McLaughlin, a@microguides.net
Printed and bound in the UK by Athenæum Press Ltd, Gateshead, Tyne & Wear.

Contents

Contributors   x
Preface   xii
Acknowledgements   xv

Chapter 1   Addiction as an attachment disorder:
                 implications for group psychotherapy   **1**

                 Philip J. Flores

                 Attachment and group therapy   1
                 Group treatment of substance abuse   2
                 Attachment-oriented therapy   4
                 Addiction and the working alliance   9
                 Conclusions   18

Chapter 2   Group psychotherapy as a corrective for
                 addictive vulnerability   **19**

                 E.J. Khantzian

                 An evolving perspective (1970–1980)   19
                 Group therapy as a corrective (1980–2000)   21
                 How do groups work?   23
                 Conclusion   26

Chapter 3   Alcoholics Anonymous:
                 group therapy without the group therapist   **27**

                 Martin Weegmann

                 AA: the historical matrix   28
                 Leaderless groups: the fellowship concept   33

AA: corrective group dialogue?   35
Group climates   37
Resistance and reluctance to AA   39
Conclusions   41

Chapter 4   Matching group therapy to patients' needs   **42**

Christer Sandahl, Monica Busch, Eva Skarbrandt, and Peter Wennberg

Group therapy in stepped care   43
Decision to change (step 2)   46
Treatment conditions in relapse prevention (step 3)   48
Group psychotherapy for demanding patients
   (step 4)   50
Conclusions   58

Chapter 5   Motivational enhancement in group therapy   **59**

Paul Jackson

Motivational interviewing: a relational perspective   61
Motivational interviewing and enhanced role
   security   65
Group therapy: removing obstacles to engagement   66
Group therapy and enhancing motivation   69
The group as a motivational matrix   71
Articulating ambivalence   74
Process or content: doing or being   76
Concluding comments   80

Chapter 6   Interpersonal group therapy in intensive treatment   **81**

Tim Leighton

Cognitive analytic therapy as a unifying model   82
Addiction   84
Elements of the treatment programme   85
12-step involvement and interpersonal group
   therapy   87
Coping skills training and interpersonal
   development   89
Managing anxiety   90
Voices in the treatment setting   92
Bakhtin and difference   93

Chapter 7	A relapse prevention group for problem drinkers	**99**
	Bill Reading	
	The context	101
	The group programme	101
	The group culture	102
	Selection and preparation of clients	103
	Structure of group sessions	103
	The format of the group	104
	Theme-centred interaction method	104
	Individual vulnerability factors on the relapse prevention curriculum	106
	A variety of approaches to implementation	107
	The relapse prevention group programme	108
	Life beyond the relapse prevention group	116
	Return to Cognac . . .	116

Chapter 8	One-off art therapy in in-patient detoxification	**117**
	Linda Vickers	
	Client group	118
	Psychodynamic approaches within multidisciplinary teams	118
	A background to art therapy group work with addictions	120
	Therapeutic framework	120
	Theories of addictions	121
	Brief encounters	122
	Visual and verbal communications	124
	'Ships that pass in the night'	125
	Interpretative approach	126
	Themes	128
	Conclusion	132

Chapter 9	Acting for Change: the evolution of a psychodrama group	**133**
	Gillian Woodward	
	Alcohol dependence – the condition or syndrome	133
	Therapeutic context	134
	Acting for Change within the new model	141
	Conclusion	144

Chapter 10   The family as group   **145**

Martin Weegmann

The case of the O'Neill family   145
Dynamic processes   152
Psychotherapeutic groups for relatives   157
Conclusion   159
Appendix   160

Chapter 11   Working with gay men in an alcohol support group   **162**

Colin Macrae

Alcohol misuse as a particular issue for gay people   162
Theoretical perspectives of alcohol problems and
    homosexuality   164
Sociocultural theories   167
The group   168
Conclusion   178

Chapter 12   Dilemmas and counter-transference considerations
                  in group psychotherapy with adult children
                  of alcoholics   **179**

Marsha Vannicelli

Importance of a continuously self-reflective stance   179
Heightened counter-transference reactions in
    ACOA therapy groups   180
The leader who is an ACOA   181
The assumption of sameness   182
Additional issues for the ACOA therapist   183
Pull towards the self-help model   185
Other issues regarding therapist transparency
    and self-disclosure   185
Other personal issues in the life of the therapist   187
On counter-transference goodness and
    availability   188
Avoiding non-therapeutic encounters   191
Conclusion and comment   192

Chapter 13   Addressing substance-related offending   **194**

Mary McMurran and Philip Priestley

Key principles of the ASRO programme   195
ASRO in practice   203
Prison ASRO   206
Common issues   209
Structured programmes for substance misusers:
    future developments   209

Chapter 14   Work discussion groups for professionals   **211**

Martin Weegmann

The daily unconscious   211
The professional unconscious   216
Supporting the helpers   217
Work discussion groups   218
Clinical examples from work discussion groups   220
Conclusion   223

References   225
Index   243

Contributors

Monica Busch is a psychotherapist and group analyst at the Addiction Centre, Stockholm.

Philip J. Flores is a clinical psychologist in private practice in Georgia, USA and a fellow of the American Group Psychotherapy Association.

Paul Jackson is a nurse therapist at the Mount Zeehan Unit, Canterbury, Kent.

E.J. Khantzian is Clinical Professor of Psychiatry, Harvard Medical School at the Cambridge Hospital and Associate Chief of Psychiatry, Tewksbury Hospital, MA.

Tim Leighton, a cognitive analytic psychotherapist, is head of professional education, training and research at Clouds House, Wiltshire.

Colin Macrae, a lecturer in nursing at the University of Birmingham, was formerly a clinical nurse specialist and team co-ordinator of an alcohol service for Central and North West London Mental Health NHS Trust, and has been involved with gay men's services since 1996.

Mary McMurran is a Senior Baxter Research Fellow in the School of Psychology, Cardiff University, a clinical psychologist, and forensic psychologist.

Philip Priestley has worked in probation, prison, and aftercare and is the author or co-author of three accredited cognitive-behavioural programmes.

Bill Reading is a service manager and psychotherapist, based at the Mount Zeehan Unit at St Martin's Hospital, Canterbury, Kent, and in private practice.

Christer Sandahl is an associate professor, clinical psychologist and group analyst at the Department of Learning, Informatics, Management and Ethics (LIME), Karolinska Institutet, Stockholm.

Eva Skarbrandt is a social worker and group analyst at the Addiction Centre, Stockholm.

Marsha Vannicelli is a clinical associate professor of psychology at the Harvard Medical School and a fellow of the American Group Psychotherapy Association.

Linda Vickers is an art therapist and psychotherapist, who has trained and worked in the UK and USA. Formerly with the art therapy department of West London Mental Health NHS Trust, she is currently based in Scotland.

Martin Weegmann is consultant clinical psychologist and group analyst with the Central and North West London Mental Health NHS Trust, working in substance misuse and psychotherapy services.

Peter Wennberg is a researcher at the Department of Clinical Neuroscience, Clinical Alcohol and Drug Research, Karolinska Institutet, Stockholm.

Gillian Woodward is an integrative psychotherapist and psychodrama therapist in private practice, formerly with the ACCEPT project in Fulham, London.

Preface

In a famous anecdote attributed to S.H. Foulkes, the founder of group analysis, he was once asked why he made the move from individual psychoanalysis to group analysis, to which his reply was that he wanted to see what his patients got up to the rest of the time. It was through the group, he thought, that a fuller picture of the life of patients became apparent.

When Bill W., co-founder of Alcoholics Anonymous, reflected on the origins of that movement, he said that all that he and the members had learned was 'hammered on the anvils of group experience'. Fellowship groups, like Alcoholics Anonymous, by definition, view progress as being possible only through human affiliation and in this way the group could be said to be prior to the individual, or at the very least helps the individual to recontexutalise his/her problems. Foulkes, with his analytic groups, took a similar view. The rehabilitative and restoring effects of group membership are now widely acknowledged or assumed in a wider range of addiction settings – many rehabilitations units work largely if not exclusively in groups, day-centres offer structured group programmes, community treatment centres frequently provide out-patient groups, such as support groups or relapse prevention groups, and detoxification wards may offer educational groups. The importance of group values or 'community as method' is well summed up in de Leon's memorable phrase: 'you alone can do it, but you cannot do it alone'. In other words, both in the self-help and professional worlds, from residential to community treatment settings, strong traditions and rationales for group therapy exist.

With respect to our own professional formations, groups have played an important shaping and inspiring role. When one of us (Martin) first came into the substance misuse field in 1990, it was to work as a group therapist and later as group supervisor within a residential group therapy programme (the Regional group Therapy Programme based at St. Bernard's Hospital, originally set up by devised by Dr. Max Glatt in the 1960's); he recalls witnessing dramatic changes in abstinent drinkers and drug-users during the course of five weeks of learning and living together in groups.

On commencing work in 1980 in a group therapy programme for problem drinkers delivered on an out-patient basis, one of us (Bill) was struck by the potential in groups for fostering a capacity for mutuality, self-disclosure and other forms of intimacy. Groups have this re-humanising effect.

Having both made contributions to developing and modernising the psychodynamic tradition in substance misuse, we stumbled upon the idea of editing a collection devoted to group psychotherapies and asking therapists with many years experience to reflect upon what they had seen. There were no apparent competitors in the UK for such a book, to be written by several authors from varied theoretical perspectives; books on groups available in the USA were usually written by a single author, developing a single viewpoint. Hence our collection is truly multi-professional.

Groups do not run themselves and group therapists are not born overnight. The chapters will indicate the carefulness and complexity involved in constructing and maintaining group work. We hope readers will derive practical as well as theoretical assistance from the book. More attention needs to be paid to the provision of training for group therapists and facilitators within this field. Group skills are complex and many-faceted, such as – managing assessment and referral to groups, creating the framework and boundaries around the group or group programme, looking after the group as a whole whilst retaining sight of the individual within, preparing people to change addictive patterns and so on. It is important for therapists to be able to facilitate good identification and feedback from fellows, thus helping sustain longer-term change or preparing patients to establish future and satisfactory, external group associations.

Our clinical experiences leave us in no doubt as to the power of the group in general and as a therapeutic agent in particular. Many of those who struggle with problems related to substance misuse will simply not recover without participation in groups in which they can both give to and receive from others in ways made possible only within this very special milieu. We have ample reason to know that, for many, the group not only makes recovery possible but also imparts a richness of experience that has a profound and lasting impact on the quality of recovery itself.

Of course, group therapy has other attractive potentials – economic and logistical to name but two. But, it is naive in the extreme to imagine that the simple gathering together of substance misusers will, in itself, produce desirable outcomes. Therapists flourish best when valued, supported and provided with an environment that enables them to express their therapeutic commitment and achieve favourable outcomes. Similarly, groups have an equivalent set of needs, requiring a respect for the conditions which will enable them to best release their healing potential and that of their members. We hope that our book will succeed in assisting others to attend sensitively to the needs of groups and to the contexts which will most enable them to succeed in their purpose.

Bill Reading and Martin Weegmann

Acknowledgements

The editors and contributors would like to thank the following people who offered help and encouragement to different people at different stages: Carrie Johnson, Stephanie Brown, Lorna Templeton, Roger Jayamanne, Christina Lee.

We would like to thank the following journals, authors and publishers for permission to reproduce the following published material:

Chapter 1 is adapted from Flores PJ (2003) Addiction as an Attachment Disorder. Jason Aronson, New York.

Chapter 2 is adapted from Khantzian EJ (2001) Reflections on group treatments as corrective experiences for addictive vulnerability. International Journal of Group Psychotherapy 51: 11–20.

Chapter 8 – The poem 'The Almond Tree', from *Rounding the Horn: Collected Poems* (1998), by Jon Stallworthy is reproduced with the permission of Carcanet Press.

Chapter 12 is adapted from Vannicelli (1991) Dilemmas and countertransference considerations in group psychotherapy with adult children of alcoholics. International Journal of Group Psychotherapy 41: 295–312.

Chapter 14 is adapted from Weegmann M (2003) Alcoholics Anonymous – encouraging greater professional interest. Drug and Alcohol Professional 3(1): 7–16.

CHAPTER 1

Addiction as an attachment disorder: implications for group psychotherapy*

PHILIP J. FLORES

Attachment and group therapy

Addiction treatment specialists familiar with attachment theory (Bowlby 1979) and self-psychology (Kohut 1978) recognize that there is an inverse relationship between addiction and healthy interpersonal attachment (Walant 1995, Flores 2001). Certain individuals, because of intrapsychic deficiencies related to genetic and biological substrates, are vulnerable to environmental influences (i.e. substance abuse) which further compromises an already fragile capacity for attachment. Because of the potent emotional rush that alcohol and drugs produce, they are powerfully reinforcing and inhibiting of the more subtle emotional persuasions in a person's life. Consequently, the vulnerable individual's attachment to chemicals serves both as an obstacle to and as a substitute for interpersonal relationships. It is rare, if not impossible, for a practising alcoholic or addict to successfully negotiate the demands of healthy interpersonal relationships. Members of Alcoholics Anonymous (AA) frequently remind each other, 'we don't have relationships, we take hostages.' Their relationships typically are exploitative, maladaptive, or sadomasochistic. The use of substances initially serves a compensatory function, providing temporary relief by helping to lubricate an otherwise cumbersome inadequacy and ineptness in their interpersonal attachment styles. Prolonged substance abuse, because of its toxicity, gradually compromises neurophysiological functioning and erodes existing structure (Parsons and Farr 1981). Consequently, any interpersonal skills they possessed early in their substance-abusing career deteriorate even further. Managing relationships becomes increasingly difficult, leading to a heightened reliance on substances, which accelerates deterioration and addictive response patterns.

---

* This chapter is adapted from Flores PJ (2003) Addiction as an Attachment Disorder. Jason Aronson, New York.

Approaching addiction from a perspective informed by attachment theory has important implications for the stance that must be taken when offering addiction treatment. Most addiction treatment specialists intuitively understand that addiction and attachment difficulties are intricately intertwined. Whether relational problems are the cause or the consequence of addictive behaviours, addicts and alcoholics are best treated by helping them develop a capacity for healthy interpersonal relationships. The underlying theme that successful addiction treatments share is consistently simple. A fundamental but profound truth is that those substance abusers who stay in treatment demonstrate the most improvement (Leshner 1997). A sometimes overlooked, but crucial, fact about substance abuse treatment is that *successful addiction treatment is dose related*. The more treatment is provided, and the longer treatment continues, the better the outcome. Disruptions in attachment to either the therapist or the treatment programme leave many substance abusers vulnerable to dropout and relapse. Consequently, treatment providers must carefully manage treatment retention. All strategies need to be geared towards reducing dropouts.

Attachment theory applied to addiction and group therapy has important implications in this age and culture, where people strive for independence, autonomy, and self-sufficiency, but all too often at the cost of alienation from self and others. Nowhere is this played out with more consistency than with substance abusers. Addicts and alcoholics are notoriously counter-dependent individuals, living their lives at the extreme ends of the attachment–individuation continuum. Autonomy is purchased at the price of alienation and the absence of mutuality in their relationships. As Nicola Diamond (1996) points out, group therapy not only represents a movement away from one-person psychology, but also contains a fundamental interpersonal conception of human beings as always being situated in relation to others. Group therapy, like attachment theory, is based on the implied notion that the essence of being human is social, not individual.

Group treatment of substance abuse

Alcoholics Anonymous and group therapy

Addiction treatment has been intricately associated with group therapy for more than 60 years. Ever since alcoholism was first recognized as a diagnostic entity, its treatment has been provided in groups. Starting with the establishment of the 12-step group movement by AA in the 1930s, addiction treatment has shared a synchronicity and compatibility with group therapy. Addiction treatment specialists have usually embraced group therapy with open arms and historically have welcomed it as an intricate and valuable part of their treatment regimen; it has never had to fight to prove its legitimacy as a viable treatment modality.

Group therapy and addiction treatment have been drawn to each other because of a very simple principle. Substance abusers usually respond favourably to group treatment and are more likely to stay sober and committed to abstinence when treatment is provided in groups. Any treatment modality that facilitates detachment from chemicals and attachment to abstinence will enhance treatment success. Remaining attached to therapy underlies a singularly influential principle of addiction treatment: as previously stated, successful addiction treatment is dose related – the longer the treatment, the better the prognosis. Group therapy, through the curative forces of affiliation, confrontation, support, gratification and identification, promotes attachment more favourably than do other forms of treatment.

Despite the wide popularity of group therapy in addiction treatment, the reasons for its preference have not always been clearly articulated or presented within a clear, comprehensive theoretical formula. A theoretical perspective is needed that explains why the inherent dynamics of the addiction process lends itself in a complementary fashion to the innate qualities of the therapeutic factors operating in a group. Such an explanation is important, because the same forces that contribute to the addictive process can be harnessed to provide its resolution if one is aware of the reasons why addiction manifests itself as it does. Attachment theory provides a theoretical foundation for such an understanding.

Enhancing treatment retention

This is where attachment theory has much to offer in understanding the strategies that must be adopted in treating this population. Foremost is the recognition that before substance abusers can become *attached to treatment* (establish a working therapeutic alliance), they must first become *detached from the addictive attachment* to the substances they abuse. Such a stance recognizes that it is extremely difficult, if not impossible, to establish or maintain a therapeutic alliance with a practising alcoholic or addict. There are other important implications for treatment if the relationship between substance abuse and attachment is closely examined. One will soon recognize that there is an inverse relationship between a person's capacity for attachment (intimacy) and substance abuse. It is rare, if not impossible, to find a substance abuser who can establish or maintain healthy interpersonal attachments. Attachment theory looks at addiction as both a consequence and a failed solution to an impaired ability to form healthy, emotionally regulatory relationships. Consequently, treatment retention is not only crucial to substance abuse treatment; it implies also that the underlying driving force behind all compulsive/addictive behaviour is related to an inability to manage relationships.

The relational models

The recent works of attachment theory and self-psychology have taught addictions specialists that dysfunctional attachment styles interfere with the ability to derive satisfaction from interpersonal relationships, and contribute to internal working models that perpetuate this difficulty. Experiences related to early developmental failures leave certain individuals with vulnerabilities that enhance addictive-type behaviours, and these behaviours are misguided attempts at self-repair. Deprivation of age-appropriate developmental needs leaves the substance abuser constantly searching for something 'out there' that can be substituted for what is missing 'in here'.

Because addiction treatment in the USA has, for the most part, been historically dominated by the 12-step abstinence-based treatment approach, in-depth psychodynamic-oriented psychotherapy has often been dismissed as irrelevant to addiction treatment. Evidence gathered from the development of the newer relational models within psychodynamic theory reflects a conceptual revolution that not only synthesizes the best ideas of psychoanalysis, cognitive sciences, and neurobiology, but also provides a credible and practical way to understand and treat addiction. The contributions of attachment theory and self-psychology have helped shift psychoanalytic thinking from classical drive or instinct theory to a relational approach with its greater emphasis on adaptation, developmental arrestment and deficits in self-structure. The evolution of the relational models has shifted the focus away from intrapsychic struggles to an exploration of the interpersonal or relational difficulties that contribute to a person's present situation. Most importantly, the relational perspective has ushered in more innovative ways for treating addiction and the difficulties that the typical alcoholic or addict brings to treatment.

Attachment-oriented therapy

Treatment that follows the guidelines of attachment-oriented therapy does not adhere to the bias of the classic psychodynamic developmental model, where maturity or mental health is equated with independence.

As Kohut (1977) and Bowlby (1980) suggest, normal development is not a movement from dependence to independence, rather it is a movement from *immature dependence* to *mature interdependence* or mutuality. This shift in perspective is especially important in the treatment of substance abusers. Helping the alcoholic or addict obtain mature dependency on people has obvious implications for treatment. The regulatory power of mature dependency or a secure attachment relationship is absolutely necessary if substance abusers are going to be required to relinquish their reliance on substances – a destructive dependency that erodes whatever existing capacity for affect regulation they originally possessed. Independence, or more correctly, the alcoholic or addict's counter-dependence, is a force that fuels the substance abuser's narcissistic position and isolation, which form the cornerstones of every addictive process.

It is important to remember that attachment theory is not so much a psychological theory as a biological theory. Natural selection favours mechanisms that promote parent–offspring proximity in an environment of evolutionary adaptation. Attachment is not just psychologically driven, but is adaptive and propelled by powerful biological needs for interpersonal closeness. From this perspective, the need for attachment cannot be reduced to a secondary drive. A primary biological function is to secure assistance and survival in the case of adversity. This is true for all social mammals and applies to parent–offspring relationships in other species, not just human beings. Attachment theory also contends that infants and their parents are biologically hard-wired to forge close emotional bonds with each other. These attachments serve important emotional regulatory functions throughout life. All social mammals regulate each other's physiology and modify the internal structure of each other's nervous systems through the synchronous exchange of emotions. This interactive regulatory relationship is the basis for attachment.

Since it is biologically impossible, even as adults, to regulate our own affect for any extended length of time, individuals who have greater difficulty establishing emotionally regulating attachments will be more inclined to substitute drugs and alcohol for their deficiency in intimacy. Attachment theory from this perspective complements Khantzian's affect regulation theory (2001). Because of their difficulty in maintaining emotional closeness with others, certain vulnerable individuals are more likely to substitute a vast array of obsessive–compulsive behaviours (e.g. sex, food, drugs, alcohol, work, gambling, computer games) that serve as a distraction from the gnawing emptiness and internal discomfort that threatens to overtake them. Consequently, when one obsessive–compulsive behaviour is given up, another is likely to be substituted unless the deficiency in self-structure is corrected.

Principles of attachment-oriented therapy

There are few things in the field of psychology and psychotherapy for which the evidence is so strong as the importance of the therapeutic alliance (Strupp 1998, Beutler 2000, Horvath 2001, Norcross 2001). There is an abundance of research evidence demonstrating that the therapist's ability to establish a therapeutic alliance is the single most important contributing factor to successful treatment outcome. Thousands of studies and the historical accumulation of expert clinical opinion dating as far back as Freud's early papers (1912–1913) acknowledge the importance of the many ways in which the working alliance determines treatment outcome. More recent empirical investigations into the ways that different attachment styles – of both therapist and patient – shed new light on the ways that alliances either fail or succeed in therapy.

These findings have important implications because they dictate to a large degree how therapy needs to be delivered when working with the addicted patient. Attachment-oriented therapy (AOT) focuses on the relationship, its implicit rules, and the transformational power inherent in any authentic intimate relationship (Flores 2003). Because substance abuse, and all addictive-driven behaviour, is to some degree a compensatory determined substitute for a person's inability to derive satisfaction from relationships and close personal contact, the therapeutic challenge of engaging the alcoholic or addict in a therapeutic alliance is both enormously difficult and enormously important.

Because the therapeutic alliance has emerged as a consistent predictor of positive treatment outcome across an entire range of different psychotherapy approaches, it has sparked an interest in the generic elements common to all forms of therapy. AOT can therefore be viewed as a 'pantheoretical' approach that transfers across all models of psychotherapy and ideological perspectives. From this perspective, AOT is not so much an approach to therapy as it is an attitude about therapy. It is less concerned with the techniques or the theoretical model that guides the therapist's interventions than with *who* is applying the treatment and in what *way* the therapist is managing the therapeutic relationship. Any approach to therapy, no matter how sophisticated or substantially grounded in solid scientific theory, will be only as effective as the person delivering the treatment. It is not so much *what* the therapist does, as *how* the therapist creates the proper emotional climate of the relationship, because it is this environment that promotes the patient's engagement in the therapy venture. Kohut (1977) suggested that the origins of the specific pathogenesis in an individual's early development is related not so much to the particular rearing practices of the parents as to the emotional climate of the home. In a similar fashion, it is not so much the specific practices of the therapist applying treatment that influence successful treatment outcome, as the creation of the proper therapeutic climate.

Attachment theory holds the view that mental health or maturity is defined by a person's capacity to move towards interdependence rather than independence from relationships. Staying connected is the primary aim of this model. Remaining in relation, even when the patient is detached, angry, or avoidant, is accomplished not by clinging to the patient, but rather by remaining empathically understanding of the patient's attachment fears and difficulties with relationships. Negotiating the vicissitudes typically involved in the give and take of any relationship eventually helps the alcoholic or addict move towards experiencing even more subtle satisfying ways of being in relation. Eventually, the substance abuser will learn how to transfer these subtleties outside the therapeutic milieu in the form of mutuality with others.

Mutuality can be defined as any growth-enhancing relationship that benefits both parties in the relationship. It is not about being enmeshed or co-dependent; it is more about the efforts to know and understand another's experience. This is true for both the addicted and non-addicted, but it is an especially important capacity for the alcoholic or addict because, as Jeffery Roth (personal communication, 2002) says, 'addiction is a disease of isolation'. Being joined by another empathically in an atmosphere of mutual respect and trust helps reduce the addicted individual's sense of alienation and aloneness. Mutuality from this perspective provides each person in the relationship with the simultaneous affect regulation that is the hallmark of emotional stability and mental health. Lewis, Amini and Landon (2000, p. 86) agreed when they wrote, 'Total self-sufficiency turns out to be a daydream . . . . Stability means finding people who regulate you well and staying near them.'

All interventions need to occur in the service of moving the relationship along. As will be discussed later in the section on negative process and repairs in ruptures of the therapeutic alliance, a key to successful treatment is the therapist's capacity and skill at working through the inevitable conflicts that arise in any relationship. This model looks at the *relational resilience* of substance abusers. What is their capacity to stay connected to others when there are disagreements and conflicts? How soon will they be able to move back into relation when there is a rupture in the alliance? AOT is focused on the ebb and flow inherent in all long-term attachment relationships.

This approach, while concerned with the dangers of enmeshment and infantile gratification, also differs from the more classic psychodynamic model with its counter-transference concerns about the therapist getting too involved. AOT is more concerned with the therapist *not* being involved enough, or being too distant. Consequently, AOT is not so much a change in technique, or even a change in theory, as a change in principle. More emphasis is placed on the importance of the relationship and the development of mutual respect, trust, and responsibility. When one can bring oneself more fully and authentically into a relationship, one not only embraces and gets to know the other, but also gets to embrace and know oneself. Knowing oneself can never be accomplished in isolation, only in relation.

Talking intimately with another about oneself is a developmental function that not all adults achieve. Communication about one's feelings in relation to another person is also a skill that many alcoholics or addicts do not possess. Knowing oneself and sharing that knowledge with another requires the capacity to put one's feelings into words, a developmental task that requires the acquisition of inner speech, or what Meares (1993) refers to as self-narrative. Attachment theory, especially informed by the work of Margaret Main (1995) and her development of the adult attachment interview (AAI), has shown a connection between attachment status in childhood and narrative styles in adulthood. Fonagy et al. (1994) write about the reflexive self function (RSF), which is the ability to think about oneself in relation to another – a necessity for intimacy. Using narratives to accurately recount one's past (insight) is a key determinant in knowing oneself and knowing others. As Holmes (1996, p. 14) says, 'Acquiring inner speech means becoming intimate with oneself; knowledge of oneself goes hand in hand with knowledge of others.' A clinical example will help to illustrate this principle.

Andrew was more than five years sober and very actively involved in AA when he sought out a psychotherapy group. A number of weeks into the group, Andrew's style of relating became painfully obvious to the group leader and the other group members. He had great difficulty relating to others interpersonally about the emotional material stirred up in the here and now of the present relationships in the group. Andrew could be supportive and compassionate of other's painful experiences or stories, but he could not stay engaged with others once the interpersonal exchange required that people relate beyond the historic content of their experience. Some of Andrew's narrative style may have been shaped in part by his repeated exposure to AA meetings, where the telling of one's stories is often stereotypically scripted, and 'cross-talk' is strongly discouraged. When Andrew spoke of himself, he could not keep others engaged. Group members would become distracted or drift off because his exchanges became bogged down in the minute details of his painful past history. People in group could feel sorry for Andrew, but they could not feel drawn in by him. It wasn't that it was unusual for new group members to feel compelled to tell their story when they first joined the group; that wasn't the problem. Everyone usually enters a group having to spend some time letting other group members know their history. Andrew's problem was that he remained stuck in his narratives. His stories became rote and stereotyped. It took a concerted effort by the group leader to steer the group away from their eventual indifference or boredom and their stereotyped responses to Andrew ('Oh, that's horrible, you had a terrible childhood, I can't believe they did that to you', etc.), and guide them to deal directly with the feelings that Andrew evoked in them. Using his knowledge of Margaret Main's work on narrative styles and attachment, the therapist was able to cut across the dichotomy between historical truth and narrative truth. By focusing on the form of Andrew's narratives, rather than their content, the group leader was able to help the group and Andrew see that Andrew's preoccupation with his history was a way for him to stay attached to his past pain and hurt in the hope of evoking protective attachment behaviour in potential caregivers. The group leader's actions in this example serve as an important reminder that therapists are more helpful when they attend as much to the way their patients talk as to what they talk about.

Addiction and the working alliance

Attachment theory applied to psychotherapy in general, and addiction treatment in particular, has important far-reaching implications for how the patient needs to be approached in therapy. It is important to remember that attachment theory is not so much a new theory as a new way of thinking about relationships, and about the crucial developmental functions attachment provides for developing children, and the important regulatory functions it provides for mature adults.

However, important as the ability to establish a working alliance is, this alone will not solve most of the dilemmas that patients, especially those suffering from addictive disorders, bring to the therapeutic encounter. A good theory and solid training in the proper application of the techniques that are guided by that theory are also essential. But as Lambert and Barley (2001) suggest, it is the therapist's ability to relate that creates the capacity for attachment and leads to the establishment of a working alliance, without which little influence can be exerted on the patient's behalf. If an attachment is not created, the therapist will be provided with insufficient opportunity to apply the technical skills that his or her theory dictates. Strupp explains why the integration of theory, technical skills, and the ability to establish a therapeutic alliance are so important:

Technical skills, I believe more strongly than ever, are the hallmark of the competent psychotherapist. They are encompassed by what I have termed the skillful management of a human relationship toward therapeutic ends. To my way of thinking, these skills are undergirded by a theory of therapy (in keeping with Kurt Lewin's dictum that nothing is as practical as a good theory) which acts as a road map guiding the therapist's interventions. One of the telling observations we made in the Vanderbilt I study (Strupp 1980, 1988, Strupp and Hadley 1979) comparing the performance of experienced therapists with that of untrained but kind college professors was the frequently encountered comment by college professors that after a few hours of 'therapy' (I use the quotation marks advisedly), they 'ran out of material to talk about.' In other words, they were adrift in a sea of material they were at a loss to organize and process. In the final analysis such a theory may be relatively straightforward but it must embody a rationale of what constitutes the 'problem' and what should be done to alleviate it. By the same token, the therapist must be cognizant of the intricacies of psychopathology, the nature of defensive operations, developmental history, and the vagaries of human communication (Strupp 1999, p. 35).

Following Strupp's recommendations, attachment theory defines the 'problem' of addiction as both a consequence of and solution to an individual's incapacity to establish healthy emotional regulatory relationships. The resolution or 'what should be done to alleviate the problem' requires that the therapist first persuade the alcoholic or addict to detach from the object of their addiction, because until they do they will not be able to attach to treatment or recovery. Creating and maintaining the attachment or therapeutic alliance with alcoholics and addicts requires a special set of skills and knowledge about what constitutes addiction, so that, unlike the kindly professors in Strupp's Vanderbilt Study, the therapist will not be 'adrift in a sea of material that they are at a loss to organize and process'.

A clinical example will show how attachment theory can help a therapist organize a seemingly unrelated sea of material when a new patient with an addiction history walks into the office.

Susan's former therapist in New York City referred her for therapy after a recent job promotion required she transfer to a new executive position at corporate headquarters in Chicago. When making the referral, her previous therapist spoke fondly of Susan, saying she had worked hard in therapy for the past five years and made tremendous progress overcoming a cocaine addiction and a very troubled childhood marked by both emotional and physical abuse.

'However,' her therapist cautioned. 'She has one persistent affliction she just can't seem to overcome. She's a compulsive shopper and she's constantly in debt.'

Susan showed for her first appointment immaculately dressed, decked out in a sleek black Armani suit, Ferragamo high heels, a gold Rolex, and a stylish leather Coach purse hanging from her narrow shoulders. A tall, thin attractive woman, Susan looked like she had just stepped out of an advertisement in Vogue magazine.

She was also an emotional mess.

Distressed to the point of distraction, she spoke discouragingly of the over-whelming stress of the recent move, her new job, the death of her father, a break-up with her boyfriend, and the loss of her therapist. Her face was drawn and taut, her eye contact poor, and her fingers revealed the bruised and bloody results of her nervous picking at her fingernails and cuticles. She was not sleeping, eating, or going to AA meetings.

'I've even stopped exercising,' she lamented. 'That's at least the one thing I've always managed to do even when I was in the worst throes of my . cocaine use.'

'Why have you stopped exercising?' The therapist asked.

Susan stared blankly at the floor for a few seconds before answering. 'I think it's because I don't want to leave my apartment. I don't want any-one to see me in this pitiful condition.'

'You're isolating,' the therapist said. 'That's deadly for an addict.'

'I know.' Susan looked up, smiled weakly at the therapist, and nodded. 'I just seem to be unable to help myself. The only thing I'm doing is working,' Susan paused and shook her head, '. . . and shopping.'

The therapist opened his mouth to speak, but Susan didn't wait for a response.

'My credit cards are charged to the max. Nieman Marcus is sending me threatening letters. Saks Fifth Avenue has threatened to close my account.' Susan frowned. 'I wish they would close my account. I owe them fifty thou-sand dollars.' Susan buried her head in her hands. 'I can't believe I've done this.' She looked up at the therapist, an angry scowl on her face. 'They're worse than the drug dealers I use to deal with. Did you know if you're a 'preferred customer', they'll assign you your own special sales-person who calls you when they get something new in to give you the chance to be the first person to see the latest from Armani.'

'They do sound like drug dealers calling to let their best customers know when the latest high quality stash has arrived from Columbia.'

'Exactly!' Susan balled her hands into a fist. 'Here I am fifty thousand dol-lars into debt with them and they're still extending my credit, and they're so damn nice and understanding about it.'

'Do you know why you keep taking their calls?' The therapist asked even though he knew what the answer might be.

A deep sadness washed over Susan's face. 'Yeah, I know. Barbara, my pri-vate sales consultant, is so sweet to me. She's the only person that calls me anymore. She's at least someone to talk to that's friendly. I know it's her job, but I really do think she likes me. And I can talk with her.' Tears welded up in Susan eyes. 'It so damn sad. I've become this pitiful that I hunger so much for someone to be nice to me.'

'No, I don't think that's pitiful at all. We all have this need, this hunger for someone to be kind to us.' The therapist leaned toward her and made an assuring gesture with his hand. *'The problem is not that you hunger for it. The problem is where you're trying to get it. It's like that old country and western song, a number of years back, you're 'looking for love in all the wrong places.'*

Susan cracked a weak smile. *'I think you're right. But how did I get into this mess and how do I get out of it?'*

'You treat this like any other addiction,' the therapist replied. *The good news is that you have a model, a template for dealing with this. You know what worked with your cocaine addiction. You just need to apply those same principles to your shopping.'*

Susan wrinkled up her face. *'I'm confused. I don't see the similarities.'*

'Look,' the therapist said as he held up his hand and began counting on his fingers. *First, you're overwhelmed by your emotions and the stress in your life. Second, you're using your shopping the same way you used your drugs – to medicate your feelings. Third, you're isolating. The only people you're really talking to or have any contact with are the dealers. Fourth, you're feeling ashamed of your behaviour, which is only further eroding your self-esteem and self-respect.'*

Susan hesitated and looked at the four fingers the therapist now held up in front of her. She slowly nodded. *'Maybe you're right.'*

'Listen, Susan,' the therapist said. *'Addiction is all about isolation and trying to manage painful feelings either or by yourself or using something other than people to help with those feelings. Because of all the losses you've had in the past few months, the people who used to help keep you stabilized are no longer available – your therapist, your boyfriend, even your home AA group. You're either turning to the wrong people, like Barbara, your Saks sales rep, or you're using things like your shopping to keep you distracted from the loneliness and isolation you feel.'*

Empirical evidence is now available to support what every experienced clinician has always intuitively known. The accomplished and skilled therapist knows that the development and maintenance of the therapeutic relationship is a primary curative component of successful therapy because it is the quality of the relationship that provides the context in which specific techniques exert their influence. Add to this recognition the emerging evidence that suggests addiction is inversely related to a person's capacity for intimate attachments, and the significance of the relationship between attachment, a working alliance, and successful treatment takes on profound implications.

Generally, addicted patients do not handle well the regressive pull that can be experienced in group if the group leader utilizes techniques that are applicable to Tavistock or classic psychodynamic theory as outlined by Bion (1961), Rice (1965) or Ezriel (1973). This is not to imply that the group leader must ensure that the group and its members are gratified in an infantile manner. Not only is this unrealistic, antitherapeutic, and ultimately impossible, it feeds the group members' narcissism and omnipotent expectations for immediate gratification. Rather, establishing a climate of *optimal frustration* provides the delicate balance necessary to ensure that enough of the dependency needs of alcoholics and substance abusers are met until they are able to gradually internalize control over their own destructive impulses and emotions.

To attain this end, group leaders must be more active and gratifying than they would be if they were treating non-addicted patients. Yalom's (1995) emphasis on cohesion as an important curative factor takes on added significance when working with this population. Following the suggestions of Pines (1998), good-enough self-object bonds or attachments need to be created with the group so the group itself becomes a self-object. Group cohesion and attachment are essentially intertwined, and are necessary if the group is to provide the support and gratification required during early recovery. Arensberg (1998) agrees when he writes, 'Obviously, for a group to work, a good-enough and safe-enough environment and group composition must exist.' The creation of a climate that fosters understanding of self, and self in relation to others, helps group members understand the ways in which their narcissistic vulnerabilities and difficulties with attachment can lead to alcohol or drug use.

In more traditional psychodynamic group psychotherapy utilizing object-relations theory, the group leader's task is to help group members work through the defences each of them uses as an attempt to manage the anxieties associated with unacceptable or threatening forms of object relations in group. These anxieties are often related to unconscious instinctual drives, and the leader's task is usually to interpret these defences and anxieties: However, drawing on Kohut (1977) and the theoretical perspective of self-psychology, it is best to not interpret these anxieties or behaviours as distorted or maladaptive, but to help the alcoholic or substance abuser understand that these reactions are related to and a consequence of unmet developmental needs for self-object responsiveness that are repeated in the here-and-now interactions of the group. This approach, heavily influenced by self-psychology therapy, is much more supportive and gratifying and less threatening or shameful than traditional approaches to treating vulnerabilities typically manifested by most alcoholics and addicts.

Group, transference, shame, and object-hunger

The exploration of the destructive forces that prevent the development of mature mutuality can take place only in what Wolf (1988) refers to as the *empathic self-object ambience*. Because the activation of shame related to object hunger, dependency, and hostility associated with the transference relationship is often too intense for the alcoholic or addict to tolerate in individual therapy, group therapy is required. By virtue of the number of group members, group dilutes the intensity of feelings that would otherwise inundate the patient in a one-to-one setting. Thus, addicts can spread their attachment to several people and the group itself. The group offers its members a way of dealing with the shame, hostility, and ambivalence in their relationships by supplying a number of attachment figures upon whom they can depend or direct their anger without too much fear of retaliation. The response of the group leader, by firm, yet non-hostile, ability to absorb anger, can lay the foundation for later identification. Consequently, the substance abuser's fear of closeness, rejection, attack, and dependency is not as severely threatened. The group provides an alternative to the substance abuser's lifestyle on the streets or in bars, and can serve as a secure-base or *transitional object* until a more stable sense of self is internalized.

Transference intensity is reduced and spread out in group therapy. The group provides a holding environment, allowing the alcoholic or addict to achieve an appropriate mutually dependent relationship with other group members without the crippling interference of their own anger, dependency, or fear of intimacy. The group helps to create a safe space between the addict and the group leader. Through identification, a more stable set of internal self and object representations (internal working models) will be incorporated.

The group format is better able to accomplish this task because it provides many key elements that individual therapy cannot provide. Group therapy can more readily do this because it gives substance abusers a far wider array of individuals upon whom they can either depend or direct their anger. By virtue of the number of group members, the group format dilutes the intensity of the feelings that are sure to be activated in any close interpersonal relationship and that have to be worked through if characterological change is to occur. This process is likely to be too threatening in a one-to-one relationship, but the group provides a safer holding environment that gives substance abusers more 'space,' while permitting them to deal with the intense hostility and ambivalence they are sure to experience as their needs for approval, dependence, and caring surface. Usually, most addicts and alcoholics cannot tolerate the stimulation of 'object hunger' or their own dependent yearnings that are activated in individual therapy as well as any in intimate relationships.

As Kosseff (1975, p. 237) outlines, the group becomes

. . . a transitional object that protects the patient from the intensity of the fear of dependency on the therapist because this dependency is transferred to the group. The group carries within it a degree of freedom or support which the dyadic relationship cannot provide while at the same time serving as a bulwark against too great feelings of frustration and fear of punishment if he should function autonomously.

A clinical vignette will help illustrate this point.

Mary, a recovering addict with nearly two years of abstinence, had been progressing nicely in her therapy group, which she had entered shortly after her discharge from an in-patient alcohol and drugs treatment programme. Along with the immediate comfort she was able to establish with the group, she also quickly developed an idealizing transference with her female group leader. Hanging on intently to her every comment, she would revel in any show of attention and support given her by the group leader. Her admiration came to an abrupt end after nearly a year in group when the group leader supported another group member's observation that Mary was intolerant of anyone disagreeing with her. Mary exploded into a rage, screaming she was 'sick and tired of people betraying and blaming her', directing most of her anger at the group leader. Attempts at containment and interpretation by the group leader proved futile. However, Mary was able to gain some solace from other group members who expressed their understanding of her feelings because they too had felt similar feelings with others in their lives. Following this emotional explosion, weeks went by where Mary refused even to look at the group leader, much less speak to her. Her only comments during the next two months were mumblings about leaving the group because she 'no longer felt safe here'. However, Mary had enough of an emotional connection with many of the other group members that she was able to respond to their urging that she stay because they cared for her and would miss her if she left. Consequently, Mary continued to attend the sessions regularly, eventually interacting more and more freely with the rest of the group members, while remaining somewhat cautious and distant from the group leader. Gradually, she was able to engage the group leader and even respond favourably to some of her interventions. Finally, one evening she was telling the group about an argument she had with her female supervisor at work. She looked directly at the group leader and openly confessed, 'You know, I think I was distorting her comments and over-reacting just like I did with you a couple of months ago.'

No interpretation was required. The group had provided her with a safe holding environment and its group members had given her enough 'good objects' to connect with until she was able to work through the intensity of the transference feelings with the group leader, who represented the internalized bad-object parental figure. If the group members had not been able to provide enough safety for Mary by their 'holding' of her, she would have likely dropped out of therapy or sought previous sources of gratification (alcohol or drugs).

Because the group expands transference possibilities, it provides important advantages for long-term recovery. As the group continues to meet and relationships develop, *affiliative-seeking behaviour* will be activated. This permits more opportunity for the elicitation and exploration of internal working models, providing group members with a more favourable atmosphere for modifying and altering the repetitive nature of their destructive ways of relating. Once the group becomes an attachment object, it offers a larger number of potential self-object candidates, creating more diverse transferences and greater possibilities for members to establish the particular *extended self-object functions* (Harwood 1986) they require (Bacal 1985). The opportunities for *adversarial* and *efficacy experiences* (Wolf 1988) are increased, adding to the possibilities for group members to experience a *self-delineating self-object function,* which is a basic requirement for the emergence of a separate sense of self (Stolorow, Brandchaft and Atwood 1987).

Figure 1.1 illustrates the expansion of selfobject transference possibilities in a group.

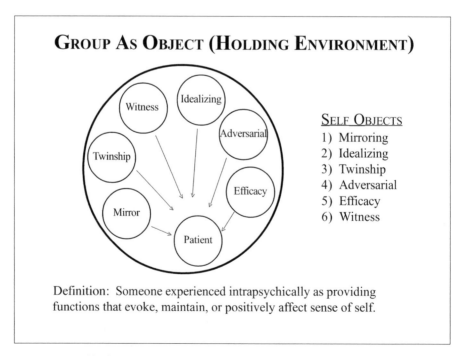

Figure 1.1 Self Object.

A clinical vignette will demonstrate how these self-object functions can be activated in a group to increase therapeutic benefit.

Betty was an attractive, energetic woman in her early thirties with one year of abstinence when she entered a long-term, outpatient therapy group. The group quickly found her to be an exciting, involved group member who was very responsive to others in the group. However, they gradually discovered her propensity to treat them as disparagingly as she treated others outside of the group. She would make hasty intense attachments, then quickly become disillusioned or bored with her new relationships. Betty repeated this pattern within the group. She was very seductive with the men and dismissing of the women. The only girl in a family with four brothers and a dominant father, she had a love–hate relationship with men while seeing women as unimportant and inconsequential. Her attachment to the group and to one of the group leaders was strong enough to permit her to tolerate the different self-object responses she evoked in others. Two men engaged her around her typical seductive patterns while another man remained consistently confrontational of her manipulations. A fourth male member stayed consistently protective and supportive of her, even during her most provocative moments in the group. Two women engaged her competitively while a third remained empathic and understanding of her difficulties with men. Another woman, Alice, became a new identified object for her. Even though Alice's demeanour was totally opposite to Betty's, Alice was consistently able to get the male members in group to respond to her in a supportive, respectful, and nurturing way because she was gentle and unobtrusive. Betty learned that all quiet women didn't have to be masochistic like her mother. Through the course of her involvement with members of the group, Betty was able to evoke the self-object responses she required to transform and alter the destructive relational patterns established in her family.

In summary, the group's value as a transitional object is in its facilitation of the identification process. It helps alcoholics and addicts:

(1) shift from a set of internalized split-images of self to a more unitary representation of self by identification with other group members; (2) shift from the part object seen as if it were the whole object (e.g. the therapist seen solely as bad object); (3) shift the fears of being engulfed by the group leader to a gradual recognition through other group members that this cannot happen because the group leader is not so powerful and because they, by sharing the leader with the patient, interfere with the patient's longing for fusion. (Kosseff 1975, p. 237)

Kosseff (1975, p. 237) sums up this process when he writes:

The group helps the patient let go of primitive idealizations of the therapist and his omnipotence by pointing out both the reality and the shortcomings of the therapist. As the patient is able to face these less positive attitudes toward the therapist, he is able 'to change places' with him and see himself in a more worthwhile light. Where the patient in individual treatment would tend to overlook differences between his view of the therapist and the reality of the therapist, the other group members jar the patient's efforts at continuing pathological identification with the therapist or themselves and force him to acknowledge, and ultimately accept, his differences from others. Where the therapist's relative silence in individual treatment may tend to foster such pathological identification, visible group behavior and interaction force objective recognition of differences. What had been a sealed-off, dead-end identification with the therapist, a giving up of the real object and a substitution of an internalized, possibly idealized object, along with a giving up of the real potentialities of the self in favor of a false compliant self, now gives way to a recognition of the self as good and different from others. As the danger of fusion and immolation with the therapist subsides, the patient develops the hope and possibility of separation and true individuation.

Conclusions

The group leader must remember that an intervention made for a newly recovering alcoholic may be totally inappropriate for an alcoholic with one, two or even 10 years of sobriety. Early interventions need to be directed toward lessening the denial of the alcoholic or substance abuser, while avoiding inducing too much negative affect too quickly. Eventually a gradual shift must be initiated, requiring chemically dependent individuals to take a cold, hard look at their character pathology and the defences that prevent them from accurately perceiving their self-defeating behavioural patterns (i.e. alcohol and drug use). Eventually they must learn how to cope with interpersonal conflicts without relying on chemicals to self-soothe or regulate affect. There are some unique features in the treatment of alcoholics and addicts in a therapy group that the group leader must be aware of if the possible curative forces available in group are to be harnessed successfully. All of the curative factors (Yalom 1995) that exist in any well-conducted group will also be available to the competent and well-trained group leader.

The long-term goal of treatment is mutuality and attachment, which helps break the substance abuser's cycle of alienation and isolation. However, important as attachment is, the maintenance of a sense of separateness is equally so. The polarity between attachment and autonomy has to be carefully managed. Secure attachment can be established only once insecure and ambivalent attachment styles are relinquished (Ainsworth 1989). If late-stage treatment requirements are successfully achieved, the substance abuser will began to understand and experience healthy mutuality. Each member can learn the important task of resolving conflicts without resorting to alcohol or drugs.

CHAPTER 2

Group psychotherapy as a corrective for addictive vulnerability*

E.J. KHANTZIAN

This chapter contains some musings and reflections on group therapy for patients suffering with substance use disorders, rather than a more academic or pedagogical approach. Based on three decades of clinical experience, it reflects a keen interest of mine, namely how and why groups help people, particularly individuals with addictive disorders, to feel better and to change. To obtain a more in-depth analysis of how and why groups work for substance abusers the reader is referred to my earlier work and that of my collaborators (Khantzian et al. 1990, 1992, 1995, Golden et al. 1993), as well as the work of respected colleagues (Yalom 1974, Brown and Yalom 1977, Vannicelli 1982, Matano and Yalom 1991, Flores 2001).

On the basis of my clinical experiences working with patients with substance use disorders in both individual and group psychotherapies, I am convinced that problems in self-regulation and the psychological suffering that ensues are at the root of addictive disorders. I have found group treatments to be pre-eminently suited to address these problems. Group work is especially effective in unearthing the nature of these problems and offers a means to relieve the distress and address the co-occurring characterologic problems that interact with their suffering. In the following paragraphs I shall describe how these ideas developed in the contexts of my clinical experience, and how they in turn generated a model for group therapy for patients with substance use disorders.

An evolving perspective (1970–1980)

When I first began teaching about patients with substance use disorders, I emphasized 'severe and pervasive co-existent psychopathology', a focus

* This chapter is adapted from a paper originally published in the *International Journal of Group Psychotherapy* 2001; 51: 11–20. The author wishes to thank Guilford Press for permission to reproduce this article here.

that shifted as I worked with more patients. I stressed primitive and narcissistic dynamics as being at the root of the impulse to use and become dependent on substances of abuse. In part, this formulation was a function of my initial experience starting in the early 1970s working with patients coming to a methadone maintenance treatment programme, patients who admittedly were more characterologically disturbed. These patients had high rates of co-morbid depression, as well as a disproportionately high incidence of personality disorder (Khantzian and Treece 1985). During this time, I continued to see increasing numbers of alcohol-dependent patients in my private practice, and with the advent of the 'cocaine epidemic' in the 1980s I was seeing more cocaine-dependent patients as well. I became increasingly impressed with the degrees of resiliency and characterologic strength in the patients I was treating, especially those in recovery (e.g. 12-step programmes). In both individual and group psychotherapy, I found it increasingly more comfortable (for me and my patients) to work with their strengths and to consider the special ways my patients suffered, and the ways they attempted to disguise their suffering from themselves and from others. This shift in my thinking increased the therapeutic alliance and, further, had special implications for group psychotherapy in my practice.

My emphasis shifted from a focus on psychopathology to more of a focus on sectors of vulnerability in personality organization. Increasingly I stressed the interrelationships between patients' distress, their characterologic defensive patterns, problems with control, and their compulsion to use addictive substances.

A close and related companion to the issues of pain and suffering in substance use disorders is the problem of control. Patients with substance use disorders have repeatedly demonstrated that a core feature of their addictive illness is their inability to control their lives in an adaptive manner. As much as a substance use disorder can be seen as a loss of control over substance use, it may also be seen as an attempt to control the addict's life – from the outside-in to the inside-out. As our patients in recovery so often remind us, 'alcohol' is mentioned only once in the 12 steps, otherwise the steps are a metaphor for life and a means to help individuals who have difficulty regulating themselves to better do so.

In my own work, spanning three decades working with patients who suffer with substance use disorders, I have evolved an understanding of addictive vulnerability as a disorder in self-regulation. The core features of substance abusers' inability to regulate their lives involves their emotions (or affects), self-esteem, relationships, and behaviours (e.g. self-care) (Khantzian 1990, 1995, 1999). When I first began to work with substance abusers I was in the middle of my psychoanalytic training, which then (and now) influenced me to believe that I could engage my patients and understand them best if I adopted an adaptive perspective. I assumed that the patients coming to the methadone programme were using opiates to cope with life problems. Because opiates are physical painkillers, I presumed they might also be a means of ameliorating psychological pain. As I continued to evaluate the nature of their suffering in greater depth, and treated increasing numbers of patients in individual and group psychotherapy in our methadone programme, I became aware of a more specific reason for the appeal of these analgesic agents: opiates increasingly seemed to me to be compelling for my patients because they had discovered the powerful anti-rage and anti-aggression action of these drugs. The predominance of these affects in the methadone patients was not surprising, given that so many of them had been both victims and perpetrators of traumatic violence and abuse.

This clinical observation was the beginning of the second stage of my thinking, and an important part of the groundwork of what I and others would increasingly refer to as the 'self-medication hypothesis'. The increasing numbers of addicted patients whom I saw in my private practice presented compelling clinical evidence that there were unique affect states with which they struggled that made the specific action of each class of drugs appealing (Khantzian 1975, 1985, 1997). The self-medication perspective, however, raised questions and inconsistencies that needed explanation. Two important ones were:

- Many individuals suffer with painful affects but they did not all self-medicate or become addicted.
- The use of addictive substances caused as much pain as they relieved, if not more.

It was in this context that my thinking evolved to consider addictive involvement as a self-regulation disorder (Khantzian 1990, 1995, 1997) and subsequently, on a related basis, also to consider the nature of the disordered person or disordered personality (Khantzian 1999) that makes it more likely that individuals will experiment, become dependent on, and relapse to addictive substances.

Group therapy as a corrective (1980–2000)

Group psychotherapy provides a special forum for these vulnerabilities and related defences to unfold and to provide corrective experiences for our patients to find relief for their pain and opportunities to change and grow. Bill, an articulate professional man, working with me in a group in which we repeatedly came around to exploring such vulnerabilities, provided the following vivid vignette to explain the sources of his self-regulation difficulties and how alcohol became a magical elixir to counter his inner distress and constricting defences.

> *My childhood was a period of isolation and loneliness – there was restriction, suppression, repression, oppression and depression. I distinctly recall my first drink, at 17 years old, and how it changed all of that. I recall the frosted highball class, the two ice cubes, unscrewing the red top of the Beefeaters Gin bottle, the cracking of the ice cubes when the liquor splashed over them, the strong odour of the juniper berries. I recall the tightening of my throat when the foreign solution burned going down – and then I recall the unfettering from my emotional chains that followed. I began to feel free – free to feel. I felt happy, even giddy – unashamed, unpretentious and uninhibited. I felt that I finally was a member of the human race, 'one of the guys', an equal.*

Fenichel (1945) quotes, from an unknown source, to demonstrate what alcoholism is not primarily about: 'The superego is that part of an individual that is soluble in alcohol'. Actually, modern psychodynamic theory (Krystal and Raskin 1970, Khantzian 1990) suggests that alcohol is at least as good an ego solvent and helps individuals who are constricted around dependency and nurturance needs to overcome restricting ego defences, as Bill's dramatic vignette demonstrates. Alcohol lessens our defensive inhibitions and our anxiety levels, enabling a 'repressed' individual to become more expressive, as Bill described. His vignette also reveals that beyond the major painful affects with which he struggled, he also experienced anguishing problems with his self-esteem and an inability to connect to others without the benefit of alcohol. In addition to the suffering entailed in the self-regulation problems with emotions, self-esteem and relationships, Bill and so many other patients like him also succumb to addictive disorders because they cannot regulate their self-care, namely they repeatedly fail to consider, anticipate, or fear the consequences and dangers of the behaviours that lead up to and are involved in substance use disorders. At the same time our patients suffer with their self-regulation vulnerabilities, they also defend against them. Their often seemingly impregnable defences disguise, at the same time as they reveal, the substance abuser's significant vulnerabilities in self-regulation.

Therapies that are effective successfully target both the pain and the defences. In my experience group psychotherapy, with or without individual psychotherapy, has been an extraordinary vehicle for achieving this end. By the early 1980s group therapy was a regular if not essential part of my armamentarium in trying to help my patients understand their vulnerability to becoming dependent on substances of abuse. In the context of a semi-structured, supportive, friendly and safe group experience I was impressed by how much my patients could reveal and teach me and each other about what the core dynamics were around addictive vulnerability. These 'friendly and supportive' elements became increasingly important operatives, and my patients had to help me and each other to loosen up and relax enough to be ourselves and to learn the value of healthy play in groups. This included the ability to laugh, as much as cry, about ourselves and our problems. I believe as practitioners we have not emphasized enough how groups are fun, uplifting, and extraordinary sources of support in engaging self with others in pursuing 'mutual concerns' (Balint 1972) and addressing what needs to be addressed in order to get better and to change.

How do groups work?

Group therapy works because it acts as a containing influence, and over time it increasingly serves as a transformative experience. In the group, members help each other to focus on what is needed to survive, given the major problems that members have with behavioural and emotional dysregulation. In my experience the natural anxiety, fear, and apprehension that are evoked in members and the leader when a group member is engaged in life-threatening behaviours, and the range of reactions that are expressed, are often crucial in motivating the patient to do something about it. Further, the understanding and non-judgmental responses from others who are experiencing similar problems positively influence the troubled member. Where friends and family have reacted with impatience, anger, or rejection, the members' commitment to each other's safety and well-being generate empathic concerns and expressions of appropriate fear and apprehension that patients cannot feel for themselves to guide their behaviour. Often, the suggestion that it is time for detoxification and confinement is spontaneously initiated by a group member who has similarly had to accept this realization, and it is often offered with hopeful and positive descriptions of their own experience. At other times the group leader enlists the patient to face the needed intervention, and catalyses a processes that encourages other patients to express their experiences and convictions about the benefits of a needed intervention, from multiple perspectives that might not otherwise be available, when it is needed so much. The group members and leader can also play a crucial role in examining distress and/or the dangerous and mindless reactions that are part of the underpinnings of addictive behaviour. In other instances when the same reactions herald potential relapse after varying lengths of sobriety or abstinence, the group members and leader may act to forestall relapse. More specifically, the members and group leader are alerted to spot the dysregulation of affects, self-esteem, relationships and self-care that are a constant threat to susceptible individuals when they are confronted with inevitable life stresses and distress.

Beyond containing addictive behaviour, groups play an equally important, if not more important, role in transforming behaviour, particularly the characterologic styles and patterns that predispose to addictive behaviours. In psychoanalytic practice the measure of improvement is not based primarily on symptom reduction. Rather, improvement is measured in terms of structural change: that is, how a person has been in their characteristic ways of relating, feeling, and behaving, and how they have changed as a consequence of treatment, indicates improvement. Do their character flaws or 'defects' that cause them to repeat the same maladaptive patterns of being and behaving that predispose them to their symptoms (in this case the addictive use of drugs) change over time, and is there an emergence of more flexible, alternative ways of dealing with life problems and vicissitudes? In this respect, effective group leaders stimulate a process to assure that the group goes beyond the important matters of safety and support, but also fosters a climate for self-examination and an understanding of how we are all more or less programmed (or not well enough programmed) to repeat and perpetuate self-defeat, or worse still, self-destruction. As one patient who suffered so much with his sadness, bitterness, and loneliness put it, 'I'm a born again isolationist.' In group, the constant challenge for him, myself, and the others was to monitor how he was constantly lapsing into taking leave of us in group even as he sat there in group, and was doing so in most of his other social circles.

In psychiatric and psychoanalytic practice we have few if any well-grounded traditions to proscribe behaviours other than confrontation. Most experienced clinicians, including myself, however, agree that as a therapeutic intervention confrontation is overrated, overused (especially in addicted populations), and more often ineffectual or damaging. Yet the need for containment and transformation for individuals suffering with substance use disorders begs for proscription of behaviours in the short term (e.g. abstinence) and long term (e.g. characterologic self-defeating behaviours) in order to get better. In the foregoing pages I have described how in group psychotherapy a kind of confrontation can evolve that preserves self-esteem and is not damaging, but still succeeds in addressing the essential need for containment and transformation. During these years, I have formulated principles about how and why group treatments work (some of which I repeat here from previous publications):

• Groups are excellent forums to foster self-examination, especially in the domain of feelings, and the characterologic defences and behaviours that mask patients' feelings.

- Groups provide powerful antidotes for problems with self-esteem.
- Groups foster effective connection with others and facilitate a process to examine how and why individuals operate to make connection unlikely or impossible.
- Groups are extremely beneficial in helping individuals to face their behavioural dysregulation and their problems with self-care.
- Groups are contexts where people seeking help can be remarkably sensitive and sensible in meeting each other's needs.
- Groups are contexts in which it is very difficult to practise 'pretend and pretence'. That is, you might not know what you are feeling (even if you are acting as if you did), or you can posture and deny your vulnerability and act as if you are OK (when you are not), but in effective groups others will gently and supportively confront your denial and defences.

In writing this chapter, I realize that much of what I have said about group psychotherapy as a corrective for addictive vulnerability is equally true about 12-step programmes such as Alcoholics Anonymous (Khantzian 1995, Khantzian and Mack 1989, 1994). Nevertheless, the two perspectives do not, or need not, compete. For reasons which are explainable or not so explainable, patients have varying degrees of acceptance of different approaches. Self-help and psychotherapeutic groups have many similar and overlapping features, upon which I shall not elaborate here. I would only emphasize that under a trained group leader, group psychotherapy has certain advantages over 12-step programmes. I offer a partial list as follows:

- Group psychotherapy is more interactive.
- A group leader can actively maintain a needed focus.
- A group leader can more efficiently maintain the correct timing of needed interventions.
- A group leader can function to stimulate needed responses and contain and forestall disruptive or counterproductive interactions.
- A group leader can set limits on destructive or unacceptable group interactions.
- A group leader can both analyse and catalyse processes that help group members appreciate the reciprocal relationship between the distress they suffer, and their characterological defences, and how this interaction is intimately interwoven with their penchant to adopt the use of addictive substances and behaviours.
- A group leader can speak instructively, authoritatively, and if necessary, even charismatically, to draw attention to what a member or members need to hear to ensure their safety, sanity and sobriety.

Conclusion

Group psychotherapy is a corrective for addictive vulnerability because a human context is created for patients with substance use disorders to play out and re-enact their self-regulation problems with affects, self-esteem, relationships, and self-care, as well as the characterologic defences that disguise and betray them. Group leaders instil confidence and hope that our patients need not passively endure their vulnerabilities. As I have already mentioned, suffering is at the core of addictive vulnerability. The worst fate, however, is not simply to suffer. The worst fate is to suffer alone. Group members learn they can help each other actively identify and modify in self and others their tendency to be unaware, deny, or remain oblivious to their pain, suffering, and defences, and the costly nature of their addictive solutions.

CHAPTER 3

Alcoholics Anonymous: group therapy without the group therapist

MARTIN WEEGMANN

Alcoholics Anonymous (AA) is a remarkably robust and quietly persistent tradition, with a current membership of around 2 million in approximately 140 countries (see Emrick 2001). Evidence has shown the historical spreading of AA beyond the wealthiest, predominantly Protestant countries (the 'first wave') to Roman Catholic and newly industrialized countries, including those in Latin America, although no one knows what future patterns might emerge (see Makela 1991). The fellowship model addresses many other addictions (e.g. drugs, gambling) as well as compulsive securities/activities (e.g. 'co-dependency', overeating); Orford (1985) lists many of these fellowship organizations. As well as standard meetings of various kinds (e.g. open meetings, step meetings, beginners meetings), we have also seen the institutionalization of 12-step ideas in many rehabilitation centres over the decades, and the development of professional '12-step facilitation' approaches for people who have not previously used fellowship groups (on the latter, see Nowinski and Baker 1992). AA and recovery ideas have entered into modern culture, insofar as most people have some kind of image of AA. Substance misusers are no exception and when asked may express strongly negative or positive views of fellowship, although many simply say that they do not think it is for them but remain appreciative of its role for others. Perhaps one finds a similar range of reactions with professionals, although there is often a lack of real knowledge and sometimes of interest in how AA works (see Weegmann 2003a). Ten years after the inception of AA, the psychoanalyst Ernest Simmel (1948) paid tribute to an organization which he believed constituted a 'mass social experiment'; he was surely right about this and subsequently the experiment has become an established tradition.

In this chapter I shall identify some features of the historical landscape in the AA story, define the concept of fellowship, and explore the notion of AA as 'corrective group dialogue'. Within the latter notion, I shall draw on some contemporary psychodynamic and group dynamic models, but also make reference to empirical research on 'group climates' and differences between meetings. Finally, I shall provide some clinical illustrations around engaging reluctance and fears of AA and show how, as a result of myself learning more about fellowships, some of my own practice has changed. Yet mine remains, as it were, an 'outside view' in not being in recovery myself.

AA: the historical matrix

There are several elements to the AA story, which I shall simplify by dividing them into the spiritual or overtly religious aspects and the secular influences. The reader interested in detailed history and excavations of these origins of AA is referred to the excellent researches of Kurtz (1979), Blumberg (1977), and Trice and Staudenmeir (1989).

Before AA, there were a number of antebellum temperance movements in America, including (after 1840) the Washingtonians who set out to reach and reform drinkers. Amongst the core temperance values were hope, conversion experiences, and the role of mutuality, that in helping others the individual is also helped. Audiences in countless cities were enthused by the speeches of lecturers, telling the stories of their former behaviours and their present redemption. The Washingtonians inspired other groups, aiming at 'moral suasion', practising 'pledge taking' and providing group support for those embarking on abstinence. After the Civil War, institutions for inebriates began to spring up, legitimizing the alcoholic as deserving of assistance, and by 1902 there were in America around 100 inebriate treatment institutions, the precursors of modern-day hospital and rehabilitation facilities.

The movement for widespread Prohibition triumphed in the early twentieth century and signalled the demise of temperance societies. However, the early temperance *ideas* did not completely evaporate, but left an imprint in culture. Trice and Staudenmeier suggested that

> a cultural legacy persisted from these early efforts: the idea that alcoholics could be helped, that alcoholism was a disease, that people banding together could help each other maintain sobriety. This provided a fertile ground for the emergence of AA in this period of reduced alternatives following the repeal of national Prohibition. (1989, p 16)

There were, however, important distinctions between the temperance movements and AA, since the founders of AA were at pains to say that theirs was not a general moral campaign, nor were they against other people drinking. But perhaps both shared a common ancestor, that of protestant religious practice and belief (see Blumberg 1977).

The link to religion is an important one, since AA grew out of and then differentiated itself from the evangelical and non-denominational Oxford Movement. The Oxford Movement was the brainchild of Frank Buchman, a Lutheran minister who laid stress on the role of 'group confession' and the promotion of spiritual reconstruction, the so-called 'Changed Life'. Members came to identify with four absolutes: absolute honesty, absolute purity, absolute unselfishness, and absolute love, which were promoted through the use of group testimony, called 'sharing'. The term 'sharing' later entered the vocabulary of AA, where it came to refer to the act of speaking and identification at meetings. Another key element in the Oxford ideas was that of achieving peace through 'handing over to God' (or 'God control') and restitution through the making of amends for past wrongs or 'sins'. Again, the central importance of reparation or the making of amends was subsequently incorporated into the so-called 'middle steps' of the AA programme.

Two men who participated in the Oxford groups – Bill W., a stockbroker and Dr Bob, a surgeon – were to co-found AA. Although soon to depart from the Oxford model and to concentrate instead exclusively on helping fellow alcoholics, these men took some of the ideas with them, such as the practice of 'sharing experience', not preaching, with those drinkers with whom they were in contact. Bill W. (1949) was later to reflect

> For our purposes, the Oxford group atmosphere wasn't entirely right. Their demands for absolute moral rectitude encouraged guilt and rebellion. Either will get alcoholics drunk, and did. As non-alcoholic evangelists, they couldn't understand that. Good friends these, we owe them much. From them we have learned what, and what not to do.

In other words, the religiosity of the Oxford groups increasingly presented obstacles. Perhaps there was, in the soil of AA, an unknowing rediscovery of some of the practices of the Washingtonians with the gathering together of fellow drinkers to hear testimony as well the more conscious influence of the values of honesty and of commitments to change from the Oxford movement.

There are many well-researched aspects of spiritual dimension of the AA story, which I will not comment on, save to mention the following:

- the influence of the psychologist William James, whose *Varieties of Religious Experience* Bill W. had read and found helpful in making sense of his own 'conversion experience'
- the spiritual/ existential ideas of Carl Jung, for whom alcoholism was a 'spiritual disease' and who corresponded with Bill W.
- the inspiration of the Revd Samuel Shoemaker, one of the leaders in

the Oxford movement. Blumberg (1977) writes of the Shoemaker's influence on Bill W., 'in the formation of AA's ideas of self-examination, acknowledgment of character defects, restitution for harm done, and working with others' (p. 2134).

Hurvitz (1974), in his valuable exploration of the links between religion and emergent peer self-help psychotherapy groups (like AA), notes the original meaning of 'religion', coming from the Latin *ligare*. He notes, 'Re-ligion literally means a reconnection that can be achieved by confession and restitution' (p. 97).

Space prevents me from saying much about the secular influences on AA and so this is a somewhat arbitrary selection, beginning with the medical influences. A medical categorization of 'alcoholism', or of 'alcoholism as a disease' became part of the ideology of AA. A great deal of the influence here stemmed from Dr William Silkworth, physician-in-charge and medical superintendent of the Charles B. Towns Hospital in New York and doctor to Bill W. Silkworth helped to fashion a disease conception of alcoholism, counteracting moral views about the nature of drunkenness, and with it the importance of a *medical* justification of the need for abstinence. Silkworth helped Bill W. in other respects – by care, by patience, by directing his interest to William James's work, and by discouraging evangelizing attitudes towards other drinkers. Silkworth had sat through and helped Bill W. in coming to terms with his 'conversion' experience. Perhaps Bill W. himself best sums up the significance of Silkworth, saying of him,

> the benign little doctor who loved drunks. He supplied us with the tools with which to puncture the toughest alcoholic ego, those shattering phrases by which he described our illness: the *obsession of the mind* that compels us to drink and the *allergy of the body* that condemns us to go mad or die. (1957, p. 13)

My concern here is not to judge the objective veracity of these thoughts (which would involve a different kind of discourse), but a more pragmatic one of how a certain narrative structure came into being and how, from the point of view of its adherents, this enabled them to solve problems.

Other, non-alcoholic, professionals played their part. In 1949, the American Psychiatric Association invited Bill W. to address them, when he spoke of 'The Society of Alcoholics Anonymous'. The word 'society' was significant, referring not only to the 'organization' AA but the implicit need to think of oneself in terms of being part of a society (or fellowship) of recovering individuals. The event was chaired by Dr Harry Tiebout, AA's 'first friend in psychiatry' as Bill W. described him. Tiebout is a good example of professional prepared to learn from his patients, to transcend the received wisdom of his own training, when, as he put it, 'I joined AA by proxy in 1939 when a patient of mine became a member of the New

York group.' He would ask his few AA patients to detail their experiences of change, and later attended many meetings himself as an observer. We must not forget that the psychiatry and psychotherapy of the day contained its own prejudices and limitations, much set in a one-to-one model of persuasion, confrontation, and insight. Indeed, Chafetz and Demone (1962) have argued that 'because psychiatry and early psychotherapy failed the alcoholic, AA came into being' (p. 161). In a remarkable succession of papers, Tiebout (e.g. 1944, 1959) speculated on the therapeutic mechanisms of AA and the resultant instillation of hope for the individual in their building on sobriety. He emphasized four factors in particular: (1) the need to 'hit bottom' (signifying that an individual had reached a crisis, whereby he/she could no longer continue on a path that had been followed); (2) humility (so that the lessons of hitting bottom could be learned from and hence form part of the impetus for change); (3) surrender (the process of 'letting go', acknowledging unmanageability, which has a paradoxically freeing effect); and (4) ego reduction (some change in the narcissistic realm, allowing a real vulnerability to be accepted and with this the need for assistance from others). Tiebout was to observe that these ideas

> had never crossed my professional horizon and certainly had never influenced my nonprofessional thinking or attitudes. Revolutionary as they were, they nevertheless made sense and I found myself embarked on a tour of discovery. (1957, p. 247)

We have already mentioned William James, who helped to popularize pragmatism in philosophy. As I understand it, one of the projects of pragmatism was that of getting away from the big, universal philosophical problems and instead concentrating on the piecemeal tackling of more local problems, finding immediate solutions which enable one set of problems to be resolved or redefined. Charles Peirce, the grandfather of pragmatism, once described scientists as being 'communities of inquirers', much dependent on and influenced by the culture of their times. William James expressed one version of the pragmatist approach in his statement: 'A true idea is a projected map of experience that leads one to wherever one wants to go' (1907, p. 37). Perhaps in their efforts to localize the problems faced by certain drinkers (differentiating from religion, distinguishing organized religion from spirituality, addressing alcoholics and not all drinkers, distancing from temperance ideas) the founders of AA typified a form of pragmatism (see the discussion by Flores 1997). The founders were inquirers, then, trying to find new solutions for problem drinkers.

Consistent with being a form of pragmatism, I think that AA helped to articulate and to address existential dilemmas, particularly around identity formation and identity renegotiation, e.g. from 'drunkard' to 'recovering alcoholic'. In this regard, I am drawing attention to work developed in detail by Kurtz (1982), who analyses the links between existential philosophy and the ideas of AA, and that of Thune (1977) who looks at the phenomenology and story-telling/creating aspects of AA. Kurtz (1982) convincingly identifies some of the core aspects of AA's therapeutic dynamic, which stems from acknowledgement of shared vulnerability. One component of this vulnerability is the concept and process of acceptance of personal limitations, aspects of what one *cannot* do or *cannot* be. Yet greater freedom of choice can result from such acceptance. In the words of David, an AA member whom I saw in psychotherapy over two years

> AA taught me the old adage, 'pride goeth before a fall'. I used to think that I could out-drink anyone else and when I first came into AA I though I could out-recover everyone else – become an expert on alcoholism, that kind of thing. Now, I simply try to be grateful that I no longer drink and can manage my situation better than ever before. For me, the key thing is being honest, not bullshitting.

Perhaps this illustrates the paradoxical release that can accompany 'surrender' (the first steps of AA have been called the 'surrender steps'), eloquently stated by Brown:

> recovery involves relinquishing the core belief of power over self and accepting the reality of loss of control over one's drinking or use of substances . . . recovering alcoholics acknowledge that they have no power over alcohol and are, in turn empowered by the truth and their acceptance of it. (1993, p. 1138)

Kurtz, in his 1982 paper, goes on to talk about how AA constructs a certain vision of the human condition, but one focused on the alcoholic and acts to ameliorate shame and denial of need.

Thune (1977), similarly, through his observations of AA meetings, explores the existential dimension of how the programme invites reconstitution and redefinition of self and world. The vocabulary of AA constructs new possibilities of living ('living sober') and he rightly emphasizes the centrality of the 'life history' to this. Through the construction of life histories, the past is reinserted and previous thought and behavioural patterns are recontextualized. The individual is thus helped to identify possible reversions to 'old patterns', or 'relapses' of thinking and thereby encouraged to move forward, building on sobriety. I recall a member of Al-Anon explaining to me that when her partner stopped drinking, the bottom fell out of her life and she found herself without a familiar role to play. Through immersion in her programme, she began to reconstruct and to reconstrue, attempting to address her own needs for growth while being vigilant of reverting to familiar patterns with her now sober partner (e.g. automatically always putting his needs first). In his summary, Thune comments that

> AA's 'treatment' then, involves the systematic manipulation of symbolic elements within an individual's life to provide a new vision of that life, and of his world. This provides new coherence, meaning and implications for behaviour. (1977, p. 88).

Summary

AA was born within the cradle of a particular time in America; it benefited from the charisma and openness of its founder members, soon establishing itself as a credible approach to alcohol problems. Of the co-founders, perhaps Bill W. possessed the imagination and vision, whereas Dr Bob had a good eye on the present and the practical (see Dr Bob 1980). Yet many other individuals were involved, both alcoholics and non-alcoholic supporters. I have suggested that a set of creative compromises was achieved, a blending of influences, involving subtle but crucial shifts and which became incorporated into the organizational aspects of AA – the 12 traditions alongside the 12 steps of recovery. Among the traditions, for example, the decision that AA should not express views on any outside issues (tradition 10) was an attempt to safeguard AA from dogmatic opinion; likewise the idea that 'God' ('as we understand him') or a 'Higher Power' (as in step 2) should be left to individual interpretation was based on the wish to be as inclusive as possible, not to exclude on the basis of belief or background.

I have touched on some of the shifts that took place, for example the move from sin to sickness, from religion (e.g. of the Oxford groups) to spirituality, and the need for a compelling group way of life as an alternative to the drink way of life. In the words of Bill W. (1949), 'We like to think of AA a middle ground between medicine and religion, the missing catalyst of a new synthesis'. AA established a novel framework, a language of recovery and reconstruction which helped the individual drinker to make sense of suffering and hence to move forward (see Makela 1996; Weegmann 2003a).The largely unrevised language of AA still reflects the compromises of its birth, incorporating the different historical elements.

Leaderless groups: the fellowship concept

Stewart (1955) draws on Freud's group speculations as a springboard to understanding the concept of the 'We' in AA, that of fellowship. Freud (1921) wrote about groups with leaders and those without and, and in the case of the latter, an 'idea' or 'abstraction' is substituted for the leader with which the members identify. From the start, attenders of AA are encouraged to listen to the *similarities* rather than the differences between people (hence the slogan, 'principles not personalities'), to listen out for issues with which they can identify, and to concentrate on a common purposes – as AA articulate it, 'The only requirement for membership is a desire to stop drinking'. People might find themselves at their first meeting through a variety of routes: they may simply turn up at an open meeting, they may be in a detoxification or rehabilitation unit and be expected to attend, or a friend or professional may have recommended it to them. The fact that a person struggling with serious drink problems could attend at almost any stage of difficulty (from still being immersed in drinking, through the earliest days of being dry, to early, medium-, or longer-term sobriety) is testimony to the flexibility and practicality of AA. There is a culture of acceptance with the implied message that any person can be assisted no matter what they bring with them through the door. Ripley and Jackson put this well, when they comment about the shift of emphasis

> from a drink-centred situation to a people-and-relationship-centred one, from bemoaning problems to attempting to deal effectively with them. The emphasis is on assets and their utilization. (1959, p. 47)

Stewart (1955) proceeds to suggest that once members and newcomers to AA start to commit, acknowledging that 'alcoholism' is the common problem, strong attachments emerge to meetings, sponsors, and shared aspirations. 'The common goal, sobriety', he observes, 'and a complex of interpersonal forces [which] gain the admiration and devotion of the new member' (p. 252). In contradicting the notion that the self can be conceived in solitary terms, AA invites a kind of resocialization and breaks down barriers which may have prevented change from taking place or having been sustained previously, barriers such as shame, self-pity, exaggerated self-sufficiency, or aggressive repudiation of owning difficulties. It is here that the concept of the 'Higher Power' is significant, conceptualized as a crucial resource in dealing with the power of alcohol(ism). From the start, this concept was opened to the individual's interpretation, though clearly some of the theistic origins of AA are evident in the language of the steps. In my psychotherapy with patients committed to AA, NA, or AlAnon, some of the interpretations of 'Higher Power' encountered (I always ask) were as follows: the AA group itself, a Christian God, a Buddhist concept of 'Good', 'friends and family', 'a simple picture in my mind of how I used to look and how I look now', 'all the nurses and services which have helped me so far', 'the words "sobriety" and "sanity"', or, in the words of a patient encouraging another to consider visiting AA, 'don't be put off by the word "God", it can mean anything from "Groups-of-Drunks" to something sublime like, "Guidance–Order–Direction"'. This, then, is a form of bringing people into affiliation, a sociotherapy not individual therapy, even though the individual is helped as a result. In a passage that could link some of the existential themes discussed previously and the ideas of humility/surrender explored by Tiebout, Stewart describes the fellowship or 'we-ness' process succinctly:

> To be a person, or to try to be, is to recognize a sense of incompleteness which needs to be compensated in fellowship. And fellowship, fostering respect for the other as for oneself, seems to flourish best in the mutual recognition of a power greater than any or all of the group members. (1955, p. 255)

AA: corrective group dialogue?

The views I develop in this section are the product of three influences:

- clinical experience with many individuals who were both using (sometimes very identified with) AA or other fellowships while being treated in professional psychotherapy, individual as well as group
- 2-year observations by the author of an open AA meeting (mainly concentrated on one meeting)
- a growing tradition of psychodynamic and integrative theory, which has attempted to conceptualize the process of change and group processes within fellowship groups (e.g. Yalom 1974, Mack 1981, Khantzian 1994a, Robinson 1996, Flores 1997).

I shall use a vignette as a springboard for my observations and reflections. Here, and elsewhere, I have used composite examples and concentrated on general themes, in order to preserve anonymity.

> *A meeting began with a reading from* As Bill Sees It *(Bill W, 1967), which addresses depression. Amongst the ideas which the chair spoke to were those identified in the passage – the pressures of 'all or nothing' thinking, the drive to try to resolve all one's life problems in one go, thus setting oneself up for disappointments or a crashing sense of defeat. The chair quoted, 'Don't be disconcerted by setbacks – just start over'. There was an element of suffering, irony and humour mixed into the story. During the sharing (when people bring in their own issues, related to their identification with the chair), there was a good deal of approbation and admiration of the chair's honesty. Others too experienced depressive bouts and imposed unrealistic demands on themselves. There was further agreement, that putting down the bottle in itself was merely a precondition for wider change and that the meeting could help people to deal with their*

emotional lives. As one person put it, using similar ideas to those of Bill W., 'the real problems for us are in the mind, not the body'. Several people thanked the chair for having spoken to issues relevant to them and that they had been glad they has resisted temptations not to attend and not to connect with others earlier in the day.

My own observations were as follows. Initially, I was struck by the *content* of what the chair was saying and that, although the language of Bill W. sounded old-fashioned in places, there were some striking parallels with cognitive approaches to depression and polarities of thinking. This reinforced my impression of the role of *common processes* between different therapies, in this example, cognitive-behavioural ideas around how individuals think themselves into corners or traps (see Weegmann's 2003b discussion of this aspect).

Next, I was struck by the process of identification with the chair and the *resonance* with certain themes. Initially, some people seemed surprised but pleased that something they had not expected to hear about (depression) was being addressed and that some of the shame and avoidance that was associated with it was openly discussed. At least two people, for example, confessed to not having wanted to attend earlier in the day but could see in themselves an avoidant pattern, the wish to stay in bed, not thinking others would be of benefit to them. Perhaps inferiority feelings came in, thinking of themselves as less than others, or the converse, that others could teach them nothing. However, through attending they had reconnected to others and to an aspect of themselves – they felt less alienated as a result. This reminded me of the emphasis within AA philosophy that alcoholism is seen as a 'lonely business' and that the alcoholics before recovery are seen as being unable to form productive partnerships. The group seemed to provide the context within which some coming together and restoration of hope could take place. Indeed, at a wider level, Ripley and Jackson (1959) refer to AA's provision of a 'consistent, integrated milieu' (p. 44).

A further dimension at this and many other meetings was the kind of *lateral insight* created by the sharing process. Although sharing begins with the chair as prompt, there is also a spreading, amplifying, or circling effect, with people taking and adding to the group dialogue. Not all the talk, for example, was of depression. One person felt able to distinguish sadness from depression, which encouraged her, while another brought in a crisis and the quite different feelings aroused by it. Having the same illness, as it were, does not mean that people will have the same experiences. I would suggest that an important component of the AA is that it helps individuals to resocialize, to engage in sober (reflective) dialogue and, hopefully, to increase tolerance – of self and of others – as a result. Commitment to the meetings, acceptance of the need to be helped, serving others ('doing service'), having something or someone more powerful than oneself, can all assist in the process. The listening process is essential to this (e.g. the idea of 'open your ears before you open your mouth') as is the decreasing of a 'first person' point of view, meaning the problematic narcissism or egocentric stance of the drinker. Khantzian and Mack (1994) have looked in some detail at how AA addresses so-called 'character defects', ameliorates excessive defences and offers possibilities for a transformation of the self.

A final observation concerned the way in which the meeting helped individuals to speak about (to identify) a particular emotion (in this case, depression), to make some sense of it (e.g. the cognitive element) and to communicate a sense that it could be contained and thus rendered less destructive (a psychodynamic element). Some could then begin to distinguish affects, such as that of sadness versus depression, self-pity versus self-sympathy. Years of drug and alcohol misuse have devastating consequences for an individual's emotional life, leading, as examples, to a narrowed range or simplification of affect (e.g. leaving an angry individual), a blunting of more subtle affects, stunted sensitivity to affective signals, and so on. Many people have commented on the consequences this can have, the difficulties it creates in terms of the 'governance' of the self (e.g. Mack 1981), and what Khantzian (2002) has aptly phrased 'disuse atrophy' in terms of knowing and being able to contain one's emotions. I end this section by underlining some of Khantzian's (1994a,b) many valuable insights. One the one hand, AA helps to tackle the negative side of the struggling drinker: 'not showing, not contacting, not persisting, not asking, not feeling, and not knowing' (p. 163). On the other hand, it creates a novel, positive resource:

> the narrative traditions of storytelling, sharing, and bearing witness to each other's distress, and the traditions of openness and honestly act as sources of comfort and support for people who otherwise would go on in their lives with their distress unnoticed, unspoken and unacknowledged (p. 165).

The tenor of Khantzian's views are clearly positive ones and it would involve an extended discussion to consider the more negative side of the coin – for example, how a particular narrative approach can limit how an individual is able to construe the world or experiences of dogmatism within groups.

Group climates

There are many other aspects to AA, and space precludes me from being able to address them. But one dimension which might strike the reader, in my appreciatory tone, is that of the variability of meetings and about what happens when an AA story becomes less than tolerant. It is important to acknowledge that styles of meeting and interpretations of fellowship do vary considerably across cultures, as amply illustrated by Makela's (1996) study of AA in six countries, and so one cannot assume the homogeneity of AA. From patients, I have heard reports of meetings that were sympathetic to other approaches (like psychotherapy), whereas others were anti-therapy or distrustful of professional services. Perhaps some of these attitudes echo earlier rivalries and misgivings (and sometimes plain ignorance) between the self-help world of fellowship groups and the professional world (see Weegmann 2003a). Some of my patients have complained about meetings dominated by a small number of people with only one message to transmit; another contrasted the quieter, reflective style of meetings he had known in one country (which he found comfortable) with the more evangelical and celebratory mood of meetings in another country (which he found off-putting). I have known some drug addicts to prefer AA because of the relatively older membership (and longer collective experience of abstinence), and a drinker prefer Narcotics Anonymous (NA) because of its more youthful, dynamic appeal. One patient felt that whether it was NA or AA was immaterial, since he identified himself as 'addict', saying that for him it was distinguishing between drugs (and alcohol being a drug) that had got him into trouble. Then, of course, even within one fellowship like AA, there are specialist groups, e.g. for newcomers, gays, people with dual diagnosis, and so on. Reactions to these can vary, however; one gay patient felt Gay AA to be the most positive group going, whereas another disliked the overemphasis on similarities when he once attended.

Montgomery, Miller and Tonigan (1991), in their empirical study, looked at four different AA groups in a southwestern US city, using a version of the Group Environment Scale (Moos 1986). Groups did have some common elements (e.g. all groups encouraged spirituality and discouraged innovation), but in other respects (e.g. degree of cohesiveness and degree of anger or aggression expressed) differed considerably. They conclude that, 'Group processes and atmosphere may differ, and members may vary considerably across groups on personality or cognitive characteristics that have been regarded as "typical" of AA members' (p. 503). Tonigan, Ashcroft and Miller (1995), in a similar study, showed how three AA groups differed in perceived social dynamics, group emphasis on the 12 steps of AA, and completion of the 12 steps. They suggest that perhaps future research may help to clarify what aspects of meetings and programme characteristics might serve particular individuals better, and why.

Resistance and reluctance to AA

As there are countless pathways into an addiction, so too there can be many routes into recovery. Of course, the term 'recovery' is itself a construct whose meaning will vary according to the values of the user or the professional. In this regard, I have found it possible to work productively with strongly anti-AA patients as much as with strongly committed AA members. Most of the people I have treated are not critical of fellowship groups, but do not personally use them. This is no more than one might expect; after all, Bill W. (1949) acknowledged, 'We of AA try to be aware that we may never touch but a segment of the total alcohol problem'. However, as a result of observing AA meetings and researching their oral and written traditions, I have become more proactive in encouraging patients to try fellowship meetings and more keen to engage with them when they express negative reactions. This is because I have hopefully learned to become more receptive myself to a world which I had not encountered in my training as a psychologist and about which, in spite of specializing in the addictions, I had scant understanding. Since I have in a separate publication (Weegmann 2003a) looked at *helpful* marriages and confluences between individuals in psychotherapy and AA, I shall here share some examples of reluctance or dislike.

The man who questioned his own views

During a community meeting on a detoxification ward, a man stated a not unfamiliar view that 'AA meetings made me depressed, in fact, made me feel like drinking'. Another patient, who had used NA, questioned him, saying 'maybe you were too much into your drinking at the time, so you couldn't take it in'. I encouraged others to share their experiences, if any, of fellowship groups and I asked the first man how long ago he had attended, and how many meetings. He said, 'a couple, maybe more, a good ten years ago'. I restated his response and asked him to now estimate the number of drinks he might have had during this time, which made him laugh with irony and shifted the tone of the discussion away from criticism of AA. Later, he spoke of having only two friends who were sober, one of whom had used AA throughout. 'How would you describe them as people, what are they like now that they are living sober?', I asked. He was positive and paid tribute to their quietly supportive presence, saying either would help him if he remained off the drink. This was useful, since it confirmed the fact that (a) recovery was possible, that (b) people might take different paths into recovery and (c), as he put it at the end of the meeting, 'it's the drinking that's really depressing. I'm sure one of my mates would be happy to take me to some meetings to try – in fact he's already offered'.

Ian: an issue of fear of groups

Ian was struggling, but managing to sustain abstinence in his first six months, angry that life was presenting him many obstacles. I tried to understand his anger, centred on disappointments with abstinence and frustrations with others (see Weegmann and Kavatha (forthcoming) for a discussion of the role of anger or rage in recovery). Fellowship groups had not been mentioned, but when I took the initiative to bring them in I was struck by his contempt. 'They are for weaklings, people who like to be told how to think, who let groups take them over', he responded. We discussed the strength of his reaction and the fact that he had no first-hand experience. In the transference, he grew suspicious that my exploration signified *my* wish that he should commit to AA. The subject disappeared for some time, but when we had looked at his negative ex-periences in most groups since childhood (at school, being bullied, and some negative work experiences with groups) I began to understand his aversion to AA groups differently. I returned and drew a link between his actual experiences and his reaction to my mention of a group, drawing attention to his image of the victim, the 'weakling' and about the defences of self-sufficiency he had built up through his drinking. We could then dis-cuss AA in less dramatic terms and I shared with him my understanding of how it might work, inviting him to visit a couple of times to make up his own mind. Although agreeable, he subsequently declined, thinking that it would not be for him. Six months later, however, during a long summer break from therapy, he said that if he found himself in difficulty, he 'could always give AA a phone'. The idea of the phone was more amenable to him than attending a meeting, as it increased his sense of control. I have no idea whether he ever did use the phone.

Sally: drifted away

Sally had discovered NA with great enthusiasm, having overcome her ini-tial fears of a 'religious group'. She had enjoyed the atmosphere of acceptance, warmth, and the fact that it helped to put her drug problems into a perspective. She was 'clean' for a prolonged period and then became involved and readdicted to drugs. She dropped NA immediately and rarely referred to it. A year later, others in her therapy group (she was by now clean again) explored the reasons why she had not returned to NA. Surprisingly, she said, 'it hadn't occurred to me' and I homed in on the apparent loss of emotional or semantic memory: she could remember meetings and acknowledge that they helped, but it sounded as though she were a different person now from the one who used to attend. It seemed that although at one level she could be appreciative of NA's role, she could not reconnect with it as a current resource for reasons I was not entirely sure of. Interestingly, although Sally did not hesitate to recommend NA to others, I sensed her fear of returning and of the process of recommitment. On a more theoretical level, Rudy and Greil (1987) have analysed the sociology of commitment to AA meetings, and refer to the 'commitment funnel' of escalating investments which arise through involvement. Perhaps getting back in felt too daunting for Sally, as well as facing her with the reality of relapse and dropping out.

These illustrations point to, among other things, the diversity of experience of fellowship groups, but also to the importance of engaging interest in such reactions, whether they are positive, negative, or unsure. I have, as a result of learning about AA culture, been more proactive in inviting discussion of the ideas during sessions and facilitate engagement in meetings for those individuals who are willing to try. It has also increased, I trust, my own humility and willingness to explore the patient's experiential world with more tools at my disposal. Professional colleagues who have joined me on observations have shared this sense of humility.

Conclusions

I have described some aspects of AA history and traced elements of the fellowship idea, suggesting that such a tradition creates new language and challenges the existing assumptive world of the problem drinker. In many ways we could look on AA as a folk experiment, and see that different climates and emphases have developed in different contexts and countries. This in itself is not surprising and the same variations in conception and culture would apply to, say, professional group psychotherapy. Although there are many alternative paths to recovery, the AA/fellowship path offers one with a high level of coherency. This might be its main strength, but to others a weakness. On the other hand, the founders of AA knew that they would only ever attract a possibly small proportion of problem drinkers. In the clinical examples, I have suggested some approaches to engaging the reluctant patient without falling into the trap of implying 'only AA or fellowship will help you'.

CHRISTER SANDAHL, MONICA BUSCH, EVA SKARBRANDT, AND PETER WENNBERG

CHAPTER 4
Matching group therapy to patients' needs

There are many good reasons why group therapy is a viable treatment modality for patients who are dependent on alcohol or drugs. In our experience, one argument that is seldom mentioned relates to the well-being of the treatment providers. Working with addicts is very demanding, especially with patients who have a dual diagnosis of substance abuse and, for example, personality disorder. In clinical work, much time and energy is spent on this group of patients. One has to cope with strong feelings and sudden changes in mood; fear, hate, mistrust, destructiveness, provocation and desperate acting-out, feelings of worthlessness, and an almost insatiable longing for closeness and care. No wonder that workers in this field are considered to be at high risk of occupational health problems.

From this standpoint, one can argue that it is good to offer group therapy, for the well-being not only of the patients but also for the staff. It is a common clinical experience that in a group one can avoid many of the difficult issues that are focused on in a one-to-one treatment relationship. The group offers multiple transference opportunities apart from the therapist: the institution, the group in itself, and the individual group members. The risk of the therapist being trapped in role-locks is considerably lower in group therapy than in individual work (Mosse and Lysaght 2002). After more than 10 years with analytically oriented group therapy for this patient group, with a good structure and a holding environment for the groups, our experience has been that the work is rewarding, resulting in change for the patients and often dramatically increased dignity. For the therapists, there have been many moving moments as well as some lighter ones.

In a study where individual therapy for patients with borderline personality disorder was compared with group therapy, Marziali and Munroe-Blum (1994) found that the two treatments were equally effective from the patients' point of view. The group therapy was naturally more cost-effective, but, more importantly, the therapists were more satisfied with their work with the patients in the therapy groups. In spite of the fact that the patients had similar problems, they felt it was easier to be empathic with the patients they met in group therapy.

Not all patients with addiction problems are as demanding as the duel-diagnosis group described, but it can sometimes be equally frustrating to work with patients who have less severe problems. One needs a long-term perspective and the ability to see the recovery as a process which includes relapses, breaks in the therapeutic alliance, etc. The group as such can provide the reliability and predictability that creates a secure base for treatment. In the group setting the patients themselves can often balance tolerance and limit-setting in a less ambivalent way than an individual therapist could. Using the group as a treatment instrument, the therapist often feels more competent and successful. This heightens self-esteem, which in turn positively influences judgment. We believe that group treatment, used systematically within a treatment programme, will help the treatment providers to avoid getting stuck in vicious circles. There is no reason to believe that such an approach will be more effective than individual therapy, but all research indicates that the outcome of treatment will be just as good.

Much of this chapter focuses on a model of working with severely addicted patients with personality disorder. Two of us (Busch and Skarbrandt) have clinical experience of more than 200 such patients in group analytic psychotherapy. We believe that the observations made, and what has been learned over the years, can be valuable for many clinicians within the field. Before going deeper into this subject, however, we should like to place it in a wider context.

Group therapy in stepped care

A group approach to treatment does not imply that the patients have no individual contacts. On the contrary, all treatment for drug or alcohol addiction must be based on individual contacts, with someone taking responsibility for monitoring and supporting abstinence. This may be a mental health worker, a doctor, a nurse, a psychologist, a social worker, or a function of being a member of AA or similar organization. Group treatment is for those patients who both need and want something more than regular social support and psychopharmacological or other forms of medication to facilitate abstinence.

What patients need is not always obvious and is sometimes contrary to what they want at a particular moment. It is our experience that a prerequisite for success is an individualized approach, adjusted to the specific characteristics of each patient and his or her dynamic relationship to the drugs of addiction. At first, this might seem to contradict a group approach, but not if one thinks both in terms of different types of group treatment and in terms of how the individual treatment goal is formulated. Patients in the same group can work towards different goals. It is important that the patient, the therapist and the rest of the group are aware of the different individual objectives. An optimal starting point for treatment is that each patient has as realistic a view as possible of what can be achieved with the treatment, and also of what is expected of them. To arrive at the point where group treatment can begin is a process that takes time.

People come into treatment in different phases of life and at different stages of dependency. The likelihood that one can help them with minimal interventions is very high if they come into treatment early, before any serious health or social problems have occurred. Employee assistance programmes, occupational health, alcohol check-ups, and similar approaches serve the purpose of identifying people in the risk zone and preventing the development of more serious problems. Other patients with established substance abuse problems may have been in treatment many times before, sometimes even with other psychiatric diagnoses. Irrespective of background, committing oneself to treatment is usually connected to some kind of life crisis. At the same time, the spectrum of the presenting problems and patient characteristics is obviously very wide. Patients entering treatment represent different populations and different phases of dependency. Naturally one has to adjust the interventions to each individual. This conclusion seems to be self-evident from a clinical perspective, but the outcome of treatment research has made it necessary to question it.

Until the publication of the results from Project MATCH (Project MATCH Research Group 1997) it was generally understood that a treatment–patient interaction effect was to be expected. The major finding from Project MATCH was, however, that matching patients to treatments added little benefit to outcome results. This project was an 8-year multi-site trial with a total of 1726 patients. Only one of 16 matching hypotheses was confirmed; i.e. patients with few or no psychological problems had significantly more abstinent days during follow-up with a treatment based on the 12-step model compared to cognitive-behavioural treatment. It should be pointed out that all three treatment models in Project MATCH (12-step facilitation, cognitive-behavioural treatment, and motivational enhancement therapy) were based on one-to-one sessions between patients and therapists, and none on psychodynamic theory. It is therefore important, despite the results of Project MATCH, to keep an open mind with regard to other possible patient–treatment matches.

There are in fact some contradictory results. Within the field of alcoholism treatment research, two randomized controlled outcome studies have unexpectedly reported differential treatment outcomes for different patient categories in two forms of group psychotherapy. In one study, positive outcome effects were found both for coping skills, and interactional aftercare group treatment for alcohol-dependent patients (Kadden et al. 1989). However, an interaction effect was demonstrated: patients who scored high on measures of sociopathy or global psychopathology had better outcomes in coping skills treatment, whereas patients low on these dimensions had better outcomes in interactional group psychotherapy. A similar pattern was observed when the same patients were categorized into two subtypes. This typology seems to be clinically relevant and has been referred to frequently (Babor et al. 1992, Schuckit et al. 1995). Patients with later onset of problem drinking, less familial alcoholism, lower degree of dependence on alcohol, and fewer symptoms of antisocial personality (type A) had better outcomes in interactional group treatment and fared less well in coping skills group treatment. On the other hand, patients of type B (earlier onset, more familial alcoholism, higher degree of dependency, and more symptoms of antisocial personality) did better in coping skills group treatment and less well in interactional group therapy (Litt et al. 1992, Allen and Kadden 1995).

In another study (Sandahl et al. 1998), alcohol-dependent patients from time-limited cognitive-behavioural group treatment and from psychodynamic group treatment had both improved both shortly after the end of treatment and at the 18-month follow-up. The patients in this study were moderately alcohol dependent and comparatively low on psychopathology. Shortly after the end of treatment no difference was found between the treatment approaches. However, most of the patients in the psychodynamic group treatment were able to maintain a more positive drinking pattern during the whole follow-up period, unlike the patients in the cognitive-behavioural treatment group, who seemed gradually to deteriorate (see Figure 4.1). The effect size was 1.19 for the psychodynamic treatment and 0.52 for the cognitive-behavioural group. The difference was statistically significant in a repeated measures ANOVA.

In this study it seemed that in the long run the psychodynamic group treatment was more effective for the type A patient group. In an earlier study (Sandahl and Rönnberg 1990), we found that a cognitive-behavioural group treatment approach (relapse prevention) had positive outcomes for a group with more severe problems.

The conclusion is that more research is needed, and that it would be unwise to abandon the matching hypothesis at this stage. One of the big mistakes with Project MATCH was that a psychodynamic treatment alternative, which some data and clinical experience seem to support as the treatment of choice for patients with less severe problems (type A), was not included. Some evidence also suggests that female patients are better able to take advantage of this type of treatment (Sandahl et al. 1998). In

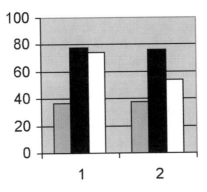

Figure 4.1 Outcome in terms of number of days of abstinence in the preceding 3 months for patients (1) in psychodynamic short-term group treatment (5 groups, n = 25) and (2) in cognitive-behavioural relapse prevention (5 groups, n = 24). Grey bars, before treatment; black bars, at 6-months follow-up; white bars, at 18-months follow-up.

this chapter we report on long-term analytically oriented group therapy, with a satisfying outcome, for severely addicted patients (more similar to type B). About 60 per cent of the patients taking part in this intervention were women, who also seemed to improve most as a result of the treatment, at least as measured by the Beck Depression Index.

On the basis of these preliminary findings we believe that it is clinically wise, in planning treatment for the individual patient, to make a distinction between two broad categories: the severely dependent patients with a higher degree of psychopathology and the less severely dependent with fewer signs of psychopathology (types A and B).

Decision to change (step 2)

When the patient has entered treatment, plenty of time should be devoted to the assessment of treatment needs. It is our experience that the assessment process in itself helps patients to better understand their treatment needs, and to become more realistic about personal goals. If the motivational interviewing approach (Miller and Rollnick 1991) is used, where results from questionnaires and other data are presented in a factual and non-judgemental way, patients become involved in the process and can formulate treatment goals that they feel to be their own and which are specific and adjusted to their own situation. Helping the patients to become clear about what they need and want from treatment, apart from being free from drugs or alcohol, can also help them to understand how they too must contribute to the treatment process. Nothing will be achieved if they expect somebody else to solve their problems. It is also helpful to see that, in the long run, abstinence is a prerequisite for working with one's whole psychological and social life situation.

Many patients have problems involving issues of authority, and find it difficult to internalize good experiences with parental figures. This is one reason why it is important to let the patients gradually discover and decide for themselves what kind of goal they want to have in relation to their substance misuse. It could be regarded as a kind of 'meta-learning' for the patient to co-operate with a therapist who reinforces the patient's use of their own judgment and the responsibility for their own choices. Irrespective of treatment condition, the patients should be supported in making personal choices regarding treatment goals. The goal of total abstinence should of course be supported when a patient chooses it, but not stated as a condition for treatment. The important thing is that a treatment goal is openly formulated and agreed. If it turns out that it does not function, it can later be changed.

Abstinence can be achieved by, for example, joining AA, or by seeing a doctor, mental health worker, or social worker regularly. It is our experience that short-term relapse prevention groups are a valuable support in this process. However, even at this stage the offer of different approaches for the subpopulations of patients is to be recommended.

On the basis of our preliminary research findings, we suggest a modified stepped care model for group therapy (see Figure 4.2). The idea is to

Step 1 Ambivalence	Step 2 Decision to change		Step 3 Coping with relapse	Step 4 Maintenance
Reactions from family or at workplace, employee assistance programme, alcohol check-up etc. Crisis	*Assessment* *Motivational enhancement*	Mild and moderate degree of dependence, relatively low degree of psychopathology (type A)	*Psychodynamic short-term group treatment*	*Outpatient psychodynamic group psychotherapy (heterogeneous groups)*
		Severe dependence, high degree of psychopathology (type B)	*Cognitive or cognitive behavioural group relapse prevention*	*Psychodynamic group psychotherapy for the demanding patients (homogeneous in terms of psychopathology)*
Outpatient clinic or other agency (e.g. AA, GP, or occupational health) supporting abstinence or controlled drinking (in the case of mildly and some moderately alcohol-dependent patients)				

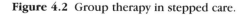

Figure 4.2 Group therapy in stepped care.

integrate, with the stepped care model (Wanigaratne and Keaney 2002) a simple matching hypothesis based on severity of substance abuse and psychopathology.

Treatment conditions in relapse prevention (step 3)

The aim of relapse prevention is to reduce substance misuse, including a reduction of frequency and intensity of relapses. For most patients, the long-term goal is to become drug free, but all experience tells us that relapse is a part of the recovery. We therefore recommend that treatment providers should maintain a factual and non-judgmental attitude to such events. The treatment goal is that the patient can learn from the experience. In this phase of the treatment, relapse prevention can offer the patients models for understanding and dealing with high-risk situations for relapse in such a way that further misuse can be avoided. We have positive experiences of both cognitive-behavioural and psychodynamic approaches of working with such a focus in short-term group psychotherapy.

Psychodynamic short-term treatment

Our clinical work in this area was developed within the theoretical frame of group analysis. Group analytic psychotherapy has much in common with interactional therapies, since it focuses on interaction and communication. European group analytically oriented therapists are somewhat less directive than American group psychotherapists, and would probably not make a point of reinforcing the expression of feelings. According to Getter et al. (1992), two activities believed to be important for interactional therapies – exploring/expressing feelings and here-and-now focus – were negatively correlated with the percentage of reportedly problem-free group members in the above-mentioned study of short-term therapies. The 'European' attitude might, in other words, be an advantage in groups of alcohol-dependent patients.

Apart from reducing the intensity and frequency of relapse, the purpose of the treatment is to increase self-knowledge and a sense of self, to allow the patients to be able to reflect on their actions and avoid being the victim of their own affects and impulses. As in long-term groups, the instructions to the patients is to try to speak of whatever comes into their mind and possibly to communicate with one another.

The therapeutic attitude may be summarized as follows:

- The therapist accepts all communication, but does not direct the group members; he or she uses verbal methods to guide the group.

- The relationship that the group members develop to each other and towards the therapist is the object for communication and analysis.
- The therapist is non-manipulative in his or her reactions, and takes transference into consideration when treating interpersonal relations.

Common themes in time-limited psychodynamic treatment for alcohol-dependent patients (which is the group we have most experience with in this type of treatment) are related to drinking pattern, drinking history, high-risk situations and relapse, relations at work and in family, memories of family of origin and, to a lesser extent, dream material and feelings in the here and now. The themes are to be discussed in a free-floating, unstructured way, one theme suddenly merging into another without any conscious effort from the therapist to control the process. The main task of the therapist is to help patients talk to each other as openly as the situation allows.

A time-limited group analytical psychotherapy for a group of patients with the same diagnosis is a contradiction in terms for a group analyst, who would normally tend to mix patients with different diagnoses and keep them in treatment for a couple of years at least. The idea, however, is to adapt group analytic principles to this different setting to create a treatment focusing on communication between group members (Sandahl, Lindgren and Herlitz 2000).

During therapy, many patients realize that they need and want more psychotherapy. Some patients prefer to continue in individual psychotherapy, but many feel that the experience of a therapeutic group was good. We recommend them to continue in any form of psychodynamic group psychotherapy for mixed groups, at the same time maintaining contact with the primary treatment provider (AA, family doctor, or similar). In this context we shall not go further into how to run long-term groups with one or two group members with a substance abuse problem. We consider this to be part of regular group psychotherapy practice.

Cognitive-behavioural relapse prevention

The theoretical model we use is based on Marlatt's work on relapse prevention (Marlatt and Gordon 1985). The clinical application in a group format was further developed and tested by Sandahl and Rönnberg (1990). The main purpose of this treatment is to strengthen self-efficacy in situations with a high probability of relapse. According to social learning theory (Bandura 1977), self-efficacy can be reinforced by focusing on cognitions and behaviours related to stimuli that precede relapse. These include:

- identification and analysis of high-risk situations for drinking

- assessment and training of coping skills as alternative strategies to relapse in risky situations
- assessment of, and working through, cognitive factors such as expectancies and decision-making.

In this highly structured programme (which includes problem-solving, interpersonal skills, skills for coping with both positive and negative moods, urges to drink, and situations of high risk for relapse), the therapists use didactic presentations, coping skills training within group sessions, and homework assignments.

Naturally, the therapists encourage discussion among the group members, at the same time being fairly active and goal-oriented, preventing the discussion from departing from the main theme for the session (which the therapist has decided). Therapist interventions usually focus on one patient at a time, rather than on relationship patterns and the group dynamics as a whole, which would be appropriate in psychodynamic treatment. For further information about the cognitive-behavioural approach within a psychodynamic framework, we recommend an excellent introduction by Wanigaratne and Keaney (2002).

Group psychotherapy for demanding patients (step 4)

Some empirical data

During 1993–2000, patients referred to the psychotherapy team at the Addiction Centre in Stockholm were included in a research project. This was in order to describe the group therapy process on an aggregate level and to evaluate the effects of the therapy provided. Three issues of specific interest from this project are illustrated here:

- a description of the patients referred to this form of treatment with respect to their personality profiles
- the development of depression during the psychotherapy process
- factors predicting premature dropout from the therapy.

The sample

The investigated sample comprised 219 individuals referred to psychodynamic group therapy because of a history of substance-abuse problems in conjunction with some form of personality disorder. A tentative estimation showed that 39 per cent used alcohol as their primary drug, 14 per cent illicit drugs, and 24 per cent legally prescribed drugs. In 23 per cent of the cases it was not possible to distinguish a primary drug because of missing data or because the person's problem was not severe enough to render a label of substance abuse. The mean age was 39 years (range 20–69 years) and 50 per cent of the sample were female.

A comparison was made between the sample referred to psychodynamic group therapy and a normal control sample (n = 212) with respect to their personality profiles. This comparison showed that the therapy sample showed substantially lower levels of extraversion, but higher levels of neuroticism and impulsiveness, after controlling for gender and age. Generally, extraversion and impulsiveness are traits that are often associated, as the concept of extraversion includes both a social component and an impulsive component. However, in this psychotherapy sample patients tended to be impulsive but without the social component that often goes with it.

Development of depression during treatment

To describe the development of depression during the treatment, a sub-sample of 100 patients with complete data were followed from inclusion to 18 months in therapy. The choice of depression as the outcome measure was made in the belief that it would provide a global measure of the person's psychological health, with strong negative correlations to other measures of psychological health. Every six months the patients used the Beck Depression index (BDI) to rate their level of depression.

For the sample as a whole there was a decrease in the level of depression from inclusion, but this decrease was substantially larger among women than men (see Figure 4.3). Furthermore, most of the improvement

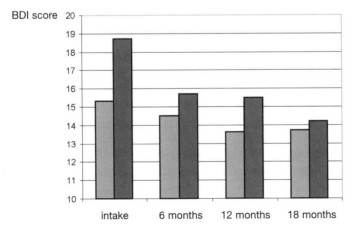

Figure 4.3 The development of depression (BDI scores) for men (n = 48, light bars) and women (n = 52, dark bars) during the group therapy process.

in depression occurred in the first six months in therapy. The improvement for depression after 18 months in therapy correspond to effect sizes of 0.42 for women and 0.17 for men. For patients with more severe depression (> 10 points on the BDI at inclusion; n = 70) the level of improvement for the whole sample was about 0.50 SD.

Premature dropout

Patients were included in a study focusing on premature dropout if they had either terminated the therapy prematurely or terminated the therapy in accordance with an initial contract set up between the therapist and the patient. An analysis was conducted of pre-therapy factors that differentiate between later dropouts and patients completing therapy.

In general, differences between therapy dropouts and completers were modest. However, subjects who dropped out of therapy showed slightly greater difficulties in handling frustration, had a more distorted body image, felt more needed by others, and reported higher levels of phobic anxiety. However, it should be emphasized that the differences were too small be used as a basis for screening and inclusion.

Clinical work

We shall describe a model that has been developed during the past 10–15 years in clinical practice by the psychotherapy team at the Addiction Centre in Stockholm. The team had the task of offering group analytic psychotherapy to patients with substance abuse and a dual diagnosis of personality disorder. At the Addiction Centre, the group psychotherapy offered by the team is considered to be an alternative relatively late in the treatment process (step 4). The patients must have been free from drugs for at least 3–6 months. Except for 10 slow-open groups (i.e. groups where patients terminate individually and new members are introduced to the group one or two at a time) the team also offers a group for female patients, young adults, families of substance-misusing patients, and children of parents with addiction problems.

The patients are referred from other departments of the Addiction Centre, psychiatric clinics, family doctors, social welfare, etc. The policy is to ask the referring agency to retain responsibility for the medical treatment. Necessary medication, extra social support, detoxification, or acute need of hospitalization is administered by the referring agency.

Fear of the group

Initially, most people prefer individual psychotherapy. For many people, especially in this patient group, a group is seen as something frightening to be avoided. What they would like is a kind, grey-haired woman therapist, with a lot of warmth, on whom they could place all their problems and from then on live a less burdened life. It takes time for patients to realize that therapy is something that will demand effort and at times give pain.

It is possible to convey to the patients that a group can in fact be warm and accepting, able to demonstrate and contain all sorts of negative and destructive human feelings; that a group can be trusted. Intuitively the patients understand that their main problems have to do with relationships; in work, family, love, and friendship. Difficulties in everyday relations will be mirrored in the group. When the problems occur in real relations in a therapeutic setting, one can find the words, understand and work through. It becomes possible to learn and test new ways of dealing with affects and coping with relationships.

If the patient is to believe the therapist that the group can provide something positive, the therapist must be sure that the groups on offer are sufficiently good and secure. As many of the patients can become very abusive and a threat to the life of themselves and others, the safety of the groups is a primary concern.

The safety aspect is one reason why our team offers slow-open groups. To start a new group is a risky enterprise, involving much hard work. In a new group, all patients are in the same phase. The beginning is characterized by a lot of acting-out and it takes long time to build trust. In a slow-open group this phase is shorter for the newcomers because there is already a culture of basic trust and a belief that the group is useful in the long run. Patients who have spent a longer time in the group and arrived at a stage of safe freedom from drugs can easily see through newcomers' manipulations and denial. No therapist can be as efficient as an experienced group member in doing exactly this kind of work. 'Old' group members who are ready to leave the group often become objects of identification, giving hope and contributing to the building of trust.

Selection of patients

The aim is to compose groups that are highly varied in terms of gender, age, problems and expression, substance misuse, and personality type. We have come to the conclusion that in groups containing only patients with addiction problems, a false sense of safety can develop. Talking about drugs can continue session after session, this of course being a very safe area for these patients. Because of this, patients with other primary diagnoses (25 per cent, on average) are also included. These patients are mainly recruited from family doctors, and most of them suffer from severe psychosomatic distress. We avoid groups containing only patients who are dependent on tranquilizers and have a stable social situation. These patients are often extremely inhibited, attending the group meetings regularly but with rigid attitudes. With one or two acting-out and difficult drug addicts in such a group, the dynamic often becomes constructive. On the other hand, a group consisting only of acting-out drug addicts would become too fragile. We also try to avoid having only one person with a severe trauma. If, for instance, somebody has experienced childhood abuse, there must be another person in the group with a similar experience.

Some patients have an extremely high degree of anxiety about being in a group. They regard it as an impossible situation and feel what amounts to terror at the thought of joining. This patient group would of course be recommended to have individual therapy. In addition, there is a group of patients with severe narcissistic personality disorder, who have difficulties in imagining that one could share something with other people. This has been the team's largest drop-out group.

When a patient is referred, a letter is sent asking the patient to contact the team. If the patient has not responded within a month, a second letter is sent asking about his or her interest in psychotherapy. It can take up to a year before a patient responds, usually a sign that someone at the referring agency is more eager than the patient. In our opinion, it is an important part of the motivational work with patients that they take the initiative in accepting the offer.

Preparations for therapy

In order to prepare the patients for therapy, they are seen individually a number of times. An extensive psychological assessment is part of the procedure, as is an in-depth interview. All this gives the therapist a good understanding of the patients. Part of the therapy is the surfacing of suppressed, denied, or avoided feelings. Together with the patients, therapists try to visualize the 'worst case' scenario.

> One woman with 11 serious suicide attempts was referred. She was of the opinion that these things just had happened, and were out of her own control. Gradually, during the assessment procedure, she realized that there was a logical pattern, which shook her considerably. At the same time the understanding of this gave her a sense of freedom. It was important to have an agreement before treatment started about what she would do if she came into a suicidal state of mind again. She promised in such a case to go immediately to the psychiatric emergency room. She talked to her referring doctor who wrote a letter to the staff at the emergency room and asked them to take her seriously, should she turn up.

Similar kinds of agreements have been made with other patients who had a high risk of destructive acting-out. This process always has the effect of increasing the patients' trust and hope.

The patients' normal ways of coping with distress, as well as alternative ways of dealing with tension and frustration, are discussed. This also helps the patients to understand more of what therapy is about and realize that the focus will be on feelings. It is often necessary to discuss the patients' fear of being in a group: 'What would be the worst thing that could happen?' 'How would you deal with that?' are examples of useful questions. It is a good idea to visit the therapy room with the patient as part of the preparation.

Part of the process is informing about and discussing boundaries, including such issues as confidentiality, giving priority to the therapy, arriving on time, telephoning in case of cancellation, and avoiding social contact with group members outside therapy. Patients are recommended to abstain from drugs as long as they are in therapy. In case of relapse, it is the patient's own responsibility to become drug free again, but it is expected that the relapse will be spoken of in the group.

The contract states that the patient should stay in therapy for at least six months. In our experience, it will take about that time before someone understands how the group can be used. When a patient decides to terminate, they must come to therapy for at least another six weeks.

Another aspect of pre-therapy preparation is discussing and formulating a treatment goal. Even if the formulations might appear banal and self-evident, it is the process in itself that is important, as it involves the patient in deciding where the main problem lies, making choices, and realizing that therapy will not achieve miracles. Patients' formulations may include, for example:

- 'I want to be able to live in a relationship'
- 'I want to be economically independent'
- 'I want to cope with my anger'
- 'I want to have a better relationship with my children.'

The initial motivational work takes a relatively long time. Much of it involves conveying respect and a view of the patient as someone who is actively responsible for their own choices. Not until the therapist feels that this message is understood will a patient be accepted for therapy. This can take 6–20 sessions, normally about 10.

The therapy process

In long-term slow-open groups, it is hardly possible to identify phases of development. Individual patients have different dynamics and go through phases at their own pace. The groups go through phases of intense work, followed more peaceful periods. Sometimes heavy feelings of hopelessness and powerlessness dominate, and at other times responsibility and activity.

At the beginning of therapy most patients in the group are dominated by fear and mistrust, though it is too early for them to be able to feel and to express this in words. Instead, there are frequent efforts to change or neglect the boundaries. The patients come late or do not arrive at all, socialize outside the group, have relapses, etc. The therapist confronts all this openly, but without any sign of moral judgment or condemnation. Such behaviour is understood as a language in need of translation. The group is supported to investigate this and try to understand what it is all about. Everything has a meaning and must be understood in its context. Often it is a question of testing the therapist. Can she be trusted? Can she bear to be with me, the patient?

The arrival of new members gives the older group members an opportunity to work through their own ambivalence to their therapeutic work. New members always challenge the group norms, in particular those who concurrently attend AA meetings. Sometimes they want more order, a time slot for each patient, etc., in order to create a safe structure in something that is at first hard to understand, even if it has been understood on an intellectual level during the pre-therapy preparation.

It is a huge step for patients in this group to come to a group at all. It has often been a long journey filled with disappointments and failures. Society and its institutions are often looked upon with great suspicion (sometimes with good reason). People they have gradually come to trust have either betrayed them or failed to live up to expectations (often as a result of idealization and the resulting devaluation). In the group new questions are triggered: 'What am I doing here? Do I want to be here? Am I allowed to be here? There is no point, I shall fail anyway. They don't like me. I don't care about them. One can always be pushed out!' It takes at least six months, depending on how badly hurt the patient is at the beginning, to feel that one can start the real work.

The group's ability to cope with various sorts of crises, for instance suicide threats, is crucial for its survival. Suicide threats are discussed in detail in the group and the therapist actively asks specific questions about 'where, how, and when'. Is hospitalization necessary, is a new contract regarding outside control necessary, etc.? Late drop-out is a further example of a crisis that has to be faced. The group has to deal with feelings of inadequacy, guilt, and failure.

Gradually, however, a certain amount of trust starts to build. A new phase can begin with acting-out within the boundaries of the group. All patients have a tremendous fear of closeness, expressed as aggression. In fear of being too vulnerable or dependent, old strategies come into play. They are torn between hope and despair. Sometimes intensive quarrels arise in the group; the risk of drop-out is very high during this period. Flight is another way of coping with threats. Often the therapist becomes a target for feelings of rage, contempt, or envy.

Drop-out related to substance misuse is surprisingly rare; often, however, it is related to fantasized or real insults, hurtful comments and sometimes feedback that is given too early in therapy. Self-image and comments on oneself are contradictory or do not fit together. The whole thing becomes too difficult, or is simply too painful.

Most of the time the patient, sooner or later, comes to terms with fear and takes the risk to stop acting and start feeling what is going on inside. It is very painful to confront all that one has avoided in adult life at the costs of broken relationships and self-destructiveness. The first time it happens it can be almost unbearable to experience the intense pain, fear, or emptiness that comes with these discoveries. In extreme cases, some patients can come close to a psychosis. During such a time, usually not more than a couple of months, the patient might need individual therapy as a complement to the group.

As this process continues, a new sense of authenticity starts to grow. Next time is usually not so overwhelming and it becomes possible to stay in thoughts and feelings for longer periods. Simultaneously, a new way of seeing oneself and understanding life emerges. This is associated with mourning and sadness. One is reminded of all the relationships one has destroyed, and close relatives that one has betrayed, but also of all the pain that one has inflicted on oneself, and of all the years that have been lost. This is a phase in therapy when the patients are less active. The therapist reinforces rest and peacefulness in order for this work not to become too intensive.

Termination

Gradually, life outside the group starts to change. Old relationships are renewed, others are terminated. This new orientation in relationships is often accompanied by a wish to take part in human life and society in a new and dignified way. Sometimes there is a wish to pay back a moral debt to society.

The patient starts to feel the need to stand on his or her own feet. It is time to leave the group, with new insights and new talents. Of course this is a challenge, and many patients feel a new type of anxiety to leave relations that have been good. It is therefore good that, in the slow-open format, they have had to confront separations throughout the therapy. Separation can be worked through many times in a slow-open group. All members can relate to the separation theme at their own pace. The first time it happens someone might be very distanced and intellectual, on the next occasion it might be possible to be less defensive, etc. This is also the reason why we have chosen to have long summer breaks, usually two months. Even if the patients feel insecure and anxious to be left for such a long period, it is a good experience of coping, which they generally do.

The process has been described as if it was a continuous one, with one distinct phase following the previous one. This is of course not the case in reality. The group develops according its own logic. One theme emerges and suddenly gets lost, followed by something that one thought had been relegated to the past, or by a sudden leap into something completely different. The process could perhaps better be described as a spiral, implying that the themes are gradually deepened when they re-emerge on different occasions.

Conclusions

In group analytic therapy the patient is seen by others and hopefully will see him- or herself. Progress, as well as failures and shortcomings, is shared in the group. The support that is provided by the group increases the personal strength of each individual. Observing how people struggle with their own difficulties serves as reinforcement for group members to take courage to try new ways of coping.

In the long run it is not possible to regard oneself as a victim. In the group it becomes clear that every choice has its consequences, irrespective of whether or not the choice was made passively or actively. At each moment there is the choice either to speak or to be silent. Either way, it contributes to the group's communication.

The group's ability to develop its communication is directly related to its capacity to help individual members to develop. To be able to leave an appropriate message, to wait and listen to the response, to check if it was correctly understood and to wait again for affirmation – this is the goal of group therapy.

When this happens, it is extremely rewarding for the therapist. But the daily life of a group psychotherapist is not like this. The group is often very demanding. As pointed out earlier, however, the group has in itself a containing function, which takes some of the burden away from the therapist. Instead, one can focus on the life of the group in which one always will discover new layers. In the group, it is easy to continue to be curious and surprised by the unexpected.

CHAPTER 5

Motivational enhancement in group therapy

PAUL JACKSON

I have no idea how an apple tree works. The quiet machine beneath the bark is quite beyond my ken. But, like the next man along, I find imagination always willing to leap into ignorance's breach . . .

The tree roots, I imagine, play a major part – managing somehow to soak up the richness of the earth. I picture this richness drawn slowly up the trunk, pumped out along every branch.

No doubt the sun and rain are also involved, their warmth and moisture in some way being essential to the constitution of the tree. But how the richness of the earth, the sun and the rain come together to produce (1) a perfect blossom, then (2) a small apple bud – well, that remains a mystery to me. (The Fifth Duke of Portland, cited in Jackson 1997, p. 3).

Over the past 20 years or so, motivational interviewing (MI) has been used in a wide variety of settings and has become well established as a primary, or component part of, interventions at many levels, to the point where it now almost goes without saying. However, to date, very few of these interventions have been implemented within the medium of the group, and Walters et al. have suggested that

We are now at a point in the investigation and application of individual motivational interviewing at which a fork in the road has been reached. Is this something that can – or should – be done in a group? (2002, p. 377)

This question in essence directs any subsequent exploration in that the focus remains very much on MI as it is conceptualized and delivered with individuals, with this perspective then being extrapolated to be added, fitted, or incorporated into a group setting. In this sense, therefore, 'can' refers more to whether MI may be offered in a group and remain recognizably 'true' to its current form. Who knows? More importantly, perhaps, since it appears that both MI and group therapy are well accepted and efficacive interventions, the answer to the question 'should it be done in a group?' should be a pragmatic 'yes'!

A helpful resource can be found in the work of Velasquez and her colleagues (Velasquez et al. 2001), who have produced a manual describing how key aspects of MI can be usefully delivered within a group setting.

In this chapter, I hope to explore some of these issues from two slightly different perspectives. First, that of those general factors in groups, many of which are not considered to be primarily motivational in themselves, which nevertheless may serve to enhance clients' motivation and commitment. Second, to consider specific attitudes and perspectives from MI as delivered with individuals that might be usefully incorporated into group settings. Hopefully this will circumvent the 'can' or 'should' considerations, which, although important, are not the remit of this chapter, and allow a focus on those factors that are naturally motivation enhancing, aspects from within formal MI, and the process of integrating these into an overall conceptualization of group therapy within the addictions.

One of the major differences in working with individuals as opposed to groups is opportunity and formality. Individuals present in many situations where the opportunity for motivational interventions presents, and the nature of this model lends itself to utilizing these opportunities. However, the mere logistics of getting a group of people together at the same time obviously requires more planning and organization, which in turn reduces opportunity and increases formality. For example, six people may have appointments with their doctor complaining of different presenting health problems to which it transpires that excessive drinking has contributed. Here the enlightened doctor has six opportunities to use motivational strategies salient to the situation and each patient's stage of change, as set out in the 'model of change' framework (Prochaska and Diclemente 1986). It would clearly be much more complex to try to recreate this scenario in a group setting, most obviously because groups require a commonality or shared theme to provide the purpose for attendance. The above six patients all have individual reasons to visit their doctor, but not reasons at this time to be seen as part of a group.

Recent analysis of treatment modalities (Miller and Wilbourne 2002) noted this in their finding that brief interventions, not necessarily motivation focused, scored higher cumulative evidence scores (CES) with people not seeking treatment for alcohol problems, as in the example above, than with specific treatment-seeking populations. There may be many explanations for this, but the most obvious might be that those clients seeking specific alcohol treatment are likely to have a more defined and established difficulty than those who, in effect, identify drink-related issues in the course of addressing other concerns. This notwithstanding, if each patient expressed some concern about their drinking after consultation with their doctor, they might then consider attending a group or meeting where general alcohol education was offered, perhaps as part of some overall health awareness, 'well-person' type of clinic, and at this point a clear commonality has emerged. However, commonality may not equal commitment, and the decision to attend such a meeting has clear motivational implications. The possible 'lag' between the motivation to attend when seen individually as opposed to being seen within a group, as well as the differing demands of each situation is, of course, a central consideration when contemplating group therapy.

In this chapter I focus on group therapy offered in formal treatment settings, both residential and day therapeutic provisions, within the field of alcohol misuse, as this is where I have gained most of my experience in the addictions. Although clients present in many different ways, at different stages of change, the commonality is that they have chosen to attend a situation in which the primary interactions will relate to their use of alcohol or drugs. This is the locus of the first conversation between therapist and patient.

Before proceeding further, I should like to define 'group' and 'group therapy' in the broadest of terms to set the context for the following discussion. I shall use Forsyth's (1990) definitions of a group as 'Two or more interdependent individuals who influence one another through social interaction' (p. 490) which in turn leads on to group therapy being, 'The treatment of psychological and social problems in a group context' (p490).

Motivational interviewing: a relational perspective

Argue
For your limitations,
And sure enough,
    They're
    Yours
                        Bach (1977, p 75)

The soul of the world is nourished by people's happiness. and also by unhappiness, envy and jealousy. To realize one's destiny is a person's only real obligation. All things are one. And when you want something, all the universe conspires in helping you to achieve it.
                        Coehlo (1993, p. 23)

Over the past 20 years or so in particular, the understanding of working therapeutically with 'change' in the addictions has evolved creatively.

Although perhaps now not so unequivocally, it nevertheless remains generally accepted that MI (Miller 1983) alongside the model of change (Prochaska and Diclemente 1986) are the major influences in both working with and conceptualizing the process of change. In this section I shall explore certain aspects of MI and related issues that I think become particularly relevant when understood in the context of group interventions and, in particular, how these issues manifest themselves within the heart of the therapeutic relationship. Miller and Rollnick (2002, p. 25) define motivational interviewing as 'a client centred, directive method of enhancing intrinsic motivation to change by exploring the resolving ambivalence'. Space does not allow a fuller exposition of the model here and I am assuming an existing familiarity with it, but for the interested reader I would recommend Miller (1983), Miller and Rollnick (1991), and Miller and Rollnick (2002).

Since Miller's original paper (Miller 1983), the subsequent process of its use in clinical practice in the addictions, development of the model, associated research and the like, have led to the approach being understood and used in many settings and contexts, but sometimes in ways that are perhaps not always in keeping with the accepted constructs of the model. In acknowledging this in the second edition of their book, Miller and Rollnick, state that

> In the eleven years or so since the first edition of this book, we have found ourselves placing less emphasis on techniques of motivational interviewing and ever greater emphasis on the fundamental spirit that underlies it. (2002, p. 33)

This is clearly very important in considering the wider context of what is, and what is not, helpful in therapeutic relationships, particularly in acknowledging the centrality of the 'spirit' of any specific approach as it is understood intrapersonally and enacted interpersonally, as distinct from the actual techniques used. Further, it is perhaps the presence of these generic, essentially transtheoretical factors, that prove to be helpful, motivational, and curative. In considering those commonalities that thread throughout motivational interviewing and all other therapeutic approaches alike, creative connections emerge.

As long ago as 1991 an observation by Saunders, Wilkinson and Allsop suggested that 'in essence it (motivational interviewing) is nothing more than the application of good counselling skills to the addictions area'.(p. 291) Further, Davidson (1996) considered that the term 'motivational interviewing' was something of a misnomer as the construct was not based on more contemporary theories concerning the psychology of motivation but was instead more accurately seen as being derived from Rogerian, client-centred counselling. However, it has also been argued that the use of terms such as 'Rogerian' and 'client-centred counselling' are misleading and serve to misrepresent this philosophy, particularly when considering the importance of empathy.

> Empathy in a motivational interviewing sense is clearly not unconditional but very selective. Workers listen for very specific things from the client, effectively seeking material salient to their next intervention. They listen in order to develop the discrepancy between current behaviour and future goals. They listen so as to avoid argument and thus 'roll' with resistance. And they listen for the clients' own statements of intended change so as to reinforce them. Rather than Rogerian, this appears to rest more easily with cognitive-behavioural techniques whereby the worker 'shapes' the client, as behaviour considered helpful is reinforced and that considered unhelpful is not. (Jackson 2000, p. 15)

Weegmann (2002a) suggests an overlap or bringing together of more contemporary psychodynamic practice and MI, particularly concerning the importance of first, demonstrated empathy and second, the commonality between minimizing resistance in motivational terms, and understanding the need and purpose of defences, psychodynamically speaking.

Perhaps more fundamentally, in that it has greater implications for how the client is perceived and experienced as a person, is not so much the Rogerian way of being in the counselling relationship, but the humanistic philosophy of personal growth and potential that underpins this concept. Miller (1983) stated his belief, taken from humanistic psychology, in the 'individual's inherent wisdom and ability to choose the healthful path given sufficient support' (p. 155) The 'healthful path' in these terms is the underlying and instinctive movement towards the constructive accomplishment of the person's inherent potential (Thorne 1989), from which several basic assumptions are made (Merry 2000). First, this actualization process is considered to be one of natural science rather than psychologically generated processes and this represents the organism's sole motivational construct. Second, the view of human nature is positive and optimistic, and although not denying the capacity for 'bad', focuses on the potential for healthy growth. Third, each person has the capacity to admit all experiences into awareness without distortion or denial and within the self are the resources necessary for personal change. Fourth, difficulties relate to a negative self-concept which is largely determined at source by environmental influences and factors, particularly those concerning relationships with others, which then sets up a pattern of unhealthy functioning.

It is the counsellor's task to attempt to provide an environment within the relationship whereby the person's innate potential for growth may best.emerge. Again, this could be understood as being the 'spirit' of MI, as it is posits an inherent motivation toward growth and the subsequent techniques used then become a way of harnessing this drive. In turn, this provides a further logic in being non-confrontational in the traditional sense, as the client's healthful drives are to be optimistically facilitated rather than the more negative view of perceived deficits, defences, and traits to be confronted and broken down so as to achieve 'the effective resolution of pathological denial' (Nace 1987).

A further perspective is offered by Bryant-Jefferies (2001) who questioned whether MI could be considered truly client centred until he met William Miller and was struck both by his way of 'being' and his fundamental respect for clients. In the light of this experience he now regards MI as 'an application of a person-centred approach rather than a strictly client-centred therapy in the non-directive sense of Rogers' (p. 16). This is an important distinction, because the implication here is that it is the 'person', in this case William Miller, who needs to demonstrate the particular qualities as a human being required to be understood and experienced as authentically 'person-centred', with the actual theory and approach secondary to this. To extend this, if it is the being of the 'person' that defines 'person-centred', not the theory, then it is not unreasonable to think integratively in terms of, for example 'person-centred behavioural therapy' and the like. This links well with the acknowledgement of those common factors across differing therapeutic approaches, the so-called 'non-specific' factors, that appear to have a great influence on outcome and relate to therapist qualities such as the ability to form good relationships, being trustworthy, encouraging the expression of feeling, having an empathic presence, and so on. As Miller and Rollnick observed, (2002), 'they are, in essence, those mysterious common healing elements that are presumed to be present in all forms of therapy' (p. 7) In other words, simple, straightforward human qualities that are central to all normal, caring relationships between people. Leading on from this, it has been suggested that at least three motivation-enhancing factors are likely to emerge naturally out of a healthy therapeutic relationship (Jackson 2000, 2003b):

- If the counsellor is warm, empathic, and accepting, the more negative view clients have of themselves is challenged, and their sense of self-esteem and efficacy might naturally be strengthened. In turn, this increases the quality of the therapeutic alliance, which also enhances the likelihood of healthy change.
- Working in this way helps in facilitating a deeper understanding of the client's relationship with the substance he or she uses, rather than pursuing a more limited interest in the way in which the substance is used.

- Entering unconditionally and empathically into the client's relationship with substances is likely to encourage the finding of words that help the client usefully articulate any ambivalence around possible change.

Motivational interviewing and enhanced role security

It is difficult to form healthy, committed therapeutic relationships if the counsellor does not feel at least reasonably secure in his or her appointed role. Clearly, role security is composed of many component parts related to personal, philosophical, practical, and theoretical factors. Role security does not mean 'knowing', but perhaps the ability to bear an informed 'not knowing' alongside the client. As Reading (2001, p. 28) observed, 'The role secure therapist is able to manifest a vital combination of attached concern and non-attached curiosity as he or she witnesses the enactment of the patient's dilemmas'. In working within the addictions, the approach of motivational interviewing seems particularly efficacious in terms of enhancing role security, and three distinct areas appear particularly relevant:

- Perhaps somewhat paradoxically, it may be not so much what the new paradigm of MI has brought to the addictions arena but, rather, that its introduction has given 'permission' to let go of an archaic, outmoded way of being with and understanding those with problems of addiction. In its place has emerged a relational perspective that asserts that factors previously solely attributed to the nature and personality of those who misuse substances are in fact often a result of the way in which counsellors have chosen to interact with them (Miller 1983). This alone is a therapeutically liberating construct.
- MI effectively covers every theoretical aspect in incorporating three discrete constructs within the overall model, all of which provide a therapeutic comfort for the counsellor. First, the humanistic principle of forward movement towards growth which provides both the intrinsic motivation to be facilitated and an optimistic perspective of the client as a person, which is undoubtedly sustaining for the counsellor. Second, the associated 'model of change' offers a logical, understandable way of describing and accounting for the complexities involved in making change. Third, MI offers a way of intervening that aims to help enhance motivation for change, or help prepare for change, while ensuring the counsellor does not carry the burden of responsibility for the change itself.

- The model places as central the need to accept, understand, and work with the client's ambivalence around making change. The normalization of ambivalence in the change process within the addictions is again therapeutically freeing for counsellors, as they are now in the position of helping the client articulate this ambivalence, rather than being charged with the thankless task of forcing them to confront and resolve it.

In bringing together the threads that unite those motivating factors that emerge between counsellor and client, the words of Rollo May (1993, p. 79) seem particularly apposite,

> It is as though the unconscious minds of the one doing the influencing and the one influenced were carrying on a conversation of which their conscious minds did not know. This brings home the eternal truism that it is what the counsellor really is which exerts the influences, not the relatively superficial matter of the words being uttered.

Or, as Yalom (1989, p. 91) states in what he calls his 'therapeutic mantra' – 'The relationship heals'.

Group therapy: removing obstacles to engagement

One of the apparent ironies of the centrality of group therapies within the addictions, is that the members of the group, those with substance misuse problems, are frequently deemed inappropriate for more heterogeneous group therapy (Yalom 1985). Further, this seems not to be based on addictive behaviour per se, but rather the perceived personality traits and characteristics attributed to these clients which mean they will, first, not be able to engage usefully in the primary task of the group and, second, are likely to become a pernicious influence militating against this task. However, whether this is a sustainable, objective observation or perhaps a rather negative, collective counter-transference enactment is not the issue at this point. What does seem evident (for all those generic reasons that are central to group therapy), is that substance-misusing clients, using groups where this substance misuse is the commonality of attendance, engage as well (or not) as any other identified type of client. A more important factor at this stage is that of trying to help the client maintain motivation to make the transition from being seen as an individual to becoming part of a group. In my experience, it is very rare for a client, on assessment or later, to express any great concern about being seen on an individual basis. However, it is almost routine, particularly with clients seeking help from an addictions agency for the first time, for them to express concern about 'having' to go into a group. This concern is equally rarely around a reluctance to address the substance misuse problem, but reflects more fundamental concerns about simply 'being' with others. The disquiet and dissonance this causes should never be underestimated, but frequently is. Fortunately, the counsellor can do much to remove obstacles to engagement in groups.

In the heyday of the jogging boom, all the old sages used to say wryly, 'The hardest steps for any runner are those that get you out of the front door in the first place'. So it is with joining a group.

- All these interventions need to be understood within the context of the worker endeavouring to maintain an empathic presence which places as central the nature of the therapeutic relationship and treatment alliance.
- The practicalities should be addressed early on, as they are often a source of great anxiety; for example, where the group is held, time, duration, general 'rules', waiting area, toilets, booking in, and so on. By all means give written information/handouts and the like, but as *an adjunct to*, not *instead of* discussing these matters. All of these conversations have to be personal, not rote and unempathic, particularly as differing practicalities have differing degrees of effect on different people.
- The counsellor should make personal and be specific as to why and how, in their judgement, entering group therapy at this time will be beneficial to the client. There is little more demotivating than being presented with vague generalities and exhortations that 'groups are helpful', so joining one is a good idea for all. Equally, the fact that a treatment agency may philosophically favour a focus on group approaches, or have only this available, does not necessarily mean this will be the most helpful intervention for 'this client' at 'this time'.
- It is important that the counsellor is demonstrably committed to the nature and efficacy of group therapy generally, and again more specifically to 'this client' at 'this time'. This is most authentic and reliably communicated to the client if the counsellor is actively involved in the delivery of groups offered. The counsellor can then operate congruently from a position of ownership, investment, and commitment rather than trying to sell something on behalf of someone else. Equally, the counsellor's own experiences of being a group member, not a leader or facilitator, can add greatly to informing this process.
- Counsellors need to be honest with themselves about the rationale for suggesting group therapy to 'this client' at 'this time'. For the counsellor, this can sometimes be a way of expressing counter-transference conflicts. For example, getting rid of a difficult client but still being seen to offer help, hoping group pressure will force change, hoping the group will look after someone experienced as overwhelming, and so on. Obviously, the list has as many possibilities as there are counter-

transference enactments. However, the client is likely to sense when the counsellor's reasoning is inauthentic and the potential rupture of the therapeutic alliance is likely to be demotivating.

- This consideration is perhaps most crucial, and failure to appreciate the interactions involved might account for a significant number of those clients who get lost somewhere between being seen individually and starting group therapy. Straightforwardly, the client's stage of change with their substance use is often perceived to equate with their stage of change in terms of treatment openness and motivation. For example, the client who has established a period of abstinence may be regarded as being more open to engaging in treatment that is offered. However, often this is patently not the case as there is frequently a discrepancy between the client's motivation and commitment to changing their substance misuse, and their motivation and commitment to entering treatment. If help is offered on the grounds of the client changing their substance use at the expense of how they might feel about entering a group per se, then the chance of missing this motivational mismatch is greater, and if the client does leave treatment at this point it will almost certainly be attributed to 'lack of motivation' about changing the substance use, rather than the possibility that this motivation remains strong, but the client simply did not want to seek further formal help at this time. It is important, therefore, that the counsellor be open and empathic with the client in exploring the possible tensions encountered within the different demands of changing substance use and that of entering the formalities of the group treatment setting. Often this requires the counsellor getting a 'sense of this' from the client which they can then help in articulating, as clients may be hesitant in expressing such reservations openly for fear of being seen as not committed, opting out, and the like. In essence, the counsellor needs to consider whether the client would have sufficient motivation for group therapy in the context of them articulating the interplay, and possible discrepancies between their change behaviour, change thoughts, and treatment receptivity. Out of this is more likely to emerge a sense of what seems right and realistic for 'this client' at 'this time'.
- Finally, at this stage of pre-group preparation it is helpful to work out with the client how they could be most usefully be responded to if they do not manage to attend, or perhaps do so for a few groups and then drop out. In part, this can be pre-empted by arranging in advance a review meeting with the client on an individual basis after the first week or so. In my experience, it is not uncommon for a client to fail to attend for groups as arranged, but still keep an individual appointment. This is obviously helpful in maintaining contact and then provides a further opportunity to work with the client on possible

obstacles to engaging in groups that may have emerged for them since making the decision to attend. Agreed responses to non-attendance might be a simple prompting letter encouraging re-attendance, a suggestion to attend a specific group on a specific day, or a telephone call. Alternatively, perhaps the client may have expressed the wish not to have any such contact in the event of their not attending. As such, the practicalities are variable and arguably not so important as the conversation itself, in which the counsellor is again demonstrating the wish to engage with the client in a realistic, supportive manner that will in turn help facilitate engagement within the group environment. Further, considering the possibility of non-attendance is not demotivating or pessimistic. Quite the opposite; it can be seen as analogous to relapse-prevention techniques that seek to minimize the possibility of a 'lapse' becoming 'relapse', all of which is motivation enhancing.

* In essence, to borrow from the observation that the best way of empowering is not to disempower in the first place (Dargert 2000, p. 153), it could be said that 'the best way to motivate is not to demotivate in the first place'.

Group therapy and enhancing motivation

People are cussed. Tell them that spinach is good for them, and that what is more you have cooked them some and they are to sit right down and eat it; the chances are that few will comply, and fewer yet will enjoy the spinach, than if you had left them to work the whole spinach question for themselves. (Houston 1987, p. 11)

Addiction disorders are essentially motivational problems. (Heather 1992, p. 828)

Perhaps somewhat paradoxically, the best way of facilitating motivation is not to make a big deal of it. As Houston notes, perhaps people will work the whole 'spinach question' for themselves if left alone.

Similarly, addiction disorders are motivational problems only in terms of where the motivation is directed. Arguably, misusing substances in the way that our clients do may require immense motivation and single-minded commitment. No, motivation in itself is ever present, it is where it is directed that becomes the problem. This is addressed in part within MI through the idea of 'rolling with resistance' (Miller and Rollnick 1991) whereby the impetus generated in resistance is not confronted, but subtly redirected towards positive change. Additionally, Wallace (1985) conceptualized another redirection of energy through what he called 'working with the preferred defence structure of the recovering alcoholic'. Here, the client is encouraged to accept the label and self-attribution of 'alcoholic' in the early stages of recovery as this then provides a non-self-blaming explanatory system for their behaviours, and facilitates a redirection of the 'drinking' energy towards recovery.

Group therapy can offer an environment where the client can both be 'alone together' and work the 'spinach question', healthily utilizing redirected energy. Similarly, if the client gets to the group and experiences an environment that they feel will be helpful in this endeavour, then they are more likely to return. In this sense, the group serves as a motivational milieu, while never being preoccupied with motivation itself in any real conscious sense. It is incumbent upon the therapeutic team to provide the environment for what Cartwright (1987) described as a 'growth oriented framework'.(p. 250) Such a milieu, he considered, demands four types of commitment from staff and clients alike, and these qualities fit readily with those humanistic growth factors cited and elaborated upon by Miller (1983) that underpin motivational interviewing. For Cartwright, these four factors were:

- commitment to personal awareness
- commitment to openness
- commitment to reality
- commitment to personal responsibility.

Now, of course, it could rightly be argued that the aim of group therapy in this context is to help the client address their substance misuse, not serve as some kind of 'psychological finishing school'. This is true, but perhaps a more helpful perspective is somewhere in the middle. That is, it is therapeutically freeing for both therapists and clients to address substance misuse problems within a growth-oriented framework. In this context, factors that have historically given rise to ideological conflict, directed the nature of interventions, and produced 'road blocks' to treatment, cease to be relevant. Instead, such matters are considered in relation to each client as a series of questions to be personally addressed in the group milieu. Questions such as 'is alcoholism a disease?', 'is abstinence the only option?', 'is controlled drinking possible?' and so on become growth-oriented struggles. That is, growth-oriented for the client at this time, not for the therapist, the group, or the agency, although all may grow in the process. Maintaining this framework is likely to be very demanding for therapists and clients alike, not least because it is recognized that each person needs to progress at their own pace. Equally, it is not advocating a laissez faire, 'what will be will be' type of attitude – quite the opposite – but recognizes Rogers' (1987) dictum that 'people are most likely to change when they feel free not to'.

The group as a motivational matrix

Groups that are run in such environments of growth and acceptance intrinsically function as a motivational matrix for their members. 'Matrix' is a word with many definitions, in both general and psychological usage, but for this purpose I use the following, from the *Concise Oxford Dictionary of Current English*: 1. A mould in which a thing is cast or shaped. 2. An environment or substance in which a thing is developed. Understood in this way, the group as a matrix does not provide or supply the motivation, but instead ensures an environment which will hold and develop that which exists and emerges naturally out of it. Further, and perhaps more importantly, such an environment also increases the likelihood of clients remaining engaged when their motivation is less, or perhaps in a state of flux. Again, this is not working with motivation direct, or conceptualizing motivation in a conscious sense, but considering those factors that emerge naturally out of therapeutic relationships, from which increased motivation towards growth is almost a by-product. The motivational matrix functions within the context of three discrete, but interactive and evolving, relationships. These are the therapeutic alliance, engagement and attachment. The matrix can be conceptualized diagrammatically, representing how motivational fluxes can be 'held' within the whole (see Figure 5.1).

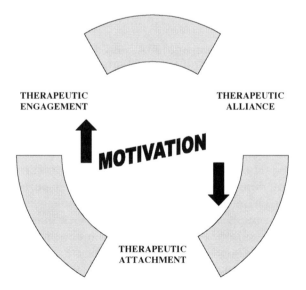

Figure 5.1 The motivational matrix.

Therapeutic alliance

The therapeutic alliance emerges out of those conversations between client and therapist concerning the presenting difficulty and out of which an agreement on how best to proceed is established. Establishing such a relationship requires the therapist to be sufficiently role-secure, interested, and empathically present. These qualities are manifest as 'therapeutic commitment' and the presence of this is more likely to promote a positive therapeutic alliance. (Cartwright et al. 1996)

Interpersonally, it is perhaps best summed up as the experience of 'being in something together' (Horvath and Greenberg 1994) that is to be maintained and developed, not just a factor specific to early interactions. Although the alliance initially emerges out of the relationship with the counsellor, as the client enters into group therapy all the members of the group serve as evolving therapeutic allies.

Therapeutic engagement

Engagement is another term used interchangeably within the treatment context. Often it is simply another word for 'attendance', which extrapolates into whether a client maintains contact with a treatment agency, nature and number of treatment contacts, and the like. Obviously this is a vital consideration, as those with substance misuse difficulties often prove frustratingly elusive. Another use of the term relates more to how 'actively engaging' the therapist is, with the aim of offering the client the experience of

> being engaged as an unique individual, with the client feeling listened to without being categorized or diagnosed. Although the 'engaging' counsellor is operating from a coherent theoretical frame of reference, that theory will not be experienced by the client as imposing treatment techniques to be employed with particular 'kinds' of client as if the uniqueness of the client was of little concern (Mearns and Dryden 1990, p. 130)

By therapeutic engagement, I mean the logical extension of the engagement described above, which results in a joint coming together or interconnection, an interpersonal 'holding fast'. It is perhaps most easily described in mechanical terms, visualizing the engagement of parts of cogs and gears at the point at which they interlock that in turn provides the shared momentum and energy for movement. It is clear that being engaged in an attending, statistical sense is not necessarily the same as therapeutic engagement, and both client and counsellor will be subjectively aware of the qualitative difference. As with the therapeutic alliance, within the group context an atmosphere of therapeutic engagement is maintained in a growth-oriented environment.

Therapeutic attachment

Within the addictions, understanding and responding to the nature of the clients' relationship with, and to, the substances they use through attachment theory (Bowlby 1979, 1988a, b) is a relatively recent development (Ball and Legow 1996, Reading 2001). In considering therapeutic attachment, I am suggesting something that arises naturally from the experience of having a 'secure base'. Reading (2001) described this process as follows:

> First, the therapeutic alliance is regarded as a situation in which the therapist functions as a temporary attachment figure, providing the client with a secure base from which he or she becomes enabled to embark on the exploratory work of therapy – a situation that has been described as being analogous to the one in which the securely attached infant is able to play and explore the environment when in proximity to the mother, or other figure with whom a satisfactory attachment bond has been established (p. 14)

In this context, the 'secure base' provided by the therapist facilitates the clients embarking into the group therapy environment, which can in turn provide a further, evolving secure base from which to explore. With this therapeutic attachment in turn comes the freedom and wish to appreciate the interpersonal relevance of the 'other'. This is both the 'other' in terms of human relationships and the 'other' in a more symbolic sense of the therapeutic environment, the fabric of the building, the ambiance of the surroundings, and so on. These ideas perhaps equate more with the experience and ethos that link with the therapeutic community ideals of social interest, described as

> the feeling of belonging, the feeling of being part of a larger social whole, the feeling of being socially embedded, the willingness to contribute and participate in the communal life for the common weal (Mosack and Dreikers 1973).

Nevertheless, such experiences are readily manifest in an appropriate group environment, and as with the notions of the therapeutic alliance and engagement, therapeutic attachment is a necessary component part that is both absorbed into, and generates, the whole. The following example will illustrate the subtle interaction of these processes.

> *I was recently in a support group, an ongoing, daily, open group that all clients can use, irrespective of how long they have been attending, where they are in respect of their treatment aims, abstinence and so on. In my experience, many addiction agencies have similar such groups that serve multiple purposes, not least in providing a safe, non-judgemental point of entry for new clients, generating the therapeutic culture and a 'secure base' from which to move on to, and return from, more specific, focused interventions. Accordingly, there is always a broad mix of clients attending at any one time.*

The group had been working hard on one of those perennial issues around exposing oneself to drinking situations when trying to abstain, and the conversation ranged over the various practicalities of this, vulnerabilities, different ways of coping, and the like. One client who up until then had been vociferously advocating the 'don't expose yourself to that situation in the first place' approach, acknowledged how envious he felt of all those who were still able to drink 'without a care in the world' as he put it. Some (though by no means all) of the group members joined with this and there followed not so much an envious attack on those who could still drink freely, but more of a wistful reflection of something held dear now lost. There then followed what felt to me like a natural, comfortable, reflective silence. In the silence I became very aware of my surroundings, the clients in the group, but then further out, noticing the sun streaming in the windows, the tree tops, and the quiet, enhanced by a bird singing. Again this felt very natural and this group 'reverie' was given words when a client simply said 'good here, isn't it'. The group smiled, agreed it was, and returned to the struggle with drinking situations.

Clearly one could analyse and conceptualize this example in many ways, but what I think is particularly relevant in this context is the experience, appreciation and enjoyment of the 'secure base'. Vitally, although I said very little, if anything, throughout this process I felt engrossed in it and there was, in my view, a deep empathic connection throughout the group; we were 'in it together'. Although they do not happen every day, such experiences are not uncommon. However, in a less intense, striking way, similar things do happen every day that are simply not obviously revealed, occurring at a lower level of consciousness.

If these factors are present, then they are likely to serve as a 'motivational matrix' that helps keep the client engaged, wanting to come back and face their difficulties even at those times when their conscious motivation to address the identified problem, their drinking, has diminished. In essence perhaps, it is the clients' equivalent of those ubiquitous but elusive 'non-specific factors'. Factors that Miller (2002, p. 33) considers are unexplainable within current psychological theory but suggests that 'Within Religious/Spiritual contexts, however, and indeed within everyday discourse, the answer to the riddle is obvious: it is love'. For our clients of course, it is this 'everyday discourse', not psychological theory, with which they engage.

Articulating ambivalence

Miller and Rollnick (2002) define motivational interviewing as 'a client centred, directive method for enhancing intrinsic motivation to change by exploring and resolving ambivalence' (p. 25). This ambivalence is specifically related to making the intended change. 'I want to but I don't want to', as opposed to ambivalence around the substance used and the actual relationship with it. This is an important distinction as often the latter is responded to as though it were the former, which is likely to leave the client feeling misunderstood and defensive. That is, if the focus remains overly on the (albeit vital) mechanisms of exploring and resolving ambivalence, an empathic understanding of the client's qualitative relationship with their substance will be lost. In essence, 'This talk of drinking is conditional: it is to help find ways of not drinking'. (Jackson 2001, p. 15) For some clients, even if motivated to change, the anticipated loss can be unimaginable (Jackson 2003a) It is the loss that is unimaginable, the absence of the substance, and although this might manifest itself in part as apparent ambivalence around change, this is an essentially limiting perception in such situations. Again, the application of attachment theory within the addictions (Reading 2001) helps in understanding the nature of these relationships, not least in allowing a more sensitive, empathic response from the counsellor.

Groups that are growth oriented in approach are particularly helpful in facilitating such exploration, in that the clients can more easily hold and articulate the differing perspectives involved, as well as using a feeling-based language. Equally, they can openly empathize with one another's loss, both perceived and actual. When these perspectives are missed or ignored by the group leader, the group often manifests an 'as if', almost depressed quality which can then perpetuate that cycle of the leader becoming increasingly active with the group seemingly equally resistant. Attending to the 'feel' of the group can help restore the empathic connection. For example, the group might talk quite animatedly and with commitment about the benefits of abstinence, their improved quality of life, emerging interests, and so on. Sooner or later, someone will make some link back to when they were drinking, however tenuous: 'bit different to when I was drinking', 'all I was interested in then was the booze' and so on. Gradually the talk will get more lively and energized, often with those previously stoically silent members adding their anecdotes. After a while it is quite likely the leader will try to direct the group back to the 'self-change' talk of earlier. However, by now the group members are in full flow and are not going to let the leader back in, which prompts the leader to confront and control more, with the group understandably refusing to be drawn, and round it goes. If the group ends on this note, the members rarely seem to leave satisfied, but instead somewhat deflated, often with little asides to one another, or to the leader: 'funny old group today', 'bet you're glad you don't have many of them'. The leader might intervene differently if they consider both the 'feel' of the group and the nature of relationships with alcohol expressed. First, in appreciating that a lot of change talk can prompt anxiety about the perceived loss required, so 'touching base', in this example revisiting the relationship with alcohol, provides both comfort and safety. However, if the leader is unempathic to this and attempts to push the group back into the anxiety-provoking area prematurely, they will of course refuse to budge. Second, the leader might comment on the different 'feel' of the two conversations. The first kind, concerning sobriety, generally tend to be more earnest, sensible, and proper, almost 'overly adult'. The others, relating to 'drinking days past', are invariably characterized by great energy, life, and an almost manic zeal, even when talking about the negative effects, such as withdrawal symptoms, DTs, loss of jobs, and so on. It is the proximity to alcohol that seems to energize, not the actual experiences described. Commenting on these differing presentations avoids the hazards of direct confrontation and helps facilitate a conversation which starts to bring the two states together; drinking and not drinking, energized and not energized. However, it is also important that the leader's intervention is empathically driven, not technique led. If it is primarily technique led, then the chances are that it will be couched in the generalities of interpreting resistance or group avoidance/flight, thus lacking warmth and relevance. If it is truly empathically lead, then the group will accommodate the technique.

Finally, I think group members leave somewhat deflated if something akin to these interactions does not occur, because their loss remains unacknowledged and expressed and they are left trying to make sense of this 'something missing'. The words of Kaplan might be helpful in setting a context for these experiences:

> Long after the return of logic and reasoning, long after we rejoin the world of the living, we are still attached to our lost ones. The human dialogue – that which makes living a life worthwhile – goes on. In the absence of this dialogue we are lost. (1995, p. 20)

Brought together, therefore, ambivalence about change is most likely to be resolved productively if the experience of the loss of the relationship with the substance is unconditionally empathized with, as well as working with the change process itself in a more integrated manner.

Process or content: doing or being

> Two monks were arguing about a flag. One said 'The flag is moving'
> The other said 'The wind is moving'.
> The sixth patriarch happened to be passing by. He told them: 'Not the wind, not the flag; mind is moving'. (Reps 1971, p. 117)

Most interventions within the addictions are based on content and 'doing', focusing primarily on the 'doing' of the substance misuse in question and the 'doing' of addressing this behaviour. By the time clients come to specialist services, there is generally a lot of 'doing' to be done. Perhaps detoxification, abstinence to be established, controlled drinking to be attempted, support to be found, different focuses of education, awareness, relapse prevention, sobriety maintenance, and so on. All 'doing' tasks. It is generally acknowledged that, particularly in a group context, this is the most helpful and least anxiety-provoking level at which to intervene initially, in an environment that is congruent, accepting, and empathic (Ball and Legow 1996, Flores 1997) As the client progresses, the groups still tend to focus on areas salient to their stage of recovery and remain content specific.

In turn, such a focus requires very specific knowledge and skills from workers in order to usefully implement such programmes. It may be, therefore, that the process of, and in, the group is never even acknowledged or considered to be of any significance. Equally, the focus may remain on 'doing', never on 'being'. The consideration of the relevance of these factors is, however, vital in contemplating the implementation of differing approaches, MI in this instance, within a group context. There are two main reasons for this. First, any intervention implemented in a group will then become subject to the multiple vagaries of the group; and second, those 'curative factors' (Yalom 1985) that are experienced as helpful and healing, all emerge out of, and are experienced through, the group process. Yalom states simply

> The content refers to the actual words and concepts expressed. The 'process' refers to the nature of the relationship between the individuals who express the words and concepts' (2002, p. 62)

He then elaborates further:

> In group therapy the difference between a group discussing 'back home' problems of the members and a group engaged in the here-and-now – that is, a discussion of their own process – is very evident. The here-and-now group is energized, members are engaged, and they will always, if questioned, remark that the group comes alive when it focuses on process. p. 63.

In a similar vein, the 'doing' qualities of the counsellor or group leader relate to skills, knowledge and interventions, whereas the 'being' refers to the human qualities, presence, and attributes that reside in, and are communicated by, the person (Spinelli 1994). In this sense, content is to process as 'doing' is to 'being'. Further, both process and 'being' facilitate best that ambiance through which the so-called 'non-specific' factors become helpfully manifest. The obvious challenge in groups emerges in attending to the vital content of working with the client's substance misuse, while remaining engaged with the process of doing this. This can be best summed up as 'work the content – tend the process'. However, as Velleman (2001) noted, 'Working with clients in a group is difficult. Many people do not do this very well' (p. 116). The temptation may become that of implementing strategies and approaches purely extrapolated from an individual context, into a group, and ignoring or attempting to minimize the presence of intrinsic group processes. Although this may be both a way of managing role insecurity and a wish to maintain the salience of a specific construct, it in turn becomes a way of nullifying that which is most helpful. And of course, ultimately the will of the group, expressed in both content and process, will always be stronger than the words of the group leader, however 'correct' these words may be. Alternatively, an appreciation of the process helps select and guide the content, both in terms of 'removing road blocks' to interventions offered and enhancing the nature of group receptivity. There are clear motivational implications here, and analogies can be made with the model of change. As we know, an appreciation of the client's stage in the cycle of change allows for interventions deemed appropriate to this stage to be made. Within groups, an empathic appreciation of the process stage of the group and a sensitivity to it allows for interventions congruent with this to be made. The earlier example about 'drinking talk' can be used to illustrate this. Interventions made at a content level were unhelpful because they were action/maintenance focused, but the group were back in precontemplation in content and perhaps contemplation in process. A clear mismatch. Action/maintenance to precontemplation/contemplation equals resistance. However, interventions empathically informed by an appreciation of the process remove group dissonance in that an understanding and acceptance of the group's wish to revisit an earlier stage is responded to as a primarily a 'being', not a 'doing', experience. The group leader is not in opposition to the group as they are able to usefully revisit precontemplation together. This facilitates the ongoing engagement and alliance, out of which the group is more likely to feel the freedom to explore other experiences that may assist growth, but are nonetheless anxiety provoking.

This also illustrates that content and process, 'doing' and 'being' are not experienced or demonstrated as discrete entities, but occur interactively, both intrapersonally and interpersonally. In a group context, therefore, it is not so much whether the content or process is being attended to in an either/or sense, but rather that a thread, interchange and openness is held demonstrably and actively between them. When these qualities are present, the group move in and out, to and fro with content and process, as a natural, unselfconscious way of being. As has been suggested earlier, motivation is also naturally enhanced in such environments, but I think two other facets also become manifest which are particularly relevant to motivation being experienced as something more robust and durable. First, emerging altruism and second, the normalizing of difficulty. Space does not allow for a fuller exposition of these factors, but both are clearly vital considerations in addressing any substance misuse problem. Whatever the aetiology, substance misuse is characterized by a turning 'away' from human relationships and a turning 'to' the relationship with a substance or substances. Appreciation of the 'other' can become all but lost. The wish to re-engage with human relationships, particularly those primary ones, is often a striking feature of those who have reduced or given up drinking. However, there is equally often a desperation to this, an attempt to fill a sudden, gaping void, that is not driven by altruism or an appreciation of the other. Within the group environment these experiences can start to emerge naturally and gently through the process that in turn allows for a gradual re-engagement with both the self and other. As a client who had established a considerable period of abstinence recently succinctly observed of himself, 'Selfish drinking, selfish recovery and, eventually, selfless recovery'. Emerging equally naturally, and allied to a more altruistic perspective, is the realization that, in Peck's (1983, p. 3) summation of Buddhist tradition applied to modern living, 'Life is difficult'. Although this may seem remarkably obvious, the acceptance of it is not, and the ability to bear life's difficulties and not misuse substances is of course central to all treatment approaches. Initially, in particular, acknowledging this allows clients to better survive the realization that stopping drinking/drug use does not stop life's difficulties, it just allows more options in managing them. However, in a growth sense there is of course a fundamental difference between 'life's difficulties' and 'life itself being difficult'. The former suggests managing and working through, the latter, acceptance of something permanent.

Where groups seem particularly helpful, and perhaps also struggle most with, is in moving towards the acceptance of this as a 'human given'. Of course, such an appreciation also facilitates the realization that life can also be rich and enjoyable. Again this requires an evolving re-engagement with the world and appreciation of the 'other' in the sense of this being a struggle for all, not that those with substance misuse problems have been solely singled out for such things. Equally, it is perhaps too much to take on consciously, and although the content busies the group with the important 'doing' tasks of making change to the substance use, evolving in the nurtured process, but most often at a less overt level of consciousness, is the emergence of altruism and the struggle with the acceptance of the difficulties inherent in a life lived.

Concluding comments

In this chapter I have attempted a tentative exploration of how motivation might naturally emerge and be enhanced through the therapeutic relationship and, more specifically, within the context of group therapy. In particular, focusing on how attending to the quality of the relationship and attunement with the processes in groups both hold and facilitate motivation towards personal growth, as opposed to the consideration of incorporating MI techniques in a specific sense. I believe that this is the most helpful ambiance in which group-based interventions with those who misuse substances can be facilitated. Perhaps an evolving perspective might be to consider further the ' fundamental spirit' that underlies motivational interviewing and the spirit that 'enhances' the therapeutic relationship, as it is reasonable to assume there will be much common ground. Finally, if I were able to summarize what I have hoped to convey in this chapter, then the words of Rogers could not be bettered.

> The most challenging new element in the group situation is the possibility of releasing the therapeutic potential of the group itself. Group therapy, and not individual therapy in a group, is the goal. If the therapist is skilful, the group itself becomes a therapeutic agent and gathers momentum of its own, with therapeutic consequences clearly greater than would result from the efforts of the therapist alone. (1987, p 305)

CHAPTER 6

Interpersonal group therapy in intensive treatment

TIM LEIGHTON

This chapter describes the integration of interpersonal group therapy and ideas from cognitive analytic therapy (CAT) into residential and intensive day treatment for substance dependence. The author has worked for many years for a non-profit organization offering a range of treatment and counselling services for people with substance dependence and their family members. These services are aimed primarily at helping people establish and maintain abstinence from drugs and alcohol.

Interpersonal group therapy has established itself as a traditional and valued element in many treatment programmes for alcoholism and drug addiction (see for example Vannicelli 1992, Flores 1997). Various eminent authors, including some contributing to this book, have described and explained the appropriateness of the model, and the modifications needed for it to be effective with an addicted population. However, it has often been unclear how it relates to the other dimensions of treatment. Our particular interest is in creating an integrative model of the rather complex experience that is intensive treatment. We want to understand how the various elements achieve helpful outcomes and how they work together, or fail to do so. The aim of this chapter is to explore how interpersonal learning as described by Yalom (1995) is facilitated through our programmes, and the part it has to play in supporting desired outcomes for our patients, which can be summarized as: the maintenance of abstinence, a more fulfilling and satisfying experience of life and relationships, and an increased sense of personal responsibility and creativity.

As this chapter is being written, we are developing a new manual for our residential programme. The design of this manual is based on some presuppositions which need to be explicit in order to understand its rationale.

- First, as far as possible, we want our treatments to be supported by the best evidence available. Moreover, we intend that our interventions should have measurable outcomes, so that we may contribute to the evidence base.

- Second, we believe in the efficacy of coherent combinations of approaches. For obvious reasons, much research prefers to focus on single, discriminable interventions. However, we think that the evidence from such studies may be misleading in that the efficacy of a particular intervention may be radically affected by the provision of supplementary interventions. A clear illustration of this is provided by the outcome evidence for cognitive-behavioural relapse-prevention programmes, which is discussed below.

- Third, we are aware that most psychological treatment effects are fugitive, no matter how skilled and successful the implementation, and that if gains for the individual are to be maintained there is a need to marshal resources to boost and support progress over time. This is why we encourage the development of an external support system through, for example, affiliation with self-help fellowships and by helping clients make use of other forms of social support, as well as helping clients to internalize treatment gains as personally meaningful, usually consciously accessible, new 'ways of operating'.

Cognitive analytic therapy as a unifying model

CAT is an integrative model of therapy which originated through the use of cognitive tools and methods to research the process and outcome of psychodynamic therapy (Ryle 1990, 1995; Ryle and Kerr 2002). Anthony Ryle developed a rich cognitive model of human aim-directed action, and CAT both acknowledges the importance of psychoanalytic and cognitive contributions and stands as a critique of them. According to Ryle:

> Neither cognitive nor psychoanalytic models acknowledge adequately the extent to which individual human personality is formed and maintained through relating to and communicating with others and through the internalization of the meanings developed in such relationships, meanings which reflect the values and structures of the wider culture. (Ryle and Kerr 2002, p. 2)

CAT has incorporated ideas from Vygotsky's activity theory, from Winnicott's concept of play, and from the work of Bakhtin on interpersonal and internal dialogue, to create a radical restatement of object relations theory. This development is well summarized in Ryle and Kerr (2002). The important implications for this chapter are that from this perspective the self is conceived of as 'dialogic', created in and embedded in an evolving 'joint enterprise' of interactions with others, and that there is an intimate relationship between 'self-to-other' and 'self-to-self'. As Ryle says, it is as though the Cartesian 'I think, therefore I am' is replaced with the Vygotskian–Bakhtinian 'We interact and communicate, therefore I become.' (Ryle and Kerr 2002, p. 59) In this model, therapy, both individual and group, becomes a culture in which new meanings can be jointly created. Here is an opportunity to understand the problem of addiction in a new way, and a model to link and make coherent sense of the previously haphazardly agglutinated collection of 'sensible approaches' to substance misuse treatment.

Key features of the CAT model are that it is collaborative, that it involves the creation of tools to describe and map 'problematic procedures', usually concerning self-management or eliciting responses from others, and that its concept of the reciprocal role procedure helps us focus both on the patient's own relational repertoire and on the patient–therapist relationship, which in a residential community with a multidisciplinary staff team can be quite complex. In CAT, issues and problems are collaboratively reformulated, though a combination of what the 'treatment culture' has to offer in terms of understandings and meanings, and what each patient brings with them, including their cultural assumptions and the personal history that has shaped these.

We hope that this will produce a much richer, more humane, and less coercive treatment experience. An example of this might be the way in which conceptual terms from AA such as 'powerlessness' might appear in the culture. This concept can be seen as a tool or sign that reflects a preexisting culture (of 12-step recovery), but whose meaning is created anew in the joint therapeutic conversation, and which is internalized by each individual as part of a personal reformulation. The enrichment of personal meaning through sign mediation enables new capacities. The interpersonal learning, so clearly articulated by Yalom as a combination of experience and joint reflection on the meaning of that experience, requires a model of internalization, realization and ownership for the patient. We believe that CAT provides this.

CAT offers a new general theory and is not simply a collection of techniques (Ryle and Kerr 2002, p. 4), but since it was developed by clinicians working with and researching a range of practical psychotherapy issues, and because those in the group around Ryle included people from various psychotherapy traditions and trainings, it provides a model of practical as well as theoretical integration. The key element, which is so appropriate and useful for addicted clients, is the explicit, joint work of identifying and revising repetitive and maladaptive patterns of thought and behaviour.

Addiction

It is problematic and potentially misleading to generalize about 'addiction' and my comments are not intended to delineate a Procrustean template into which all those with substance misuse problems are to be crammed. However, many of the clients who are admitted for residential treatment have suffered damage to their personal relationships as a result of their addiction problem and feel isolated, lonely, and frightened, as well as secretive, ashamed, and untrusting of others. Some have a history of highly unsatisfactory relationships in their primary family before the development of chemical use problems, and may have suffered considerable mistreatment, neglect, or abandonment. People who are in varying degrees frightened, ashamed, underconfident, or demoralized will have developed strategies, including ways of relating to others, in order to deal with and manage these feelings, and to minimize the risk of exposure. The way that addicted clients often present to helpers has given rise to some stereotypes which have a core of truth and can be useful. It is common to come across clients who appear to be very compliant in conversation with therapists and peer helpers, who will agree with every suggestion, and who seem to have great difficulty acknowledging their ambivalence or their destructiveness. These clients may appear to have lots of 'insight' and to be 'making progress', but they are then seen to behave in ways which contradict this, often in a very self-defeating manner. They are sometimes just as bewildered by this as the therapist might be.

We typically see clients presenting either as an 'addicted self' whose position is to undermine and rubbish the client's own attempts to recover and the efforts of others to offer help and support. Or, more often, we may see (and the client may experience themselves as) what we call the 'pseudo-responsible self' who is sincerely help-seeking but who cannot acknowledge, or even have access to, the attitudes and thoughts represented by the 'addicted self'. In turn, the 'addicted self' refuses to acknowledge the authenticity of the 'responsible self'.

The usual problems that our clients bring are, couched in the terms of the current traditional approaches:

- considerable pressure from family, friends, or employer to modify or abstain from chemical use
- commonly, a degree of ambivalence about this goal
- a high level of psychological and often physical 'dependence' on their substance use
- an inadequate understanding of their personal 'high risk situations'
- skills deficits in coping with such situations.

Typically, they have rather low levels of social support, and their social functioning may be impaired. Most of our clients have a long history of problematic substance use, are usually not in stable supportive couple or family relationships, have had an involvement with the criminal justice system as a result of their drug use, and have limited financial or social resources. They may have poor mental health, childcare issues, and other complex needs.

One very influential and rather well-researched approach comprises coping skills training for relapse prevention, based on a cognitive-behavioural model (Marlatt and Gordon 1985, Monti et al. 1989). According to this model, learning and implementing successful coping in high-risk situations leads to higher self-efficacy, which in turn makes relapse less likely. Various forms of skills training programmes have been devised and many outcome studies have been carried out, often demonstrating an apparent beneficial effect (reviewed in Carroll 1998). However, it seems that the demonstrated acquisition and use of such coping during treatment programmes, together with increased self-efficacy scores, more adaptive cognitive styles, and similar treatment outcome measures, make a surprisingly small contribution to the variance in drug use outcomes after a year or so. For example, Allsop et al. (1997) show an impressive difference in favour of a skills-based relapse prevention programme at six months after treatment, compared to a relapse discussion group or to no explicit addressing of relapse issues, but find that all significant difference has disappeared by 12 months.

Although we are convinced of the value of coping, and are persuaded by the evidence that those who are resilient to relapse tend to use specific cognitive coping styles, we are interested in why many clients, often those 'low in social functioning' (Longabaugh and Wirtz 2001), or those who feel hopeless, unsupported and alienated, fail to benefit from coping skills training in the way that is predicted by cognitive-behavioural theory (see also Morgenstern and Longabaugh 2000). We hypothesize that for vulnerable clients, such learning may have to be 'scaffolded' by a supportive 'culture' made up of therapists, recovering peers, mentors, friends, and family, perhaps for a very considerable length of time. There is recent evidence that the most powerful single predictor of relapse may be a state of demoralization or depression (Miller and Harris 2000). If this is so, better treatment outcomes may well emerge from programmes that are successful in addressing hopelessness, isolation, and alienation.

Elements of the treatment programme

We have identified seven major elements of our treatment programme. The programme is characterized by an integration of therapies that are usually seen as individual, such as the development of coping skills, with those that are clearly relational or social. We have further specified measurable proximal outcomes for each of the elements. We hope this will facilitate future research into the relationship between treatment process outcomes and longer-term alcohol and drug use outcomes.

These elements are:

- A focused **induction programme** which will help new clients explore how the treatment programme might be of use to them, to develop their motivation, and to clarify the level of fit between their personal goals and aspirations and the goals of the treatment. Considerable attention will be given to helping clients understand and prepare for interpersonal group therapy.
- An introduction to, and training in, the use of the **12-step recovery resource**, including the philosophy of the 12-step programme and the social support available from Alcoholics Anonymous (AA) or Narcotics Anonymous (NA) meetings.
- An element aiming to improve **interpersonal relating and the self-to-self relationship**. This is primarily achieved through interpersonal group therapy and the monitoring of individually identified problematic interpersonal and self-management procedures.
- **Exploration of personal meaning and purpose**. This aims at reducing feelings of emptiness and boredom and increasing hopefulness. It involves an exploration of beliefs and values and may or may not include a spiritual aspect, depending on the individual client's inclination. The exploration and development takes place in a group and community context, with many opportunities to share beliefs, attitudes, and opinions with other people and to understand how one's behaviour in relation to others sheds light on personal meanings and values.
- A **cognitive-behavioural relapse prevention** programme, using an individual analysis of relapse risk and aiming at developing coping skills to address risky situations. The skills training takes place in a series of topic-specific workshops in which a group of clients learn together.
- **Health and well-being** – an educational programme designed to increase health behaviours, improve sleep pattern, teach relaxation skills, and inform the client about the benefits of good diet and exercise. Also included is information about the management of and reduction of transmission risk for viral infections, particularly hepatitis C and HIV. In addition there is an opportunity to try a variety of complementary therapies.
- **Family work** – an opportunity to help family members assess their relationship with the addicted person, how they have adjusted to and

coped with the problem, and what kind of adjustments might be desirable to facilitate better relationships in the future, to start the process of healing past hurts, and to anticipate possible snags or setbacks. Family members also have an opportunity to learn about the treatment process.

As well as these seven core elements, for those clients who have complex needs or are dually diagnosed there would be an individual programme of assessment, and additional treatments or interventions would be considered. This might include education and training; for example, about how to take necessary medication in an effective manner and how to rebut misinformation that they might encounter, such as 'You can't be properly clean and in recovery if you are taking medication.'

As this overview clearly shows, the 6-week residential programme is a highly complex experience with a very broad menu of possible interventions. In this chapter I focus on the links between interpersonal learning and the elements of treatment, and I hope to show that the programme design as a whole is coherent and integrative. Needless to say, the success and coherence of the treatment from the point of view of the individual client depends entirely on the creation of an agreed and relevant treatment plan, based on a collaborative assessment of the client's needs.

12-step involvement and interpersonal group therapy

Encouraging people with alcohol and drug dependency problems to attend and get involved in AA or NA meetings is enthusiastically endorsed by many addictions professionals, but regarded with considerable scepticism or reservations by others. The evidence for the efficacy of 12-step recovery is partial, contradictory, and open to starkly differing interpretations. There is controversy about retention rates, success rates, and whether the philosophy of the 12 steps is empowering or fosters dependence and helplessness. 12-step recovery has certainly been promoted with ideological fervour in the USA, and its proponents often appear to believe that it is 'the only way' to recover from addiction. Our experience in the UK also shows clearly that those who are attracted to these self-help fellowships generally find them very helpful and supportive, and in recent years a series of studies from various countries have consistently shown that regular involvement (as opposed to simple attendance) in AA or NA is associated with a range of good outcomes (e.g. Fiorentine 1999, Tombourou et al. 2002, Kaskutas, Bond and Humphreys 2002).

We are generally satisfied that, for most of our clients, the 12-step fellowships provide a safe and supportive resource, provided they learn to use them in a constructive way, and provided the more vulnerable clients develop the ability to recognize and protect themselves from limiting or even damaging experiences in these groups.

Caldwell and Cutter (1998) find that:

> AA is by nature . . . characterised by multiple and spontaneous interactions that require some measure of openness and the ability to relate with different people. Individuals who are uncomfortable with such intimacy may lack more extensive and diverse relationships, and, therefore, less opportunity for 'identification' and a weaker connection with AA. They may also be unable to experience a feeling of 'belonging' or share their feelings ('catharsis'), important dimensions of the 'therapeutic' value of groups (Yalom 1985). Lacking these positive experiences, they are much more likely to leave AA. Qualitative findings from this study support the assertion that individuals who value, and are emotionally able to take advantage of, the opportunity to share their feelings with others are more likely to be involved with AA. (Caldwell and Cutter 1998, p. 226)

Participating in interpersonal group therapy within a short-stay therapeutic environment provides an ideal opportunity for clients to learn and develop such abilities. Moreover, the patterns of relationship that are revealed and illuminated in the group therapy provide vital clues about how someone is likely to relate to others outside the therapy situation, including in AA or NA groups. Typically our clients have great difficulty with trust and intimacy, and often appear either very cut off and defended, or else wide open and unboundaried. They often report repeated experiences of being let down and betrayed by those they have trusted, and seem highly sensitized to any hint of unreliability in those they allow themselves to depend on. Feeling let down may well provoke an overwhelming feeling of disappointment, which in turn produces angry and destructive behaviour, often directed against the self. One individual may feel that their intimacy needs can be met only in an intense, exclusive, and sexualized relationship, and will make every effort to actualize this. This may be responded to with compliance and collusion, or with rejection and ridicule. Others may believe that all trust and dependence on others is to be rigidly avoided, and another may devalue any help offered and dismiss any attempt by others to reach out to them.

More apparently 'adaptive' interpersonal styles, such as entertaining or impressing others, offering help and support to others but finding it hard to receive anything, or distracting oneself and others from painful feelings, are revealed in the group therapy process to have negative, limiting, or self-sabotaging results.

Conversely, what each person really has of value to offer is often recognized and acknowledged in the group for the first time. This is vital, of at least equal importance to the recognition of problematic interpersonal behaviour. Our clients are usually very troubled and doubtful about the acceptability of 'just being themselves' and are often quite aware of putting on a 'front' to elicit predictable responses from others. When such a person is unguarded and unaffected, perhaps offering simple concern towards or interest in another person, or when they speak out what they really feel or think, it is often as though this action is countered by an undermining or threatening internal voice, and signals from others are quickly read as critical, disapproving, rejecting, or ridiculing. In a group situation, in which a culture of honest, warm, and respectful feedback is encouraged, clients are often amazed to learn what the group members value in them, and this positive feedback can precipitate and strengthen a supportive inner voice for the client. Later in the chapter I consider the dialogue of 'voices' in a community of people attempting to recover from addiction, from a Vygotskian–Bakhtinian perspective.

Coping skills training and interpersonal development

A programme of structured workshops designed to explore and developing coping skills might be seen as quite a different kind of activity from interpersonal group therapy sessions. Indeed, the specific tasks of such workshops, accomplished with informational presentations, worksheets, group 'idea-storming' and discussion, and rehearsal of skills, do require a different kind of interaction, and a different leadership style. But opportunities for interpersonal learning are by no means absent from this setting. In fact, there will inevitably be plentiful examples of interactions that can be usefully reflected on within individual counselling sessions, in the client's journal, and in group therapy sessions. Clients may eagerly participate and either experience gratification from this or suffer anxiety about the appropriateness of their contribution. The latter is an example of a 'snag' in CAT terms: 'I should like to participate, but if I speak out freely I risk ridicule or disapproval, or I might harm others by smothering and depriving them.' This can lead to a dilemma: 'Either I keep quiet and get nothing (and maybe contemptuously dismiss the programme as worthless), or I participate and feel exposed and anxious.' The exits from these involve mutual feedback and reflection, taking risks and receiving encouragement from a culture that affirms such risk-taking.

Other responses in the workshops might include undermining or disruptive behaviour, attempts to impress or 'trump' other participants, or seeking approval from the group leader or from the peer group. These patterns might be quite subtle, particularly if the workshop is well conducted and most participants are to some extent enjoying the experience and recognizing the relevance of the workshop material. It is also important to distinguish between behaviour that signifies anxiety at a group level, indicating that the group of clients feels unsafe and uncontained, and behaviour that is primarily a manifestation of an individual's interpersonal repertoire.

Managing anxiety

Our client group shows high levels of anxiety. Average score at intake on the trait scale of the State-Trait Anxiety Inventory (STAI-T) is 56 (SD = 11.3). The average score on the Beck Depression Inventory (BDI) at intake is 21, indicating a high level of distress. Christo and Sutton (1994) found that in a group of UK NA members it took an average of 3–4 years of abstinent recovery for the initially high anxiety scores and low self-esteem scores to reach levels comparable with those of a 'normal' control group. Traditional psychodynamic therapy, which aims to loosen intrapsychic defences by encouraging regression, is by its nature anxiety-provoking, and psychoanalytic pioneers soon found that those with addictions did not usually benefit from analytic treatment, and were often made worse by it. Of course, many modified psychodynamic treatments have been developed which have shown much more promise (e.g. Khantzian, Halliday and McAuliffe 1990), but I believe that where such treatments fail to be helpful it is often because the client cannot tolerate the anxiety involved, resulting in frequent early dropout, or a blocking of the therapeutic relationship. This is typically followed by an increase in addictive behaviour.

Some of the research evidence comparing group interventions is worth reviewing in the light of this consideration. For example, Kadden et al. (1989) found that although interactional group therapy and cognitive-behavioural coping skills training groups, offered in an outpatient setting to recently abstinent alcoholic patients, were both helpful, they also found that for patients with more psychiatric problems or higher sociopathy scores, skills training groups were more effective than interactional groups. This difference was still found at 18 months follow-up (Cooney et al. 1991). Interestingly, the same research group found that responses to a pretreatment drinking situation role-play exercise predicted differential treatment outcome, with higher anxiety and self-reported urges to drink after the role-play predicting a more favourable outcome with skills training groups than with interactional groups (Kadden et al. 1992).

A review of similar studies on group therapy (e.g. Yalom et al. 1978, Brandsma and Pattison 1985, Vannicelli 1992) and of the reported outcomes for various forms of individual psychodynamic therapy for clients with substance use disorders (e.g. Woody et al. 1983, 1985, 1986) suggests to me that such therapies are indeed useful and effective, but only if clients are provided with sufficient support and structure. The more a client lacks external support and connection and internal capacities to manage and modulate feeling states, the more the treatment environment needs to provide structure and support. This is not to suggest that such therapies are contra-indicated for more vulnerable clients, but that they should be provided in a containing and structured environment, at least to start with, and that they work well when combined with other forms of therapeutic activity such as skills training workshops, discussion groups, and shared group leisure and social activities. It is vital that the therapeutic team should be aware of and be able to titrate excessive anxiety at both the group and the individual level.

Successful group therapy in an intensive setting with clients who are at a point of painful emotional crisis and transition depends on the treatment team being able to provide both the required clarity and structure, and a flexible and responsive level of support. This requires therapists who have a clear understanding of the group therapy task, particularly the ability to monitor the points at which the group can take responsibility for its own functioning and those when active help needs to be provided.

Further, if the therapists have an understanding of the elements of treatment as coherent and linked, and if they are able to facilitate a similar understanding in the clients, and help them link their interpersonal experiences in the various treatment settings to agreed problematic procedures in their own lives, then the power of the group therapy will be maximized.

My experience has been that if such group therapy is provided within a structured and containing environment, clients will routinely report in their post-treatment evaluations that 'group therapy' was the most important and helpful part of the treatment experience. It clearly often produces a strong feeling of cohesiveness and bonding, and we are not infrequently told by clients that they have experienced an unprecedented freedom to experience or express feelings in the group. This is equally true of clients who have high levels of measured psychological distress, those who might experience themselves as quite fragmented or dissociated, and those who at the beginning of treatment may have expressed considerable anxiety about group situations. If a client early in recovery receives a good experience of interpersonal group therapy in a safe and containing environment, then there is a good likelihood that as they progress in recovery they will be able to benefit from interpersonal work in much less structured settings.

It is important that the therapist team and the patient group do not develop a culture of determinedly 'breaking down defences'. Therapies that prematurely threaten what Wallace (1985) has called the 'preferred defense structure of the alcoholic' are counterproductive with this client group, and are potentially abusive. It is also always important in my view to maintain a focus on how the therapeutic work is linked to the alcohol and drug use. If a conscious 'addiction focus' is lost, then we often experience the paradoxical, confusing, and demoralizing situation of what looks like productive and insightful therapy accompanied by apparently split-off continuing addictive acting-out. Moreover, if addictive behaviour does occur, the opportunity for it to be understood, anticipated, and gradually replaced by a reliable and adaptive alternative repertoire can be lost. In common with colleagues, as a general psychotherapist I have repeatedly discovered that even in clients without marked substance dependence, problematic substance use (or other related behaviour such as binge eating) is quite capable of seriously undermining therapy (Ryle 1997), and that if this does occur it should be consistently and firmly addressed.

Voices in the treatment setting

In my view, the Vygotskian concept of the 'zone of proximal development' (Vygotsky 1978, p. 86) is crucially useful in thinking about psychotherapy. This idea, which was developed in the context of pedagogy, proposes that an individual child possesses a set of capacities to act in the world which have been acquired socially. These capacities depend on the transfer of cultural signs (words, gestures, concepts) which are used as 'tools' to mediate behaviour and achieve tasks. The transfer occurs through joint activity, and the gradual emergence of shared meaning. Part of the process is a stage in which children can be heard talking to themselves when learning something new, and this conversation is a recognizable version of talk between adult and child, in which 'mummy's' or 'daddy's' voice is in the process of becoming the child's own.

It is possible to measure a child's capacities when particular tools have been assimilated and mastered to establish 'what she can do on her own'. Vygotsky understood that beyond this there was a zone of transition in which a child is able to achieve things in joint activity with a more competent other or others, which she is not yet able to do by herself. This is the zone into which individual mastery will eventually extend, and is known as the zone of proximal development.

It is not difficult on reflection to imagine that such a process of learning and acculturation does not end with childhood. Helping adults to change might also be facilitated by the creation through joint activity of new tools with new meanings. However, an implication of Vygotsky's ideas is a tendency to sameness: clearly an acculturated individual on this account is one who tends to share meanings as closely as possible with others in the culture. As Cheyne and Tarulli point out, Vygotsky emphasizes the sharing of epistemological space, and assumes that dialogue is 'basically a cooperative enterprise aimed at an ever greater agreement' (Cheyne and Tarulli 1999).

However, as we all know, things go wrong if we apply these assumptions to the therapy process. If the process of assisting change is simply envisaged as the transfer of skills or wisdom, and the therapeutic relationship seen (explicitly or implicitly) as analogous to a teacher–pupil or parent–child relationship, we soon discover disruptive, resistant, challenging, and mischievous voices appearing in the dialogue as well as disappointed, critical, and dismissive ones.

Bakhtin and difference

Mikhail Bakhtin's concept of dialogue, along with the difference between his understandings and those of Vygotsky, can, I believe, help us to think about and create a more effective treatment based on therapeutic community and group therapy. Bakhtin emphasizes difference and the distinctness of the other (e.g. Bakhtin 1990, p. 87). For Bakhtin the utterances of inner speech (conscious thoughts and feelings), just like interpersonal utterances, are dialogic in that they always respond to previous utterances and anticipate the evaluative response of the other. This other may be internal or external, actual or potential, perceived or hidden. Thus the dialogical self is understood as a community of voices. The communication may be conflicted, distorted, or misdirected in various ways, but for Bakhtin the productivity and creativity of dialogue depends on the different standpoint of the other. To quote Cheyne and Tarulli again: 'It is in the struggle with difference and misunderstanding that dialogue and thought are productive, and productivity is not necessarily to be measured in consensus.'

A further idea, that of the third voice, needs to be introduced before I can illustrate the application of this perspective to the treatment group situation. Despite the importance of self–other differences, people clearly have a strong need to achieve understanding and validation from others, and Bakhtin points out that implicit in any two-person dialogue there is a 'third voice' which represents a reference point or authority.

(Bakhtin 1986, p. 126). So, for example, if a psychologist (first voice) is teaching a client (second voice) to 'think more rationally', the 'third voice' might be that promoting the value of science, or rationality, or 'evidence-based practice', from which the first voice derives its legitimacy and to which the second voice is supposed to defer.

Other typical 'third voices' might decree 'what we do in this family/in this country/in this treatment centre', etc., 'what God wills', 'standards of reasonable or civilized behaviour', and so on. As we can see, the type of relationship we are thinking about, for example psychologist–client, treatment staff member–resident, group facilitator–group member, inherently contains an asymmetry of power and authority.

This type of dialogue can be described as 'magistral', where the first party or group is in the role of master or tutor, and the second party or group is in the role of pupil. Obviously the tutor does not act in a vacuum. She inevitably has an agenda or curriculum, and there will inevitably be 'authoritative utterances that set the tone . . . works on which one relies, to which one refers, which are cited, imitated and followed.' (Bakhtin 1986, p. 88). This applies even in the case of 'client-centred' counselling where the magistral genre is less manifest.

This type of dialogue is keenly entered into by both addictions therapists and clients: 'Tell me what to do to get better.' In April 2003 I saw on British television a well-known addictions therapist who said that he had enjoined his celebrity client, who had a cocaine problem, to 'take the cotton wool out of her ears and put it in her mouth', and this injunction was enthusiastically endorsed by the client. Many treatment programmes include series of 'lectures' and promote certain kinds of beliefs and slogans. Treatment groups often look to the leaders to instruct them, and feel abandoned and incompetent if they do not receive guidance.

However, the asymmetry of this type of relationship produces, partly out of its success in developing more competent and knowing apprentices, a different kind of dialogical genre. As the second voice questions the first, a Socratic dialogue emerges which challenges the authority of the third voice. This Socratic dialogue tends to resist consensus and mistrusts 'expertise'.

An example of this emerging Socratic dialogue occurred in the treatment centre recently. The senior counsellor was giving a talk to the client group about 'shame'. A female client asked: 'What is the difference between shame and embarrassment?' The counsellor began to explain that in his view these were on a continuum, and described how when we feel embarrassed we may attempt to pretend through our speech and actions that we are not discomfited, but that we may find ourselves blushing and thus reveal our feelings to others. He then asked the group how people respond when they see someone blushing, and there was agreement that we often respond with sympathy. At this point a client of Afro-Caribbean origin said: 'But this only applies to white people!' The counsellor then asked this client to explain how embarrassment was experienced and shown by people who were not white. At this point several members of the group interrupted to say that the counsellor was blushing bright red! He invited the group to say why that might be, but they asked him to say. He reflected that he had become aware that he might have said something insensitive or racist, and that he was feeling embarrassed. Various insights and connections were made. The group realized that they did indeed feel sympathy for the counsellor. He, in turn, explained that his feelings of shame might after the session provoke thoughts that he had 'blown it' and was useless, but that it was possible to interrupt and challenge this. Needless to say, this dialogue, in which the counsellor was honest and undefensive, challenges the omniscience and authority of the 'expert'. As Jauss says (Jauss 1989, p. 210) after the confusion in which the dialogue does not go 'according to plan', 'it produces a meaning that is the result of mutual enquiry, and that emerges out of a knowledge of one's lack of knowledge.' It may be worth pointing out that this 'Socratic' genre is different from the 'Socratic questioning' of cognitive therapy, which is dialogue of a distinctly magistral kind.

The progression to a productive Socratic dialogue is not easy for any of the parties involved. It is characterized by an openness to emerging truth which may be very anxiety provoking as it may require acceptance of complexity or challenges to received wisdom. The 'junior' parties may oscillate between a feeling of being 'misunderstood' or not heard, and a desperate need for clear definitive answers. The 'experts' may be loath to give up their authority and certainty. If the experts give up their authoritative position they may be seen as, or actually be, floundering and confused and the clients will feel uncontained and unsafe. If they insist on their authority they may be seen as hypocritical or misguided. Under such circumstances there is a danger that the dialogue will move from the healthy and collaborative Socratic questioning to something much more cynical, mocking, and undermining. This has been named Menippean dialogue by Cheyne and Tarulli (1999), after the Greek satirical dramas of Menippus.

Anyone who has worked in or been a client in an intensive group-based treatment setting will have no difficulty in recognizing these genres. They can of course be observed in interpersonal relations, but in my view these dialogues are also taking place *within* individual selves (self-to-self). When clients are in Menippean mode, staff members may experience challenging individuals or groups as misbehaving nuisances. They are thought of as manipulative and threatening. We can also hear various third voices here: 'Addicts are not to be trusted', 'They are sick, deviant, and immature', and attempts are usually made to re-establish a magistral type of relationship. From the other direction, the clients find it harder to trust the staff and very often express considerable hostility and blame towards them. They too often feel that unruly elements need to be ejected and order restored, or else decide that the environment has nothing to offer them, and feel impelled to leave.

Most therapists in the field of addiction treatment, reading and understanding the above paragraphs, would, I believe, agree with me that the brute re-establishment of magistral dialogue and the screening out or ejection of difficult customers who threaten this is not the right solution. We work within a social context in which our clients are stigmatized and labelled as deviant, and we observe that society tends to deal with such deviance first with remedial education, then by medical or quasi-medical therapies, and if those fail, with the sanctions of the criminal and civil law.

All of this has had little effect on the carnivalesque drama of relapse and failure which is so often experienced by those dependent on drugs and alcohol, their family members, and those who try to help them. At the individual level this may be partly explained by the same kind of conflicts I have described at the interpersonal level in a treatment situation also occurring in the inner dialogue of a person struggling to recover.

So what is to be done? We know that many people successfully extricate themselves from addiction, and achieve long-term change. In our treatment settings we are not so much concerned with those who have the resources to do this without intensive professional help. As I have said above, our typical clients are clearly under-resourced emotionally, psychologically, and materially. We know from a well-conducted study (Georgakis 1995) that about two-thirds of those admitted to our residential treatment centre are likely to be in sustained recovery 30 months later. About half of these were 'instant responders', and the other half lapsed or relapsed at least once in that time. The other third experienced more or less no benefit from the treatment, and typically continued to use in a problematic manner for the whole follow-up period. Most of these were early drop-outs or were asked to leave treatment. Since 1995 our drop-out rate has been relatively steady, but staff have felt that more effort has been needed year by year to maintain a healthy culture in the centre. The proportion of younger clients, those with dependence primarily on illicit drugs as opposed to alcohol, and those with complex needs, has increased significantly. Our continuing concern is to extend whatever is beneficial about our treatment to more people, and to have some positive impact on those who may not achieve in the short term the abstinence goal to which they had committed at the point of admission.

How can we maintain and encourage a healthy, change-promoting culture, and protect the safety of our group of residents without always striving to re-establish a magistral, didactic kind of relationship which we know is counterproductive? It is my opinion that the key is interpersonal group therapy, and the integration of that group therapy into the therapeutic community. Somehow, the maintenance of the culture must be seen as a joint enterprise, for which staff and clients share the responsibility. This enterprise should, I believe, be consistently encouraged and regularly discussed. It is easy to blame the other party: 'The residents aren't taking responsibility', 'John doesn't want recovery, he shouldn't be here', 'Why don't the counsellors do something?' (about the using in the house, about threatening behaviour, etc.), 'Why are the staff inconsistent and unfair?', 'Why are the residents so demanding and ungrateful?' and so on. It is helpful to come to realize that there are no perfect answers, no last word, no systemic or management solutions that will make these problems go away. But if the clients can't do something or don't know how to do it, the group facilitators must come forward and help, often very actively and visibly.

From a Vygotskian perspective, as counsellors and therapists we should be committed to maximal involvement of our clients in the therapy task, even at the point when the task situation is not fully understood by the clients. I believe we need to provide a 'scaffold' of dialogue in which we are very attentive to the performance of our clients, and supply interventions which nudge the clients towards higher levels of competence in the therapy task, so that eventually they may take responsibility for their own functioning. In the therapeutic community or group situation, we are aided in this by the extension of the scaffolding to the peer group, as they support each other, both as more experienced role models helping and guiding the newcomers, and in a more equal relationship in which mutual vulnerability is shared.

From a more Bakhtinian perspective, I feel that therapists do well to understand the value and productivity of difference, and to model a culture in which tensions and conflicts are not resolved in an authoritarian manner. Maintaining this in a counselling or treatment situation is difficult and requires thought and persistence, but this is what we are paid for. All our clients are going to have to integrate such tension and conflicts within their own selves and in their intimate relationships in order to forestall Menippean chaos in their own world. Many of them come to us with a strong tendency to criticize, demean, and oppress themselves, and it is possible to change this.

I particularly did not want to write another chapter on the technical application of Yalom's model of group therapy with this population, as I know this will be addressed thoroughly by other authors in this book. I hope that this chapter has succeeded in combining a fairly straightforward account of how the elements of our treatment programme relate to each other (and the place of group therapy within this process of integration), with a more philosophical, discursive and, I hope, thought-provoking section in which the treatment process is illuminated by a Bakhtinian–Vygotskian perspective.

CHAPTER 7

A relapse prevention group for problem drinkers

BILL READING

During a recent visit to a distillery producing cognac, I was interested to learn that during the process of production the eaux-de-vie (alcoholic spirits resulting from the distillation of wines from the Cognac district which will eventually be blended to become cognac itself) are stored in wooden casks for maturation. At the point of entering the vats, the eaux-de-vie contain 80 per cent alcohol by volume. During the period of maturation in the wood a number of chemical changes occur, including the spirit's acquisition of flavours and tones imparted to it from the wood itself. While the liquid spirit is held safely within the casks, its alcohol content slowly diminishes as alcohol vapour is able to migrate through the wood and escape into the surrounding atmosphere in the form of 'the angel's share'. It is at the point where the alcohol content of the spirit has fallen to 40 per cent that the resultant cognac becomes ready for bottling. Once bottled, the cognac loses little further alcohol.

This insight into these production methods struck a number of chords in me with regard to my experiences of treatment provision for drinkers over many years. I was especially aware of a parallel between the safe holding provided to the spirits in Cognac in such a way as to allow some of the alcohol to be released and the way in which many drinkers seem to require a period of safe holding within the therapeutic environment as they become progressively more able to disengage from alcohol. The parallel seemed to hold particularly for that aspect of treatment which has become known as 'relapse prevention'.

The notion of relapse has long been intrinsic to operational and theoretical models of addiction. It features prominently in the traditions of fellowship movements such as Alcoholics Anonymous (AA) and has become much discussed within the current emphasis on cognitive-behavioural approaches. However, only in the past 20 years or so has the topic of 'relapse' emerged from a position of relative obscurity to the point where it is now a topic for systematic study in its own right.

Although it can be argued, for instance, that all good past interventions in the addictions have been geared towards preventing relapse, it is now legitimate and helpful to regard 'relapse prevention' as having come of age as an area requiring separate study and therapeutic application.

The use of the term 'relapse' may carry the risk of connotation with a quasi-medical paradigm, thus inviting a potentially unhelpful set of inter-actions between passive ('ill') clients and relatively potent ('well') others. However, I would argue that the preference of many clients and their helpers in continuing to use this label attests to its validity as a metaphor for the situations in which they find themselves. In my own experience, it is entirely feasible (and perhaps ethically essential) to respect the autonomous choices of clients, while employing the metaphor of relapse and enabling the client to benefit from some of the ideas from 'relapse prevention'. In this respect, a concept shares with many other things in life (including drugs themselves), the fact that it is the use to which it is put that provides the best measure of its helpfulness, or otherwise.

For working purposes, I shall assume here a conventional definition of relapse within the addictions: *substance use which is harmful to the client after a period during which such harm was reduced or eliminated.* For some, this may involve a return to pretreatment levels of substance use or harm, whereas for others the occurrence of increased harm may be more associated with 'lapse' rather than 'relapse'.

I shall describe the development and implementation of a group therapy programme for problem drinkers attending for help as non-residential clients at a statutory community alcohol treatment unit in the south-east of England. The programme utilizes the healing group processes so ably described by other authors in this volume, and its content largely comprises the delivery of important tenets of relapse prevention in a form suitable for this therapeutic medium. Particular group exercises are described in some detail along with a consideration of the approaches used in delivering them to the clients. Although it would be possible to replicate the exercises elsewhere, the aim has been to provide an example of the way in which a particular programme was devised and applied in the hope that the account given will assist others in designing other programmes similar to that described yet sensitive to the needs of particular client groups and local environments. Alcohol was the primary drug of choice of the clients for whom this programme was developed, but it is expected that any insight into the programme under discussion will have validity for those experiencing difficulties associated with the use of drugs other than alcohol.

The group sessions themselves are each organized around central concepts within relapse prevention: for example, high-risk situations, lessened cognitive vigilance, etc. For the purposes of this chapter, I have assumed that readers will be familiar with these concepts, although definitions will be offered on some occasions. Readers wishing to study these concepts in more general form may wish to consult one of the many texts which outline them more fully (e.g. Marlatt and Gordon 1985, Wanigaratne et al. 1990)

The context

The group was developed within Mount Zeehan, the headquarters of a community alcohol service serving a general population of some 700 000 people, with a lower age limit for service eligibility of 16 years. Clients are offered individual, family, and group treatments, with many accessing combinations of two or all three modes. The service is predominantly client centred, with particular emphasis being given to attempts to assist clients in constructing and implementing their preferred solutions to personal difficulties associated with alcohol use. No single aetiological model is employed; the core therapeutic principle of the service has been the need to recruit, train, and retain workers who are highly competent and able to express high levels of therapeutic commitment. All workers are required to be trained to at least diploma level with fluency in motivational enhancement therapy and competency in routine individual, family, and group-work skills. Most of the 15 clinicians employed engage in further study in related areas of specialization, including gestalt, systemic, psychoanalytic, and cognitive-behavioural therapies.

The service operates a strict requirement for workers and clients to be free from the effects of alcohol and non-prescribed drugs at the time of any therapeutic encounter. This requirement exists primarily to facilitate an optimal and safe therapeutic ambiance and to express the service's commitment to the autonomy of the individual. Those for whom drug-free attendance is genuinely problematic can expect to receive appropriate temporary assistance in the form of detoxification as a prelude to adequate therapeutic engagement. The service regards itself as having neither a right nor a responsibility to pronounce on the choices made by clients outside the therapeutic situation. The use of prescribed psychoactive drugs is rare.

The group programme

Mount Zeehan offers a wide range of group-work options. The relapse prevention programme was devised to complement and extend an existing group programme of two groups daily over a 3-week period: an initial information-giving week (the 'education group', using discussion guided

by structured input) followed by a 2-week awareness-building programme (the 'awareness group', using structured, written exercises as a
prompt for group discussion). The existing group programme was seen
as less relevant to the needs of those requiring help with the tasks of
maintaining change, in contrast to the needs of those at earlier points in
the model of change. The relapse prevention group was offered as a
closed group of fixed duration for those who had usually completed both
the education and awareness groups, though it was possible to achieve
membership via other routes on condition that potential members were
assessed as having achieved a position of 'active change with at least provisionally formed personal drinking goals'.

In addition to the 'phase-appropriate' role of the group within the
overall group programme, it was hoped that the emphasis on self-help
within relapse prevention would assist clients in planning their successful
exits from treatment and looking to sources of support beyond the treatment situation for needs identified yet not entirely fulfilled. Historically,
Mount Zeehan had given detailed attention to refining processes conducive to client engagement, but had given relatively little attention to the
question of how we might assist clients in being able to effect an exit
which would consolidate rather than threaten the gains made during
treatment. We were particularly mindful that for many clients a difficulty
in negotiating endings in a satisfactory manner seemed to be one of the
central difficulties (e.g. Elliott 2003).

The group culture

In keeping with other groups offered within the service, the relapse prevention group programme was conducted in a supportive atmosphere
within which more expressive/interpretive interventions could be made
when appropriate (see Flores, Chapter 1). More particularly, the notion of
the 'secure base script', a notion deriving from attachment theory (Shaver
and Mikulincer 2002), seemed particularly consonant with the needs of
clients attempting to maintain and enhance existing areas of change.
Secure base script describes a situation in which an individual is consistently able to engage in a sequence of three simply stated yet vital
operations for dealing successfully with his/her problems:

* the ability to acknowledge and communicate personal distress
* the ability to identify that a problem requires solving
* the ability to seek the support of others.

It is easy to see the ways in which heavy or prolonged use of alcohol is
likely to inhibit an individual's capacity to operate effectively at any of the

three stages. Equally, the script provides an accessible guide to some of the needs that may surface as clients attempt to negotiate their lives with less reliance on alcohol, and points towards interventions which may assist them in this respect.

Selection and preparation of clients

The following criteria were agreed for potential members:

- reasonably well-formed drinking goal (i.e. reduction, changed context, or abstinence)
- evidence of commitment to maintain or enhance changes already made
- ability to attend sessions as agreed
- willingness to undertake written or behavioural assignments between group sessions
- acceptance of group rules (no alcohol or non-prescribed drugs at point of attendance, confidentiality, taking personal responsibility, honesty).

Almost all clients will have had previous experience of groups, including those with current or past participation in fellowship meetings.

Each cohort of clients has comprised a mixture of those who are currently aiming for total abstinence (temporary or permanent) and those wishing to continue using alcohol, albeit on a reduced basis. The resultant mixture of individual approaches has consistently proved to be far more creative than problematic. This outcome is clearly associated with the fact that all clients attend sessions in a non-intoxicated state and also that an ambiance is fostered within which respect for the position adopted by others is combined with encouragement to explore reactions to difference within a respectful and encouraging environment.

Structure of group sessions

The programme comprises a total of ten 90-minute sessions. Trials of different modes of delivery showed that it was preferable to have two sessions within the first week to facilitate initial group formation, with a maximum of one session per week in subsequent weeks. The gap of at least a week between sessions is sufficient to allow time and experience for the completion of assignments, and has proved helpful in providing a bridge between members' lives inside and outside the group experience. Members have frequently described the way in which anticipation of attendance at the next group meeting has, in itself, proved helpful in handling tricky situations between sessions. The group is facilitated throughout by one staff member, with the occasional presence of a second therapist in a training capacity. Supervision is provided routinely, with the option of using a one-way screen for live observation where required.

The format of the group

Each group session takes as its theme one or more of the essential concepts of relapse prevention models, with these falling within the three routine domains:

- awareness building
- identifying skills repertoires, deficits and areas for improvement
- achieving a balanced lifestyle.

We have found it helpful to encourage clients to consider an additional domain for attention: that of *individual vulnerability factors* (see section below).

Theme-centred interaction method

Cohn's theme-centred interaction method (TCIM) (Schaffer and Galinsky 1974) has proved to be a very suitable model for conducting the relapse prevention group. TCIM has been offered as appropriate to group-based activities of all kinds, whether convened for therapeutic or other purposes. In addition to usual group rules on confidentiality, no violence, etc., TCIM sets five additional ground rules:

- being one's own chairman
- speaking for oneself (use of first pronoun)
- giving the statement behind one's question
- disturbances take precedence (preoccupied individuals cannot participate fully in the group)
- speaking one at a time.

TCIM group-work centres on the identification of a theme for discussion, with this theme being stated in active and personal terms. For example, the theme of 'triggers' for drinking might be introduced as 'things that trigger my thoughts of drinking'. The primary task of the group leader is to assist the members in being able to interact on the set theme, often by steering the members back when they have moved too far away from the theme itself. The theme is best explored within three domains which are regarded as forming a triangle within which interaction can occur (Figure 7.1).

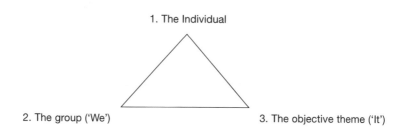

1. The Individual

2. The group ('We')

3. The objective theme ('It')

Figure 7.1 The 'I–We–It' triangle.

It is the therapist's attention to what is termed the 'I–We–It' triangle that has seemed especially well suited to exploration of themes within the relapse prevention group. The task of the group leader is essentially one of attending to the group process in terms of its location within the 'I–We–It' triangle, an approach which helps to avoid the extremes of excessive personalization ('hijacking') or avoidance through excessive objectification or intellectualization. Additionally, the leader will make frequent and explicit references to the group process with this, in turn, fostering an enhanced sense of the members' awareness of the containing and supportive potential of the group.

The following vignette provides an example.

(The group theme has been set as 'How I cope with feelings without drinking'. The members have spent time considering questions such as 'what is the difference between thoughts and feelings?', 'can you change your feelings?', 'do feelings have to be justified?'. For the past few minutes, Elizabeth and Joe have been involved in an exchange, with other members remaining silent.)

Elizabeth *(to Joe): So you think that you don't have to look at your feelings at all?*

Joe: *You've got to be positive and get your thinking straight.*

Elizabeth: *So you'd rather be in denial then?*

Joe: *I didn't say that, I just think you have to put the past behind you.*

Leader: *Maybe, Joe, what you're saying makes sense for you but it might be different for others?*

Joe: *I suppose so . . . but I still think Elizabeth's feeling sorry for herself.*

Leader: *I wonder if other people here are coping with feelings by sitting out of the discussion and leaving it to Joe and Elizabeth to do the talking at present . . .?*

The relapse prevention group can be seen as offering a curriculum of themes which have useful potential for exploration by the group members, e.g. cognitive vigilance, feeling in control, covert antecedents, etc. TCIM offers a structure for helpful interactions on such themes, and the outline of particular group sessions provided below illustrates the way in which these curricular items have been framed within the group programme. In addition, this approach can be employed in a more fluid manner, sensitive to particular themes as they emerge within a particular cohort of members. A recent example occurred when several group members had spoken the difficulties encountered in talking to other people about their drinking. As is usual practice, the leader first identifies a useful theme for exploration and then asks members to reflect on the theme for a few moments prior to engaging in discussion:

> **Leader:** *It feels as if the subject of people's self-image is around in the group today. Perhaps you could all take a moment to think about this theme – 'how my drinking affects the way I relate to other people'.*

It may be helpful for the identified theme to be displayed in written form to assist the group in keeping to task. There are inevitably a number of themes active within a group at any given point, and the group's purpose (in our case, that of preventing relapse) should act as the best guide to which of these simultaneous themes is most worthy of group attention. Workers vary greatly in their ability to identify themes active in group (or individual) sessions and thus isolate those suitable for more sustained focus. However, I have also found that workers can be helped to 'think thematically' – for example, simply though encouraging them to list themes as they presented, as the therapist subsequently reflects on the course of a therapeutic session. The use of transcripts, audio recordings of sessions, and process notes has been particularly useful in this respect.

The 'I–We–It' triangle provides the group leader with a useful model for considering and guiding the group's process in the more general pursuit of its task, even when not specifically focused on exploration of an explicit theme. Once again, this involves the leader's ability to help the group to focus its attention on all three points of the triangle in a balance suitable for the group's current task or narrative.

Individual vulnerability factors on the relapse prevention curriculum

The relapse prevention literature and research findings provide us with a set of considerations which have general validity when attempting to frame the circumstances, aptitudes, and lifestyle factors that are likely to be relevant when a given individual attempts to avoid getting into difficulty again with their drinking. For example, we know that those who 'relapse' will frequently cite 'unpleasant feelings' as having been important in understanding their shift from less-problematic to more-problematic drinking. However, 'unpleasant feelings' may encompass an enormous range of possibilities which may require vastly differing remedies (e.g. emergence of past trauma, inability to handle feelings of excitement, poverty, lack of purpose, unacknowledged anger, low self-efficacy in a the face of a high-risk situation, etc.). Assisting clients in effecting a detailed analysis of what may make them vulnerable to relapse as unique individuals provides the basis for a personally tailored version of the otherwise 'ready to wear' approach which comprises mainstream relapse prevention.

> *Susie had kept a diary of her cravings for alcohol during the course of the group. She was able to identify that these occurred only at times when she was about to see her boyfriend. She was both shocked to observe a pattern which had become extremely clear when presented in written form, and at a loss to account for a craving which occurred only at what appeared consciously to be a time of pleasurable anticipation. She was later able to identify that past experiences of loss had disposed her to insecurity as to the future of the relationship. This insecurity was accompanied by a dread of communicating her fears to her boyfriend lest this act itself might drive him away from her, just as she had accounted for past losses as having been triggered by her unbearable state of need.*

This vignette illustrates a situation in which the client's ability to achieve a more precise appreciation of her relationship with alcohol has clear implications for the tasks that she may need to address in order to reduce her own propensity for future relapse.

A variety of approaches to implementation

TCIM has comprised the central model of technique used in administering the programme, but a selection of other approaches has also proved useful – as illustrated within the group exercises described below. The devices and models most prominently employed in addition have included:

- solution-focused brief therapy
- rational-emotive therapy
- role-play
- cognitive-behavioural therapy
- behavioural rehearsal
- standard questionnaires
- written handouts/information leaflets
- journals
- written and behavioural assignments between group meetings

- craving/drinking diaries
- didactic input.

Perhaps one of the most important factors in the rise of relapse prevention to its current status has been its potential to assist workers in developing a systematic understanding of processes involved in relapse. Given that clients themselves may struggle to make sense of their experiences of relapse, relapse prevention models have provided therapists with an explanatory framework which, at the very least, fosters a sense of enhanced understanding, and thus of an enhanced sense of role security. An equivalent process can be observed in the client group whereby it has seemed helpful to inform clients about key aspects of relapse prevention (comprising the 'It' dimension of the 'I–We–It' triangle) through didactic approaches such as talks and written handouts, as a prelude to personal scrutiny of the concepts involved. Once again, TCIM is well suited to enabling the clients to effect the shift from a relatively generalized and objective concept ('It') such as 'coping skills within high-risk situations' to group exploration ('We') of highly personal and relevant themes ('I') such as "what skills I need to be able to use when I'm tempted to drink again'.

Although it is expected that particular items of the relapse prevention curriculum will have general usefulness, the aim of TCIM discussion in this context is to offer clients the opportunity to consider these items in terms of their potential usefulness rather than to introduce these ideas as representing some body of knowledge whose assimilation is necessarily desirable. Many clients have reported that some of the concepts involved lack relevance for them, or that they may, indeed, be unhelpful in their impact. For example, clients who prosper within the 12-step paradigm may regard discussion on the transitional nature of the relapse process as hostile to a view that is better supported by an 'all or none' approach, although some in the same category might regard a decision not to attend a fellowship meeting as comprising a lapse. The relapse prevention programme presents clients with a menu of concepts and potentially useful ideas within a setting conducive to safe and productive exploration. It is for individual clients to select those items that may or may not prove helpful in their individual situations.

The relapse prevention group programme

Although the outline of the programme given below might be replicated as described, its actual delivery is necessarily different from one cohort of clients to the next. For example, the content of a session as described may require distribution over two or more sessions, and the generation of themes for discussion needs to be conducted in accord with the needs of

particular groups at particular points in time. The duration of the programme can be extended where necessary.

Descriptions of specific sessions is followed by a list of observations
made by therapists who have delivered the programme in the past.

The pre-programme meeting

A meeting is held with all prospective members, in which the purpose and
format of the group is explained. The purpose is simply described as
being that of avoiding or minimizing the potential for relapse. Early
emphasis is given to the notion of maintaining or enhancing change, in
contrast to an emphasis on contemplating change. Clients are invited to
consider what they would like to achieve as a result of membership of the
group. The requirement for members to undertake written or behavioural assignments between sessions is made explicit, along with the need for
a commitment to attend all sessions. A written timetable is issued to those
wishing to proceed. The first session of the programme takes place within days of this inaugural meeting.

Session 1

- Explanation by leader as to the form of group sessions, namely:

    - agreement regarding group ground-rules
    - each session to start with a brief period of members 'checking in'
      where required
    - systematic introduction to main concepts in relapse prevention
    - use of questionnaires or written assignments
    - use of TCIM
    - use of role-plays.

- Members are asked to give a description of their current and recent
  drinking status, along with a statement of their individual drinking
  goals. All members are invited to give feedback on individual presentations.
- Leader gives general definition of relapse and asks members to reflect
  individually on the theme 'what the idea of relapse means for me',
  before theme-centred discussion.
- Leader introduces distinction between the concepts of 'lapse' and
  'relapse'. Members are invited to engage with an appropriate theme
  exploring personal meanings of these terms.
- Leader distributes written instructions (see Figure 7.2) for a written
  assignment to be completed in preparation for group exercise in
  next/subsequent session.
- Leader closes session.

Describe the last occasion when you relapsed or had a problematic period of drinking. Try to give particular consideration to:

1 How you were feeling.
2 What your thoughts were like
3 How you were getting on with other people

In writing this account, try to focus on what it was like for you:

1 Before the episode
2 At the beginning of the episode
3 During the episode
4 At the end of the episode
5 After the episode

Figure 7.2 Instructions for written assignment.

Therapist's observations on session 1

- *It is helpful to attend to members' emotional reactions to invitations to participate in group tasks.*
- *Some clients may not consider their drinking to fall within episodes of problematic use, e.g. habitual drinkers.*
- *Members can be invited to consider their reasons for rejecting any specific suggestion or idea, especially where such rejection occurs rapidly and with emotional arousal suggestive of possible defensive exclusion.*
- *The leader advises members that their written accounts will be seen only by its author who then chooses what he/she wishes to reveal later to the group.*

Session 2

- Members check in.
- Each member reads aloud their account of their last relapse or problematic drinking episode.
- Leader creates space for questions, clarifications and other responses from members on hearing accounts given by particular members.
- Leader instructs each member to return to their written account and to highlight or mark all points of choice contained within it.
- Each member reads the account aloud again, including points of choice that have been identified.
- Leader creates space for questions, clarifications, and other responses from members on hearing accounts given by particular members.
- Leader introduces the notion of the experience of control as a factor in

relapse and invites members to consider this in the context of their respective written accounts – e.g. 'is there a point at which your experience of being in control changed during that episode?'
- Theme-centred discussion – e.g. 'how the choices I make affect my feeling of control'.
- Leader gives assignment – clients to complete the Inventory of Drinking Situations (IDS) (Annis, Graham and Davis 1987).
- Leader closes session.

Therapists' observations on session 2

- *Although written exercises such as this have value in enabling more coherent and systematic exploration, it is important for the leader to remain sensitive to the anxieties that the prospect of self-disclosure within the group may provoke for individual members.*
- *The return to accounts of relapses, with points of choice highlighted as described, seems consistently to identify previously unrecognized transitional stages in members' eventual relapses. Although the aim is to assist clients in recognizing additional points at which opportunities for other choices might be made in similar situations in future, the leader needs to be sensitive to the potential for increased feelings of guilt and anxiety.*
- *Clients vary tremendously in the range and extent of their reactions to the notion of control as a factor in relapse precipitation. For some, excessive drinking may be equated with an enhanced sense of control, whereas for others the opposite holds true. Others still may consider that their personal control is never impaired and that to assert differently is to do nothing other than to make excuses for otherwise unacceptable excesses.*
- *The IDS is a 100-item, self-completion questionnaire which measures the extent to which clients drank heavily in a number of given situations. Subscales for a total of eight situations are located within one of two categories:*
  - *Personal situations: unpleasant emotions, pleasant emotions, physical discomfort, testing personal control, urges and temptations*
  - *Social situations: conflict with others, social pressure to drink, pleasant times with others*

  Computer scoring of the IDS generates a profile of the client's situation-specific drinking behaviour.

Session 3

- Members check in and hand in completed IDS questionnaires so that individual profiles can be available for the next session.

- Leader introduces a cognitive-behavioural model of the relapse process charting the following transitions: perceived self-control/high-risk situation/ineffective coping skills/low self-efficacy/initial lapse/rule violation effect + perceived effects of substance/increased likelihood of relapse.
- Members invited to comment on or question elements of the above model.
- Theme-centred discussion – e.g. 'what could alert me that I am at increased risk of relapse?'
- Members given Relapse Precipitants Inventory (Litman et al. 1983) for completion before next session
- Leader closes session

Therapists' observations on session 3

- *It may be helpful at this stage to introduce members to the basic tenets of cognitive-behavioural approaches – first, that the way in which we think about ourselves will affect how we feel and behave and second, that it is possible to change ways of thinking in order to achieve different feeling and behavioural outcomes.*
- *The leader may wish to emphasize that the identification of high-risk situations may provide opportunities for avoiding them, or the development of strategies to manage them effectively.*

Session 4

- Members check in.
- Members score RPI and review scores in light of leader's explanation of scoring system.
- Leader distributes IDS profiles.
- Members discuss IDS profiles.
- Theme-centred discussion – e.g. 'situations that could trigger me to relapse'.
- Assignment for next session – members to review description of past relapse episode (see sessions 1 and 2) and other, similar experiences with a view to identifying early warning signs that there is increased risk of lapsing or relapsing.
- Leader closes session.

Therapists' observations on session 4

- *The RPI is a 25-item self-completion questionnaire which gives an overall score of proneness to relapse as measured across four categories of potential relapse precipitants: unpleasant affect, external events, social anxiety and lessened cognitive vigilance.*
- *A variation in distributing the IDS profiles exists in the form of*

inviting members to guess the identity of the member to whom a profile belongs. This approach seems both to assist more detailed understanding of the dimensions being measured and to facilitate more intimate group interaction.

Session 5

- Members check in.
- Members discuss early warning signs identified from last assignment.
- Leader introduces notion of 'cognitive vigilance' and the role of reduced vigilance as a potential factor in relapse.
- Theme-centred discussion – e.g. 'how I can make sure I don't get too complacent about my drinking'.
- Assignment – members to compile a list of their main high-risk situations and the skills they will need to manage these effectively.
- Leader closes session.

Therapists' observations on session 5

- *It can be helpful to ask members to describe ways in which they have been able to maintain a sense of vigilance in the past.*
- *Many clients are able to describe ways in which they have tricked themselves into reducing their vigilance in past situations. The notion of the 'drinking self versus the sober self' can provide an accessible metaphor for the struggle to avoid such self-deception (Cartwright, personal communication, 1980). Within this model, the drinking self is regarded as being committed solely to increasing the person's use of alcohol, regardless of the harmful potential of so doing. One of the main strategies of the drinking self is to play tricks on the sober self in order to undermine any attempts at moderation or abstinence.*

Session 6

- Members check in
- Members feed back on the skills required to manage high-risk situations identified in last assignment.
- Individual members asked to list, in writing, resources or means by which required skills can be acquired or enhanced.
- All group members asked to give feedback and suggest additional alternative possibilities for skills enhancement to each individual after their presentation.
- Individual members asked to respond to suggestions or comments of other members, including likelihood of pursuing potential resources.
- Leader introduces notion of individual vulnerability to relapse.

- Assignment – members to identify sources of individual vulnerability and potential remedies.

Therapists' observations on session 6

- *The idea that' skills' are required to manage difficult situations may require illustration, for example, to introduce the idea that capacities such as acknowledging feelings of discomfort, asking for help, and expressing oneself in the group itself can be seen as requiring the use of skills.*
- *Where clients seem unable to identify useful skills, or remedies for skills deficits, the leader may invite members to explore the possibility that this may reflect an ambivalence to the possibility of change. Similarly, it can be helpful to invite members to identify and express the reasons for rejecting particular possibilities or suggestions from others.*

Session 7

- Members check in.
- Members share lists of individual vulnerabilities and potential remedies.
- Group feedback on individual presentations.
- Group leader gives introduction to the idea of lifestyle balance as a factor in relapse prevention.
- Theme-centred discussion – e.g. 'getting balance into my life'.
- Assignment – members to list typical activities over the course of one week (i.e. what it is that each member tends to do each week).

Therapists' observations on session 7

- *The idea of individual vulnerability to relapse may exist in any number of domains within the client's life, e.g. poverty, wealth, past experiences of abuse, maladaptive defences, spiritual need, etc. It does not imply that the individual is necessarily vulnerable per se, but rather that the client is likely to have idiosyncratic propensities which require attention in order to minimize personal relapse potential (see Reading and Jacobs 2002).*
- *It is helpful to consider individual vulnerability as operative at three points: predisposition ('triggerability'), precipitation ('triggers') and persistence (continuation of behaviour once triggered).*

Session 8

- Members check in.
- Members are asked to read aloud lists of weekly activities and to consider where to locate each activity on a continuum between 'wants' and 'shoulds'.

- Leader invites members to consider the suggestion that overemphasis on 'shoulds' may act as a relapse precipitant.
- Theme-centred discussion – e.g. 'enjoying myself without alcohol'.
- Leader introduces idea of covert antecedents/'seemingly irrelevant decisions' (SIDS).
- Assignment – members asked to list the ways in which past experiences of SIDS have proved to be significant precursors to lapsing or relapsing.

Therapists' observations on session 8

- *Of course, many activities will not fit easily into either of the categories of 'shoulds' and 'wants', or may best be described as embracing elements of each of these possibilities.*
- *Implicit in the question of the 'wants' that members experience is the notion that alcohol itself may have been an important means by which wants and other areas of need were fulfilled. For many, the reduction or cessation of alcohol use may reflect response to what 'should' happen, which will often exist in conflict with what the client may ideally want to happen. Although such dissonance may be commonplace in early help-seeking, relapse prevention holds that maintenance of change will be most effective where the change itself is experienced as becoming progressively more characterized by the client's sense that this is what they want, rather than (or as well as) what they 'should' do.*

Session 9

- Members check in.
- Members discuss list of SIDS from last assignment.
- Theme centred discussion – e.g. 'who can help me avoid making mistakes in the future'.
- Assignment – each member to write a short essay entitled 'how I intend to set up my next relapse'.

Therapists' observations on session 9

- *Attention to covert antecedents or SIDS can be linked to the strategies that individual members believe will help them avoid similar mistakes in the future.*

Session 10 (final session)

- Members check in.
- Clients read essays resulting from last assignment.
- Leader focuses on task necessary for group closure or plans for future, less frequent meetings.

Therapists' observations on session 10

- *The essays have proved to be an enjoyable and illuminating experience for members, often bearing witness to the fact that despite rational perspectives gained from relapse prevention groups and elsewhere, members can recognize their potential to make choices which overthrow such insights.*
- *Members and leaders may elect to convene continued meetings of the group with variable levels of structure or openness. A gradually reducing frequency of group meetings has sometimes seemed a helpful way for the group to proceed towards termination.*

Life beyond the relapse prevention group

It is expected that participation in the relapse prevention group programme will have resulted in members becoming more aware of what will be required in order for them to advance their collective and individual recoveries. The need for continued further attention to skills, awareness, lifestyle balance, and individual vulnerability factors will, necessarily, require a long-term commitment to change. In some respects, members may identify areas that are appropriately addressed within the treatment setting, for example skills training, marital or family therapy, psychotherapy, aftercare groups, and cognitive-behavioural therapy. Perhaps one of the most important outcomes of such a group is to offer members the opportunity to acknowledge that they may have relied excessively on alcohol to meet, distort, or deny their true needs. A high-quality, long-term recovery is most likely where such people find personally meaningful ways in which hitherto neglected areas of need can be pursued. A move away from the addiction treatment setting may be central to this end.

Return to Cognac . . .

Once the cognac has been carefully stored in its cask, it must be allowed time to give the angels their share of its alcohol and find its own true character. Although the processes required in the early stages are almost identical from one year to the next, each year produces its own unique vintage.

CHAPTER 8

One-off art therapy in in-patient detoxification

LINDA VICKERS

> The hospital – its heavy freight
> lashed down ship-shape ward over ward –
> steamed into the night with some on board
> soon to be lost if the desperate
> charts were known. Others would come
> altered to land or find the land
> altered. At their voyage's end
> some would be added to, some diminished.
>
> Jon Stallworthy, from 'The Almond Tree'

This chapter examines a short-term weekly art therapy group taking place within an in-patient detoxification unit. I shall discuss the potential benefits of art therapy, looking at the particular difficulties and needs of substance misusers. Using case examples, I shall illustrate how experience of an art therapy group can enable exploration of motivations and choices in the early stages of detoxification. I propose that art therapy is appropriate for this client group, allowing individuals to moderate their interactions with others, as well as tentatively to explore underlying issues which come to consciousness during the withdrawal process. The role of the art object in art therapy is as a means through which the individual is able to regulate distance between self and others in a group setting; the art-making process being primarily solitary, and the art product being a symbolic communication to the group, which is often less threatening than verbal exchanges. I shall discuss my adaptation of psychodynamic models (as used in longer-term therapy groups) to accommodate the needs of this client group and setting; and posit that a positive experience of group work during detoxification may provide motivation to persevere with treatment, and to build on embryonic insights in later therapeutic work.

117

Client group

Although addicts are generally socially marginalized and are considered problematic individuals, they are also an engaging client group to work with. Because of the complex nature of addictive personalities, theoretical assumptions are constantly tested in clinical practice. The challenge for clinicians is the multifaceted nature of addictions, as explained, for example, in the pioneering work of Dr Max Glatt, whose work in the field helped to get alcoholism universally acknowledged as a disease. He first came across 'drinkers' in the 1950s while working as a psychiatrist at Warlingham Park Hospital, Surrey, when he observed someone who was 'noticeably different from the other [psychiatric] patients' and who 'displayed none of the attributes that society associated with drinkers' (Glatt 1998, p. 2). Glatt's constructive approach was instrumental in his development of treatment in the field. There are, of course, also inherent frustrations that come with the territory. The prevailing ambivalence of addicts towards giving up their habit can be challenging, and even more so for those staff whose input is required on a daily basis and over a prolonged period of time. Staff working in the field are put under pressure 'do something' with clients who are insufficiently motivated to give up their substance. Notably, in my work as a psychotherapist within the UK National Health Service, there is a policy of refusing treatment to 'active addicts'. My experience of working therapeutically with substance users has therefore been confined to art therapy; which, as I discuss in this chapter, seems to be a particularly useful treatment option.

Psychodynamic approaches within multidisciplinary teams

The difficulty in finding a consistent model from which to work reflects the complexity of the subject. Although it may be possible to attribute certain traits to people who struggle with addiction, these may be indistinguishable from difficulties that are intrinsic to the addiction itself. Waller and Mahony (1999, p. 2) cite studies by Lavelle, Hammersley and Forsyth (1993), who argue that the hypothesis of an 'addictive personality' has produced 'contradictory evidence with methodological flaws'. It is clear from the popularity and success of the 12-step approach of Alcoholics Anonymous (AA), for example, that their philosophy offers stability among the chaos caused by addiction. However, like Beasley, I would query the concept of substance misusers constituting one homogeneous group suffering from one 'disease'. Without doubt, AA is of incomparable benefit to substance misusers, and has arguably been of more assistance than specialized clinical treatment, but as Glatt (1998, p. 2) points out, there is a danger in taking just one party line: 'Anyone can become an alcoholic. It follows that there are very different personalities among them, so to think there's only one method for treating all alcoholics doesn't make sense.' This concurs with my lasting impression of 'individuals in the groups' rather than remembering each group as a whole; and perhaps reflects the difficulty in establishing a cohesive structure for treatment.

Although there is no consensus about causes of substance misuse or models of treatment, contemporary models advocate multidisciplinary team working. Group work reflects the contemporary view of addictions as being multi-influenced by social, psychological, physical, and moral factors (Orford 1985). Winship posits group work as central to the treatment of addiction because it is fundamentally a 'social' problem, in that the 'interpersonal field of human relationships underpins the cause of addiction'; hence 'group therapy has evolved as a core treatment intervention'. This said, he also asserts that 'the social context of addiction does not preclude the constellation of biological and cognitive factors, which should also be considered, such as genetic disposition and disease concept'. As he shrewdly observes, most problem drug users have in-depth interrelational problems, since 'It is clear that their [substance] use did not arise out of nothing. It is not a case of a recreational pursuit that has gone wrong' (Winship 1999, p. 51).

A multidisciplinary group ethos is also adopted in the information leaflet made available to service users being admitted to the detoxification unit. With the more immediate medical and social care that is provided by other members of the team, there is scope for the art therapy group to be more enquiring. However, working psychodynamically within a multidisciplinary team requires the therapist to be aware of the impact on the institution. Integration seems to be the key here, requiring the therapist to be sensitive and in dialogue with the philosophy and methodology of the institution. Groterath (1999, p. 20) advocates the need for therapists working in addiction treatment centres to give up the pretension of being exclusive, and to 'be constantly aware of their intervention being only one factor in a complex system of therapeutic factors'. A behavourist approach to abstinence, for example, could conflict with a psychodynamic exploration of a person's addiction; and this highlights the need for constant feedback among the team. Even if psychotherapeutic methods used in the creative therapies prove to be well employed in group settings and combine easily with other modalities, there has to be agreement between disciplines on compatibility of therapeutic method. Cantopher (1999, p. 43) points out the tendency for alcoholics or addicts to develop 'strategies to avoid experiencing the impact of one particular therapeutic style or treatment'. A multidisciplinary approach is more able to safeguard against such defence strategies, because it offers many therapeutic strands.

There is a tendency for sessional staff to work in isolation from the staff team, often exacerbating divisions between staff and patient groups. It is important for the art therapy group to be presented as an integral part of treatment, and for this reason the attendance of a member of staff who acts as a link with the ward team during handover is essential. This arrangement also offers an educational experience of art therapy, and provides opportunity for action research. Because of the rotating schedule of nursing staff, the link worker changes from week to week, although this is less problematic than might be thought because of the fluctuating patient population.

A background to art therapy group work with addictions

The modality of choice for substance misuse clients is group work, and most art therapy practice is conducted within groups (Skaife and Huet 1998). In the early days of the profession, art therapists worked with large groups of patients within the open art studios of the large psychiatric hospitals, a trend discussed by Edward Adamson (1984). As a result of working within psychiatric institutions, art therapy was exposed to approaches used by other professionals, including that of occupational therapy, which influenced the development of practice using theme-based or projective art groups (for example, Liebmann 1986). In recent times this model has been replaced by group analytic art therapy and group interactive models (McNeilly 1983, 1987, 1990, Waller 1993) which have developed in response to a broader client group and government initiatives for care in the community.

Therapeutic framework

Although art therapy services have been developed extensively within psychiatric settings, there have been far fewer interventions in substance misuse and, indeed, few art therapists list addictions as an area of specialism in the register of the British Association of Art Therapists. Waller and Mahony (1992) reviewed the use (or non-use) of American and British art therapy in centres for drug and alcohol patients. From the limited literature available, they discovered that the stated theoretical orientation of the art therapist was not borne out in the description of practice. Consequently, practitioners new to the field may find that the employment of a theoretical model is an obstacle to working with group dynamics as they occur in practice. Despite these problems, there is a need in psychodynamic work to establish some kind of therapeutic boundary within which material can be safely explored, and as Walsh (1995) notes, the therapist's responsibility is 'to hold the meeting at a specific time and place'. Within this defined context, the patient may explore the space and the limits of its boundaries. Winnicott (1971) is a primary source of reference for art therapists, with his ideas of the therapeutic framework and transitional object – in this context the art object – providing the foundations of a sound framework for preliminary art therapy sessions. To some extent I would see a one-off session as analogous to assessment, its basic aim being to explore the patient's difficulties as much as possible, and to consider how best to proceed with future treatment. In addition, these encapsulated sessions are a means of assessing and developing clinical practice: through looking at common threads that run through the work, one is afforded an opportunity to form a realistic working model.

Theories of addictions

For motivational purposes I have found it useful to draw on the observations of other creative therapists working in the field of addictions. Moore's review of the literature on art therapy with substance abusers (1983) considers art therapy groups to be a particularly appropriate treatment tool given the characteristics of addicts. Traits include loneliness, low self-esteem, an inability to communicate in a genuine way, and the loss or lack of a sense of control. Groterath, discussing the creative therapies, proposes that addicts have a fear of being judged and tend to re-enact a tribunal situation within verbal psychotherapy:

> This phenomenon has been called therapeutic resistance by some, and 'non-treatability' of addicts by others. The important thing is that we have noticed that even so-called 'untreatable' addicts react positively and often in a highly differentiated way to psychotherapy as soon as the 'stage' shifts . . . and instead offers a more permissive 'stage'. That is what the arts therapies do – with colours and forms, movement, music and play. Furthermore, in that they involve not only the mind but also the body of the patients, these methods more closely connected to the vital expressions of the individual. (Groterath 1999, pp. 21–22)

An element of play is introduced into the therapeutic environment, this being a necessary component of human development (Winnicott 1971, Brown 1998). Cantopher identifies the tendency of resistant patients and those in denial to dislike art therapy intensely. However, as he points out, if they survive the initial discomfort, they come to value this form of therapy. Over a long period of time they have become used to covering over their feelings with substances through intellectualization or with denial. (Cantopher 1999, p. 43).

If patients are to gain some understanding of their experience, an essential task of the therapist in a one-off group is to encourage resistant group members to endure the discomfort.

In relation to addictions, the model of narcissism is of particular interest to psychotherapists and art psychotherapists alike (Albert-Puleo 1980, Springham 1992, 1994, 1998, 1999). Narcissistic disorder is thought to have its roots in childhood when the infant fails to receive adequate nurturance from parental figures. If a pattern of neglect is established, the child will oscillate between attention-seeking behaviour and withdrawal into their own emotional world. In adulthood, alcohol and drugs facilitate this withdrawal from consciousness. Cantopher observes that 'a person starved of attention and affection will not have learnt how to give these commodities to others. Hence their emotional life is largely internal and mediated through substances' (1999, p. 37). Albert-Puleo (1980) considers art therapy to be a particularly useful intervention in the treatment of pathological narcissism because it facilitates both public (patient and therapist/group) and private (patient and image) experiences within the therapy session. Springham, an art therapist who has used this model extensively in his work with substance misusers, supports this view and suggests that:

> the narcissistic model of dissonance between public and private selves and its resulting need to hide and be seen at the same time, is a helpful one. Art therapy uniquely combines private and public experience and in so doing matches the narcissistic wounds that have the real spur to seek proper help and this type of 'sobering experience' has obvious implications for longer term treatment. This is the essence of good 'problem clarification', and for me this is the strongest argument for including art therapy on such drug and alcohol programmes. (Springham 1994, p. 40)

Given the special need for defences to be protected during the very early stages of detoxification, this would appear to be a useful treatment model, and Springham's research (1994) in the area seems encouraging in terms of developing an appropriate therapeutic approach.

Brief encounters

In introducing art therapy sessions to the substance misuse team, I had reservations about how useful one-off therapy sessions could be. My main concern was that too vigorous a psychodynamic approach could be detrimental to patients at such a vulnerable stage in treatment. A survey of some of the literature on time-limited therapy (Yalom 1985, Feltham 1997, Mander 2000) indicates consensus on the need for adaptability in approach. Discussing acute in-patient group psychotherapy, Yalom (1983) suggests that the therapist should take into consideration the needs of the patient (intrinsic factors) in the context of the setting (extrinsic factors), since the interface between these two aspects is likely to influence the therapeutic value of the group. Yalom proposes that in this situation the therapist emphasizes the here and now, and should encourage the group to use the experience of the present as material for reality testing their assumptions. In terms of the developmental sequences or tasks of groups, he describes the initial stage as time for 'orientation, hesitant participation, search for meaning and dependency' (Yalom 1985). The more challenging and confrontational elements of later stages, which allow 'negative' affects such as anger and jealousy to be expressed, are unlikely to emerge in the context of a one-off session. However, there is a difference between such affects being seen and the challenging and confrontation of them. At the detoxification stage, for example, there may be a lot of anger present which is not necessarily confronted. When the therapist is used to working psychodynamically, the scope to work with transference material is also curtailed. Mander (2000, p. 23) advocates that brief interventions 'require a careful and deliberate decision about how much, if at all, to interpret or foster identified transference'. Feltham (1997, p. 59) suggests flexibility, arguing that the 'optimal attitude for effective time-limited counselling is . . . one of openness to possibilities, willingness to explore some of the techniques offered by approaches other than one's own and commitment to action research with clients'. This is a useful guiding concept during the establishment of one-off art therapy sessions, and implies a need for interpretative responses to unconscious material to be moderated in these brief interactions.

The 20-bed ward where I am based has a constantly shifting patient population, with admissions and discharges taking place on a daily basis. As a consequence, the membership of the art therapy group changes from week to week, with patients rarely attending more than one session. Given that psychodynamically oriented work is traditionally provided on a longer-term basis than the duration of a one-off session, it is important to look at the limitations, as well as the scope, of the one-off situation and to be realistic and flexible in method. As stated in the patient information leaflet, the remit of the unit is 'to provide a supportive environment to begin physical recovery and an opportunity to *begin looking at* [my emphasis] the changes that need to occur in order to begin a drug and alcohol free lifestyle'. Given the immediate physical and social difficulties that the patient will be dealing with, therapeutic interventions need to be realistic and respectful to the treatment setting. Treatment can be as fundamental as supporting the client in being able to sit still and work through withdrawal, making it possible to begin to look at future treatment options.

In a longer-term treatment programme of art therapy, a more challenging approach may be appropriate, as long as the therapist holds an awareness of the anxiety that is experienced by the patient and moderates interventions accordingly. Cantopher (1999) ascribes this anxiety to the fact that over a long period of time the addict has become used to covering over their feelings with substances, intellectualization, or denial, and observes that 'Art therapy seems to cut through these defences, to get through to feeling, and in due course sometimes to understanding.' This fear of exposure was illustrated by one man's image of a can of worms, which he said symbolized the thoughts and feelings that had overwhelmed him once the anaesthesia of alcohol had worn off. The safety of expression through the artwork was meant he was able to display his image, without prematurely verbalizing painful insights. The artwork provided him with a screen of safety from which he was able to moderate his interactions with the therapist and group. Albert-Puleo (1980, p. 47) views this process as a constructive approach, in that the artwork is the focus, which can be talked about, allowing repressed material to be brought more tolerably to consciousness.

Visual and verbal communications

Patients' resistance to verbalization is certainly heightened in shorter-term therapy – for example, in acute psychiatric settings and time-limited outpatient groups – and although I observe the usual performance anxiety around initial mark-making, this is relatively unproblematic in comparison with the resistance to viewing and discussing images at the end of each session. There is a particularly marked resistance in the case of substance misusers, and from a narcissistic viewpoint, Springham suggests that patients may adopt a solitary approach, turning away from relationships, and entering their narcissism during art-making. He cites Lachman-Chapman (1983): 'image production in art therapy reduces potential shame at expressing such archaic longings for merger with an all empathetic object' (Springham 1998, p. 151–152) and goes on to describe how patients new to the art-making process are also often surprised at the power of the art object upon completion:

> the permanence of the art object and the disclosure it carries, can later be a source of anxiety for the patient when it comes to the group discussion of

the images. Returning to the relationships with the other group members once back in the circle, the patients often seem disturbed by how absorbed they had been with their images. There are now anxieties about how the images will be received and what others, primarily the therapist, will see in their work. . . . Patients need to be helped greatly at this juncture because they are anxious that their images will have breached their own 'false self'. (Springham 1998, p. 153)

Consequently although the therapist's presence may be minimal during the period of art-making, comparable to Winnicott's (1971) parent 'being there' while the child plays alone, the therapist is required to be more active when the patient emerges from their narcissistic withdrawal of art-making.

Figure 8.1 Ships that pass in the night.

'Ships that pass in the night'

The peculiarity of time-limited therapy was aptly depicted by one group member who made a drawing of two ships passing in the night, the name of the unit and the patients split between the two vessels. Showing his image to the rest of the group, he reflected upon the transitory nature of the ward and his difficulty in forming close attachments with people who would soon be gone. The theme of 'being in the same boat' prompted supportive group discussion between those with similar problems, which was reminiscent of the 12-step support groups. However, there was also an awareness that the time spent together was brief. Consequently some group members made this an obstacle to sharing their inner worlds, while others used the relative anonymity of the setting as a means by which to explore their difficulties in greater depth. One group member expressed her anxiety about the future, which promoted discussion about future options and choices. Clearly, the image was symbolic of the group and acted as a springboard for discussion around present and future hopes and fears. From a psychodynamic perspective, I was interested in the patient's expressed unwillingness to form attachments with the other group members, his rationalization being the transitory nature of the setting. Given my interest in attachment theory (Bowlby 1988a,b), and narcissism (Albert-Puleo 1980, Springham 1992, 1994, 1998, 1999), in a longer-term group I might have challenged this patient on his patterns of relating to others. However, what seemed most pressing at this point, was to encourage and develop dialogue based on the group's homogeneous qualities, and to address the more immediate anxieties regarding survival on the ward and after discharge.

Interpretative approach

Evidently substance misusers are ambivalent candidates for psychotherapeutic work, giving mixed messages about their commitment to treatment. This will often result in a confrontational approach being employed by staff in their attempts to gain control over this difficulty with their patients. Waller and Gilroy question the usefulness of confrontational methods without a frame of reference:

> Whilst intuition and pragmatism may provide what the client needs in a treatment situation, unless there is a conceptual framework to provide a rationale for interventions and therapeutic technique, the therapeutic relationship is open to misuse and abuse. (Waller and Gilroy 1992, p. 181)

Specific to art therapy is the use of the artwork as an object of transference, which provides a means of communicating with the patient in a less confrontational and more playful way. The artwork provides the means by which the patient initially encounters their fears and later negotiates new terms of reference. Its methodology also differs from other psychodynamic therapies, because of the presence of both visual and verbal material, as well as its diverse historical development. Waller describes its ability to get underneath addicts' characteristic verbal defences and intellectualism; and how in practice it is far from the popular image of 'a gentle relaxing pastime, nor an opportunity to dissect the artwork of one another' (Waller 1999, p. 62).

Resistance to the therapist's interpretation of transference material is common, but is a particular consideration for one-off sessions, where it is important to have sufficient closure at the end of each group. Waller (1999, p. 67) discusses the difficulties inherent in conducting one-off sessions, where powerful material needs to be contained and processed; and speaks of the necessity in 'overcoming the myth that art therapy [can] work magic in just one session'. Springham also acknowledges the constrictions of time-limited work for group analytic interpretation, and suggests that adjustments be made to the group aims to accommodate this:

> Rather than pursuing the aims of longer term work, e.g. the identifying and working through of personal problems via the relationships within the group, the short-term group here limits its objectives to 'problem clarification'. In other words, if through attending the art therapy the patient has a conscious experience of his/her previously unowned emotional needs, and the defences employed against them, and this then leads him/her to seek longer term help through either AA, rehabilitation centres or long-term therapy, then the intervention is considered to be successful. The difficulty in the task is that denial is the universal symptom in addictions and these patients tend to minimize the depth of their needs. (Springham 1994, p. 36)

Unrealistic expectations are indeed problematic, with many patients believing that the 2-week detoxification programme will be sufficient to cure them. A task of therapy at this stage is to address conflicting agendas – to challenge overly optimistic assumptions, and look at the patient's situation as it really is.

Whether or not the therapist makes an interpretation explicit, I feel it is useful to hold an awareness of transference material, and to introduce this to the group if and when this seems appropriate. Particularly in the case of time-limited work, my approach is one of 'suspended inquiry' (Betensky 1987), in which the meaning of the artwork is allowed to begin unfolding. My intervention in response to the artwork will often explore structural elements of the art, such as space, colour, line and shape, thus facilitating the patient's perception of their artwork. Ideally, in reflecting on their subjective world, the patient is able to bestow meaning on their art, and thereby self-awareness. I strongly encourage that initially the patient actively participates in searching for their own meanings, and discourage premature interpretations from others. In the therapeutic setting, there is always a risk of the therapist being cast in the position of 'the one who is supposed to know', particularly when dependency issues are a concern. Indeed, Winnicott (1965) and Casement (1985) promote the idea of the fallible therapist as a means by which the client is able to reach independence. Winship (1999, p. 48) describes this process as the 'value of being wrong, where the client and the therapist can exist in a real world and the client's image of the therapist as the all-knowledgeable being who will save them is confronted'.

Once the patient has begun to make associations, that is, to reflect on the process and product of art-making, there is opportunity for a more challenging, interpretative intervention. Here, I find it useful to refer to the notion of the *manifest vision* (the image as it appears) and the *latent vision* (the image as it is perceived at an unconscious level). The task of the art therapist is to explore possible meanings through encouraging links between structural qualities of the artwork and unconscious material. The same process is feasible in a one-off session, but is likely to be less developed and complete in its explorations. The therapist needs to maintain an awareness and sensitivity to the patient's readiness and ability to look at unconscious material. The benefit of art therapy is that defences can be protected by the artwork. The art object provides a tangible aesthetic level at which to relate, while therapist and patient maintain an awareness of underlying messages. However, in practical terms, during one-off sessions it is the manifest image rather than the latent vision that is more willingly focused on, and is the springboard for verbalization in the group. Looking at the manifest artwork which has been produced over a 3-year period, I propose to examine common themes as a means of illustrating concerns of substance misusers going through a detoxification process.

Themes

Although there are many more common themes than I am able to discuss here, those presented are representative of the frequency with which they have occurred over the duration of sessions: death, narrative, and landscape. In discussing each of these, I shall give a picture of the interrelation between the manifest and latent aspects of the material, and the potential for the patient to reflect on their meaning within a group context.

Death

Death as a theme is presented in a variety of forms, with a preponderence of corpses and graveyards depicted in the artwork, a fact unsurprising given that death is an anxiety for many of the patients being admitted to the unit. Indeed, many have been forced to receive treatment, having seriously compromised their health, and this will often be a topic of discussion amongst group members, along with vivid stories of almost fatal experiences. My counter-transference responses to these stories has tended to be one of disconnection, raising the question for me as a practitioner of whether patients are truly connecting with their experience. These images are usually presented as being either an expression of resignation to die, or as a declaration of abstinence, with the artist's intrinsic message being that they have a progressive disease which has to end in either abstinence or death. These patients' verbalizations have an inauthentic quality, in that the latent message conflicts with what is manifestly presented. As Beasley points out

> what initially appears as an authentic confrontation of one's situation is actually interpreted deterministically . . . . Both selves, addict and ex-addict remain sedimented. There is an inherent dissociation in the patient's deterministic beliefs, which precludes true reflection upon available choices. There is a security in being defined, because the person is able to flee personal responsibility. (Beasley 1998, p. 64)

My aim in working with themes of this nature, therefore, is to challenge fatalistic views, and to focus on the patient's ambivalence to giving up a cherished habit, a change that will inevitably involve a mourning process.

Narrative pictures

Despite the themes of death discussed above, I would say that there is a prevalent sense of vitality within the groups, albeit accompanied by much bravado and recounting of stories. Parallel to this is the substantial production of images, which I describe as 'narratives', in that they depict the individual's life story as they would like to present it to the group. These images are relatively undeveloped with a cartoon-like quality, often accompanied by labels or titles as a guide, and are used as a prequel to 'telling the story'. The dramas that enfold in these images help to maintain the addict's identity of being helpless, and often provoke sympathetic responses from the other group members as well as competitive story-telling. Unquestionably there are many contributing factors leading to substance misuse, but these narratives often depict only external agencies considered to have led to addiction, while omitting personal responsibility. This is analogous to the determinism of the death images described above. One man, for example, drew a picture of a bleak inner-city council estate surrounded by pubs, and insisted that he would be unable to maintain abstinence unless his housing situation was changed. Although the desolation of his situation was not in question, his inability to take responsibility for his habit was marked by his insistent focus on purely external factors, and my oral observation of this was deflected by the group as a whole. The tactics of the group to homogenize through common experience and to isolate the therapist is not unusual. Springham (1998, p. 149) suggests that this is an indication 'that the patients can only relate to a mirror image of themselves and here one is reminded of the mythological Narcissus forsaking all others to gaze lovingly at his own reflection. This can leave the therapist feeling irrelevant and useless, just as the nymph Echo did'. This defence mechanism on the part of the group displays an inability to engage beyond the 'false self' level. The false self defines itself so strongly that disclosure of the true self is prevented.

Landscapes

Finally, I shall discuss the prevalence of images of landscapes and desert islands, most of them idyllic, which are often accompanied by a professed belief that 'all will be well' when such a place is reached, perhaps a counterbalance to the fear of damage and dying in the previous discussion. The prevalence of this type of image is also noted by Springham (1999, p. 153) who agrees that they 'occur with far more regularity than with any other patient groups'. The incongruity between this idealized place and the patient's actual circumstances – on a locked detoxification ward – seem to indicate an inability to deal with the reality of the current circumstances. One man produced such an image in his session – a desert island – and in displaying the completed image with the group, expressed his belief that if he were to live in such a paradise, he would not need to drink. This fantasy was punctured by the comments of another group member who had in fact tried living in a tropical place, and had spent the duration drunk and with little memory of the experience. As Springham (1999, p. 153) points out, these images serve as 'a profoundly useful tool in the therapeutic process [in that] they communicate the nature of the ideal object and unrealistic expectations that must eventually come into the therapeutic discourse'. However, this is not to say that all aesthetically pleasing art objects should be viewed as an indication of pathological narcissism, as clearly there can be healthy and positive creative expression. Lowenfeld and Brittain (1982, p. 30), for example, argue that 'aesthetic experiences are greatly related to a harmonious feeling with our own selves'. For Springham (1999) it is that rather than facilitating therapeutic engagement, these 'paradise pictures' are obstructive, in that the therapist is unable to compete with the unrealistic expectations of perfection disclosed within them. As an example, two very different types of landscape were produced in one of my sessions: one of a man running down the road away from the 'demon drink' to a better place (Figure 8.2), the other of opposing landscapes within a single image – one 'good', the other 'bad' (Figure 8.3). The first person assumed unrealistically that he merely had to run away to avoid his drink problem; the second man was able to express painful and ambivalent feelings about his situation, identifying the bridge in the middle of the picture as the precarious point at which he currently stood. He was able to acknowledge his difficult location in the picture, which although painful, was realistic, unlike most of the (idyllic) landscapes presented. As a result, this patient was able to begin thinking about his next step, and to recognize possible pitfalls. As Winship (1999, p. 47) rightly points out, 'we do a client a disservice if we do not point out just how bumpy the road is to recovery. . . . The temptation is always to try to make things better, but it is better not to do so. It is better to model a survival of the "shittiness".'

Figure 8.2 Running away from the demon drink.

Figure 8.3 Two landscapes.

Conclusion

In introducing one-off art therapy sessions to the substance misuse team, it became necessary to return to the fundamentals of art therapy in order to make it accessible to patients and staff, and to create the space that would allow the exploration of client group characteristics as they arose in clinical practice. Comparing the material presented by the detoxification group with that from other clinical areas, it is clear that there are themes common to substance misusers, and that these factors will have an impact on group interactions. Understandably, any one-off art therapy group session is likely to provoke anxiety in participants, and will require sensitivity and adaptability on the part of the therapist. Indeed, it is evident that substance misusers are a particularly complex client group who, somewhat paradoxically, are as well suited to art therapy intervention as they are inaccessible to it. Engagement in art-making may be a relatively painless process for these individuals, who are readily absorbed in their creative process, but the group format – an approach proven to be a successful treatment modality – is also an arena where a patient's resistance is put in play. The task of the therapist is to engage with this phenomenon, with the aim of guiding the patient to the next stage of recovery.

CHAPTER 9

Acting for Change: the evolution of a psychodrama group

GILLIAN WOODWARD

This chapter tracks the evolution of a psychodrama-based group called Acting for Change through two different phases of development in a therapeutic day community. It describes a change in treatment approach, away from a model based on insight and underlying issues to a more contemporary psychodynamic model where the emphasis was on self-management, negotiation of boundaries, and containment. It explores how this change was reflected in the psychodrama group and in the roles of the therapist.

Alcohol dependence – the condition or syndrome

> Hell is our natural home. We have lost everything. We live in fear of living. Alcohol was my only friend. We found ourselves in alcohol and then it turned against us and tried to kill us. No other friend would do that to you. But we kept drinking because we had to. (Denzin 1987, p. 15)

Although it is not the purpose of this chapter to launch a discussion on the nature and causes of alcoholism or serious alcohol dependence, in order to put the group Acting for Change into context it is helpful to say something about my view of the condition.

Alcohol dependence appears to develop in response to a combination of influences: early object relations, psychodynamic roots, politico-sociocultural factors, and genetic disposition. In its acute form it might be seen as a form of regression to infantile fixation points and the acting-out of distress arising from early unmet needs. This distress is initially alleviated by the anaesthetizing properties of alcohol, but as the addiction progresses a second level of distress is created: physiologically, mentally, emotionally, and spiritually. Symptoms may emerge, such intense anxiety, extreme mood swings, or paranoia, which can be easily confused with deeper, more fixed problems, such as bipolar disorder. As a psychosocial therapist working with highly dependent, newly abstinent clients, one of the frameworks that I have found useful has been Elliott's (1997, 2003) description of four fundamentally psychological problematic characteristics, which closely resemble features of borderline personality disorder:

- the speed and intensity with which a new dependency is formed
- the tendency towards extremes and splitting
- the preoccupation with boundaries, limits, and authority, and a rather 'adolescent' feel to the relationship
- low self-esteem and below-average tolerance of emotional discomfort.

To these I would add shame and the drive to self-sabotage.

Therapeutic context

The centre

Acting for Change (1994–2001) was just one of the groups on offer at an agency called ACCEPT, situated in south-west London, whose mission was to provide, 'an innovative, multi-faceted community service enabling individuals to develop a fulfilling lifestyle free from problematic alcohol use by being at the heart of decisions about treatment'. It offered a range of services: an abstinence-based group therapy day programme and therapeutic community, and a solution-focused counselling service to drinkers, relatives, and friends.

The clients

Although referrals were mainly from social services, they could be accepted from any source including family doctors, the probation service, or self-referral. The clients on the group programme numbered up to 24, averaging one third women, up to one quarter gay, and, for brief spells, up to one quarter from minority ethnic communities. With the development of care in the community in the UK, there was an increase in clients with co-morbid mental health problems. Many clients arrived with multiple social problems as well, such as poverty, children in care, and criminality. Consequently, the client group as a whole was more challenging and complex than in the early days at ACCEPT. The only clients who were excluded from the day programme were those uncommitted to the goal of abstinence, those who threatened violence, and those who were using alcohol to medicate chronic mental illness such as schizophrenia.

The original model

ACCEPT was founded in 1974 when there was little alternative to hospital or Alcoholics Anonymous (AA). There was a large treatment centre, a tremendous diversity of groups and activities, and about 30 group facilitators. The structure remained constant but over time, for economic reasons, there was a reduction in the scale of activity, which was down to one third of its original size by the time I joined in 1992. There was a wide range of clients and a healthy balance of levels of functioning from some individuals who were still actively participating in society, perhaps performing well in demanding jobs, and others who had a much heavier burden of deprivation and social problems. Clients were required to attend a 4-day week and could stay on the day programme for up to 8 months.

The treatment emphasis at this time was on underlying issues, deep psychodynamic exploration, and the promotion of insight alongside some skills-based work. It was informed by psychoanalytic tradition. Discussion about aspects of alcohol dependence as a condition was almost taboo, and generally regarded as stereotyping and unhelpful to clients. The ethos was critical of the philosophy of AA, where members are encouraged to concentrate on the common characteristics of alcoholism. ('listen for the similarities not the differences'). Some counsellors regarded AA as shallow and mechanistic, insufficiently open to individuality and to the perceived need for insight into the psychodynamic roots of the problem: indeed, some clients were referred to as 'refugees from AA'. The group Acting for Change started in this clinical context.

Therapeutic roles

A useful framework for psychodrama interventions with newly abstinent clients is the role theory of Moreno (1964) and Clayton (1992). Building on this work, I define the therapist's roles relevant to psychodrama (and indeed other group work) as: *excavator*, *container*, *parent*, *advocate*, and *cheerleader*.

- **Therapist-as-excavator.** The therapist is the facilitator of in-depth exploration of the roots of current problems, encouraging the detailed examination of early experience in order to promote insight into underlying issues. Psychoanalytic interventions may be used, such as analysis of past trauma and interpretation of the transference.
- **Therapist-as-container.** Much distress is caused by loss of control, spilling out of feelings, and consequent fragmentation of self. The therapist can help moderate the high levels of anxiety by embracing and

holding in the Winicottian sense of psychically putting one's arms around the client and providing a calm, safe, non-judgmental space for the, sometimes desperate, feelings of rage and fear. The therapist seeks to be both 'empathic and mistrustful' (Yalom 1985), always reminding the client of the danger of acting-out with the readily available weapon of destruction. In the role of container the therapist works with the fear of abandonment by facing the inevitable separation from the pro-gramme and therapist-carers right from the beginning. The therapist is a guardian of boundaries, reminding the clients of their limits and those of the therapist. In this role they help the client work through anger and to modify the defiant or avoidant behaviour which can lead to despair and relapse. The therapist interprets the splitting and con-tains the swings between idealization and devaluation of both the therapist and the client's self.

- **Therapist-as-parent.** As serious alcohol dependence can have life-threatening implications, the therapist has to actively emulate the role of nurturing parent. The therapist cannot be imbibed, but is compet-ing with the instant gratification and relief that drugs or alcohol offer. In the parent role the therapist needs to be perceived as loving and unshakeable in the face of repeated self-destructive acting-out by the client. Within the developmentally needed relationship, the therapist exercises benign authority and resists the invitation to punish the client. However, the parent must not sidestep the 'depriving role' but freely acknowledge it, firmly maintaining the boundary of abstinence. The therapist works with the fear of separation and places emphasis on building activities outside the therapy, helping the client to expand positive external resources to counteract negative patterns.
- **Therapist-as-advocate.** In role as the client's advocate (Miller 1987), the therapist may help the client to identify abuse by caretakers and work through the necessary stages of understanding and mourning. The therapist works with the concept of the *inner child*. For example, Mary spent several sessions with her inner child at different ages. She held a remembered imaginary child-self on her lap to comfort her. Through this training in self-soothing, she arrived at an understanding of her terror at being left alone with her deaf sister for hours on end by her parents at an early age.
- **Therapist-as-cheerleader.** This is a term coined by solution-focused therapists (e.g. de Shazer 1985). The role refers to a motivational dimension of the work. The solution-focused approach assumes the concept of the person as 'larger than their problem'. Through carefully guiding questions it helps the client own their own strengths and suc-cesses, even when the situation may feel hopeless, for example, 'what is it about you that enabled you not to drink for the last two days?'. The

counsellor and client set goals by imagining a future in behaviourally observable terms. This is particularly effective in helping deeply shamed clients to build self-esteem. The cheerleader is an 'instiller of hope', reminding the client of times s/he has felt hopeful and effective.

In my exploration of how the approach at ACCEPT changed. I shall focus on the roles of therapist-as-excavator and therapist-as-container.

Psychodrama and therapeutic roles within the old model

With the old treatment model it made sense that I directed psychodrama with the emphasis on my role as excavator or co-excavator. All the clients were fulltime, and I had a core of clients who had become familiar and comfortable with psychodramatic techniques and expected to dig deep. We often concentrated on childhood issues and the development of insight leading to a catharsis.

Warm-ups (i.e. preliminary activities to put clients gently in touch with salient issues) could be highly exposing; for example, each client standing in front of the group and laying out all their 'baggage', i.e. their current issues, dilemmas, and moods through making noises or a posture to demonstrate their feelings.

The scenes chosen by the protagonist (the particular client exploring their issue) would often be highly emotive. A client might, for example, remember a childhood Christmas and reverse roles with one of their presents. Jack talked to the Action Man he received at the age of four while remembering breaking him into small pieces, and was horrified to get in touch with the rageful, spiteful part of himself. Or a client might recall a family photograph, then choose someone in that photograph to speak to using another member of the group as 'auxiliary', i.e. to act as that person. Flora, in speaking to her brother, became distressed at the memory of his abuse of her. Sometimes we would encourage constructions of family 'sculpts' (i.e. the group representing the family by simply standing or sitting in positions which represented the emotional closeness or distance), and the protagonist would speak to each member of the family about the impact of their drinking on that person. The psychodramatic process often went in a triangle (Figure 9.1).

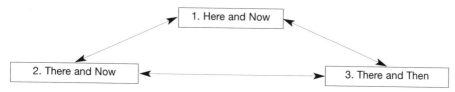

Figure 9.1 The psychodramatic process.

In the sharing after the warm-up, a member of the group might express some dissatisfaction with a boundary or rule at the agency (Here and Now). This could remind someone of a difficulty with authority outside, such as an employer (There and Now). From there we would go back to an authority figure in her past with whom she had been in conflict, for example her father (There and Then). The main focus was the uncovering of feelings and experiences 'There and Then' and the resolving of present conflicts through insight into underlying issues.

The setting

A room was specially set up for psychodrama with cushions on the floor and became known as the 'soft room'. All group members, except myself and those involved in the immediate enactment, sat on the floor. We created a stage area so that the enactors and myself, as director, were some distance from the rest of the group.

Noel's psychodrama

The warm-up consisted of each member of the group (nine people) imagining going back in time to childhood and meeting an important toy or pet, then reversing roles briefly with this toy or pet in front of the whole group. Noel recalled a pet duck and the group volunteered him as protagonist.

The psychodrama consisted of three brief scenes. In the first the '4-year old Noel' plays with his pet duck around the pond at the bottom of the large expanse of lawn in front of his house. Behind him, in the house, the scene is chaotic and unpredictable, with a drunk and abusive father. The adults are apparently unaware of Noel, or uninterested. He and the duck have fun splashing together. Noel tries to get the duck to fly and even tries to fly himself. The duck is his best friend. Later the duck disappears, to Noel's great distress.

In the second scene, family Sunday dinner, Noel breaks down in tears at the sight of his pet which is now cooked and waiting on the dinner table. The whole group is moved and outraged. In the last scene we move to Noel in the present, isolated in his London flat.

In the sharing stage, several members of the group were in touch with hurt and wrongs from childhood. Noel and the group members used other, open-talking groups on the programme to explore the issues which have arisen. The duck recurred as a motif for love and loss in Noel's therapy for several months.

This kind of probing and exposure was clearly dramatically effective in terms of identifying underlying issues. Because the method put clients dramatically and rapidly in touch with their pain, it could also be particularly gratifying for the therapist. It can stimulate significant and helpful insight and catharsis. However, it may work against the client if catharsis occur before adequate core strength and self-care mechanisms are in place. As we know, individuals with addiction problems can be particularly perceptive, emotionally literate, and cooperative with insights. They may appear to be progressing in a way that can be sadly misleading to both parties. Indeed the focus on insight, seductive as it is, can become, on both sides, an avoidance of more urgent aspects of self-care. Along with the staff therapy team, I found myself paying too little attention to the condition of vulnerability with regard to extremes of feeling of the newly abstinent client. In Noel's case, a number of the clients were visibly distressed and crying (the cathartic aspects then considered to be helpful to them). Looking back, it is hard not to shudder while questioning how much these kinds of experiences could have triggered relapse.

Although I do not reject the insight approach, my considerable experience of other approaches, especially AA with its emphasis on practical, strategic self-management and recognition of alcoholism as a condition with a life of its own, led me to feel frustrated at having to leave this wisdom outside the door while working with my clients; wisdom such as a focus on the similarities of feelings and behaviour of individuals in advanced stages of addiction, and the traditional teaching and advice in response to these. As is sometimes observed at AA meetings, 'they say AA is brain washing, but perhaps my brain needed washing!' My own observation is that people really only properly individuate again in the later stages of recovery from serious addiction.

These restrictions changed with the appointment of Barbara Elliott as director of ACCEPT, as she instigated important modifications and changes in the programme and the therapy team.

The new model

Building on the understanding of the aforementioned characteristics of the newly abstinent client, we instituted some changes of emphasis in the programme:

- Clear boundaries and containment throughout, and especially during the first phase of the switch in dependency from the substance to the therapy. Full attendance was required for the first 2 weeks.
- The emphasis was on holding on to the clients, helping them to stay with the programme despite the discomfort.
- In the early stages particularly, less attention was paid to the content of what the client brought (though of course this was still regarded as important), than to how the client was using the structure (Elliott 2003).
- The community group and the client reviews were a particularly important forum for acknowledging dissatisfactions with boundaries,

ambivalence about being in treatment, and swings in feeling about the therapy and the persons administering it.

More didactic and cognitive elements were introduced, offered in the informative sessions such as the alcohol and therapy seminar, the self-management group, and relapse prevention.

- Exploration of relationship issues, in the men's and women's groups, Experiences of Childhood, Growing through Loss, and Acting for Change. The deeper and more detailed exploration of these issues would generally happen in the weekly second stage – long-term, more analytic groups which overlapped with end of the day programme and could support the client for anything up a further 2 years.
- A client role of increasing responsibility and active decision-making regarding treatment and outside activities, encouraged by an open-ended programme. Clients were supported in their 'self-prescribing', i.e. choosing their own programme from week to week in the client review through feedback from peers and staff.

The emphasis was on helping the client to avoid relapse at all costs by giving full recognition to the fragility of the newly abstinent self. Intense emotional pain was avoided as far as possible in the early months. The unconscious was far from ignored, but was explored less in terms of early experience, and more in terms of unconscious motivation (Figure 9.2).

Conscious motivation (known to client)	Unconscious motivation (unknown to client)
My life is being ruined by drinking	I am in pain
I have lost/may lose my spouse, child, home, sanity, life	I feel depressed, anxious, empty, bored, lonely, terrified, frustrated
I don't want to destroy myself	I have little/no tolerance of these feelings
I want to stop drinking	A drink will stop these feelings I want a drink

Figure 9.2 Conscious and unconscious motivation. From Elliott (1997).

Insight into the deeper reasons was of course regarded as necessary, but as a slow, ongoing learning process. It became clear that a number of clients were able to recover just by understanding immediate triggers, and that they might never get to the roots of internal conflicts. Group analyst Caroline Garland (1982) vividly describes this change in emphasis:

I should like to offer a gardening analogy. Faced with a chaotic and aban-doned flowerbed, the gardener may either spend his time pursuing the root systems of the weeds that infest his chosen patch, or adopting an alternative strategy altogether, he may plant ground cover between the plants he wants to preserve, and allow the new and healthy growth to encroach upon the territory originally occupied by the weeds. Both approaches concur in agreeing that the weeds are unwanted, but the approach to eradicating the problem is radically different: one involves direct assault, the other the nurturing of alternative elements of healthy growth that simply begin to occupy enemy territory.

The new programme moved from a wide-ranging, eclectic therapy to a more integrated, coherent and strategic model able to incorporate wisdom from other therapies and 12-step programmes. It was underpinned by complex thinking from literature on borderline personality disorder, group analytic psychotherapy, cognitive-behavioural approaches and principles from early therapeutic communities which strive for the autonomy and independence of their clients. There was considerably more emphasis than in the original model (where the 4-day programme allowed little time for developing outside activities such as voluntary work or college courses) on bringing about significant changes in life outside the therapy.

The change in approach worked. Outcomes improved, with numbers of successfully abstinent clients rising to over one half rather than one third as witnessed in the old model, and in other agencies, a year after leaving the day programme. This was confirmed by attendance of a second stage group, or by follow-up letter and interview.

During this transition, my therapeutic role shifted from therapist-as-excavator to therapist-as-container. We concentrated on the Here and Now and the There and Now, rather than the There and Then.

Acting for Change within the new model

The new client group, who could now choose to come in as little or as much as they chose, or 'prescribed' themselves, therefore attended most of the groups less regularly, and had also started to voice more of their misgivings about the psychodrama group. There was also a new group, the Creative Group, which rotated fortnightly with the psychodrama. This meant fewer culture-carriers with any confidence or sophistication in terms of psychodramatic technique. Any given client might not be around for more than several weeks, attending Acting for Change perhaps only two or three times in all.

As time went on, it became clear that even to stand in front of the group and say something was too much for many of them because of their painful self-consciousness and the fear of being embarrassed, feelings along the continuum of shame. The numbers in the psychodrama group dropped, so rethinking the delivery was imperative.

I first reassessed what Acting for Change had to offer that was different from the other groups, especially as we were now working with less spontaneity and catharsis. What seemed of real value was the externalization of internal issues through enactment. Psychodrama is immediate in the way it can expose internal splits. Even a simple role reversal with a rebellious or wise aspect of the self to explore the dilemma 'to drink or not to drink' is immensely effective.

The group

As already explained, as psychodrama director/facilitator I had no guarantee of even a core group of attenders, and with new clients joining the community every week the group composition was never the same from session to session. Group size could vary from two to ten. I was now more highly aware of the fragility of the newly abstinent self. If painful buried feelings were stirred up prematurely, clients were more at risk of relapsing and dropping out. I would not always have a second chance to work with a client's distress.

The setting

We stopped using the cushions as seating and kept them just as props, reverting to a horseshoe of chairs with the director's chair and another two available for role reversal, a little separate from the others but still within the circle. This was to allow some enactment space if needed, but with everyone still close to each other, thus making the group more intimate than before and as unprovocative of anxiety as possible.

The warm-up

At the beginning of each session I would use either a non-threatening group warm-up and/or a pair warm-up. Warm-ups in pairs are particularly helpful to needy clients as the guaranteed attention goes some way to meeting these emotional needs, with less exposure.

An example of an effective group warm-up would be group members placing themselves around the space as though it were a swimming pool, in order to represent their level of engagement with the therapeutic work: clients might also place themselves physically in relationship to a bottle (a chair), or along a line of chairs, a continuum of enthusiasm about being there at all, hence encouraging the exploration of ambivalence about the desire to drink and about the usefulness of the therapy.

Community issues as warm-up

As members of a therapeutic community, clients are likely to be relatively 'warmed up' to ongoing issues most of the time. If an issue was very live

I might choose a related theme for the group and announce that theme to the community in advance, thus preparing clients rather than relying on spontaneity. The team would discuss ways to link the themes of the groups to current community issues. An example of this would be a period of greater upheaval than usual, such as a member of staff leaving. To address this theme, clients might lay out a block of chairs to represent the organization. They could thus express their feelings directly to it. They might then reverse roles with the agency. We used this technique also when clients were about to leave the day programme and needed to communicate their mixed feelings of anger, grief, and achievement.

Some of the most useful psychodramatic work was undoubtedly when these themes were carefully linked. Feelings such as anger against staff, could be safely expressed and then further, explored and contained in, for example, the self-management group.

Different forms of enactment

These warm-ups might become the main action of the session; for example, each client might talk to the 'bottle' and reverse roles with it briefly. A particular client might review their position in relation to the bottle and decide to change it. Each enactment remained within the framework of a vignette, i.e. one or a limited number of scenes within the same time zone, usually the present or the future. There was always time for discussion after any enactment to further explore the issues that had emerged for the whole group.

Two other forms of enactment useful to clients were the externalization of internal splits and role training. Much of the work with splits was simply about raising personal awareness of ambivalence, such as whether to recover or not. As we know, some addicted clients experience such swings in their perceptions of themselves and others that they are close to what cognitive analytic therapy refers to as 'dissociated self states' (Ryle 1990). For example, Stephen presented two typically extreme and contradictory views of himself as a 'completely useless waste of space going nowhere' and as 'much more clever and successful than most other people, wasting his time in treatment', and 'needing to get back to his high-powered job'. He used cushions to represent each 'self' and spoke as each, then reversed roles with auxiliaries representing those different positions. In another session, four clients spoke as their ideal confidant(e), i.e. a wise and totally caring person who was commenting on their well-being. Janet became her (deceased) kindly uncle who congratulated Janet on entering treatment and cautioned her about the pitfalls ahead. He represented a higher/wiser self. In the vignette 'To drink or not to drink' Paul argued with Alcohol, one minute his friend and comforter, the next his enemy and destroyer. He eased some of the conflict by physically moving Alcohol to the furthest end of the room.

Sociodramatic techniques (i.e. those that are based on group issues rather than individual issues) can be used to involve the whole group in an enactment: for example, the group may be invited to interview someone in the role of Alcohol. Alcohol may be put in the 'hot seat', i.e. personified, enacted by a client, and in the process interviewed by the group. Alcohol may attempt to 'seduce' the client. After the client has responded the group may act as consultant, advising, for example, as to how to take a firmer stand against it, with individual members sometimes 'coaching' the protagonist by actively demonstrating how to do it differently.

The structured work of role training, with its clear boundaries, is ideal for this client group. It is particularly helpful if individuals need to stay in thinking mode and not immediately get in touch with strong feelings they may not be able to deal with. It is also a liberating and optimistic tool. To illustrate: a whole session can be taken up with brainstorming past and current roles and putting the collective input up on a flipchart. Josh, for instance, identified a progression from Withdrawn Child to Star Performer Teenager, to Rebel Problem Drinker Adult. Jack noticed Rescuer all the way through his life, with Mr Pissed-Off lurking in the wings. In subsequent sessions clients might think of a role they would like to be in, then speak from that role. A particularly effective exercise has been to get every member of the group to speak as their best possible self in a year's time.

The sharing

Every enactment is followed by personal sharing, each member saying something about what they have identified with in the drama. The group may (extending the usual psychodramatic format) offer strategies for the protagonist/client to take away.

Conclusion

Psychodrama draws to a close with the sharing. This chapter draws to a close with the experience the writer has attempted to share with the reader and practitioner; the exciting, difficult, and profound process of going through such a change in therapeutic approach. It was profound and difficult in the shedding of certain personal constructs and embedded views of how to be an effective therapist with seriously alcohol-dependent clients. The change involved a move to the depressive position (Klein 1963) of more realistically holding the good and the bad in ourselves and in our clients. What has been exciting has been the challenge of personal and professional growth and the tangible benefits we witnessed in so many of our clients.

CHAPTER 10

The family as group

MARTIN WEEGMANN

This chapter concerns addiction in the context of family systems, how an addiction(s) is maintained in family life and the consequences of that addiction on the system or other members. In the first part of the chapter I shall describe a family in detail, as portrayed in the play *Long Day's Journey into Night* (1956) by the celebrated Irish-American playwright Eugene O'Neill. As I argue, there are good reasons why O'Neill's work is relevant and illuminating of families and addiction. The play is a powerful insight into family process, the role of substances within it (alcohol, morphine) and the human consequences for the individuals concerned. A rich harvest awaits the reader who attends to the detail and nuances of the play, which is all the more powerful for being a reflection of O'Neill's own family.

In the second part, drawing on themes in the play as well as other clinical examples, I identify some possible dynamic processes associated with addiction in families, particularly the role of shame, blame, and splitting. The list is not an exhaustive one, nor is it confined to addiction in families.

Finally, I shall describe a service and group therapy intervention for relatives and concerned others who have been affected by someone else's addiction.

The case of the O'Neill family

For a psychotherapist, one of the most compelling aspects of the plays of Eugene O'Neill is their well-known biographical dimension (see Gelb and Gelb 1960, Goodwin 1988). O'Neill experienced alcoholism, and his brother, Jamie, died from it. In his own case, after a brief psychoanalysis he remained sober for the remainder of his life, with the exception of two relatively minor relapses. Just as alcohol had been an escape, so he claimed from 1924 that 'Writing is my vacation from living'. His acting father was also a heavy, daily drinker and his mother became addicted to morphine following its prescription to her after Eugene's birth. In turn, similar drug and alcohol problems afflicted his children, with whom he had alienated and problematic relationships.

With the deaths of his parent and Jamie (who had drunk himself to death in 1922), Eugene was freed, 'to explore the dark side of his family life . . . ' (Dymkowski 1992, p. ix). One product was the masterpiece, *Long Day's Journey into Night*, which portrays his own family with no attempt at subterfuge, a brilliant portrayal of family secrets and conflict. In this and many of his other plays, O'Neill showed himself well able and well placed to transform his own experiences of addiction and despair in the service of creative expression. Indeed, perhaps it is because he was able to see the potential for 'giving up' within himself and certainly in others, like his brother, that he was able to write with such conviction. As a testimony to the suffering behind *Long Day's Journey*, O'Neill's dedicatory note to Carlotta, his third wife, talks of, 'this play of old sorrow, written in tears and blood' and that it enabled him to face his family, 'all the four haunted Tyrones'.

The play: a preamble

From the outset, one's sense of Tyrone family atmosphere is one thick with tension, with James Tyrone (hereafter Tyrone) locked into an adversarial stance with his sons, particularly his elder son Jamie, and with worry focused throughout on his wife's physical and mental state. Tyrone's wife Mary starts to use morphine in the play and is worried about the health of her younger son Edmund who, it transpires, has consumption. As the sons enter the scene, Mary plays the intermediary, trying to quieten her husband's criticisms at the same time as trying to contain Jamie's thinly veiled contempt for his father.

Act I

Unable to be direct about Edmund's health, Tyrone hints there may be 'something else' affecting his cold and that the family doctor will be consulted shortly. However, as Mary leaves the room, Edmund and men discuss the doctor's view that Edmund has consumption. Jamie is critical of the 'quack doctor', who has been consulted only because he is cheap and whose judgement therefore cannot be trusted. At this point, tension shifts away from concern over Edmund to the potent issue of money, with mutual recriminations between Jamie and his father. Jamie is accused of being irresponsible, of having thrown his life away on 'whisky and whores'. Jamie, for his part, resents how he felt forced by his father on to the stage as a fellow actor. Their history, what Jamie calls 'ancient history', with these resentments and grievances, is invoked. Tyrone portrays Jamie as an ungrateful, useless son. Jamie, at one point during the quarrel, shrugs his shoulders, 'alright, Papa, I'm a bum' (p. 28). The father, not wanting to be portrayed as miserly, turns again on Jamie, blaming him for leading his younger brother astray, being a bad role model, killing Edmund's already weak constitution and exclaiming, 'you've been the worse influence for him. He grew up admiring you as a hero! A fine example you have set him!' (p. 29).

With a lull in hostilities, they acknowledge concern about the impact of Edmund's health on his mother, if she knew: 'I wish to God we could keep the truth from her but we can't if he has to be sent to a sanatorium'. (p. 32). Here, as at other junctures throughout the play, there is a temporary pulling together between them in the face of an awful situation. With this shift in focus to the mother, Jamie has sensed that her behaviour has changed recently and starts to wonder, although Tyrone downplays his worries.

Later, while Edmund and his mother are alone, she begins to express some of her long-term grievances: of not having had a 'proper home', always being on the move as a result of following the acting life. Further, with her husband being an actor, a profession associated with disrepute, she has missed out on friends, and Edmund and Jamie had lost their chance to associate with 'nice girls'. Edmund, partly protecting his father, lets slip that his mother's mental state in the past made it difficult for people to come round. He immediately realizes what he has said, making Mary predictably defensive, knowing that he is trying to get at something in her past or, more sensitively, her present. She complains that all the family are now viewing her with suspicion and that she feels alone in the household. There is a sense of two people worried in different ways, Mary about her 'baby' son's physical health and her son because of his mother's possible return to addiction. They resort to a mechanism of reassurance, Edmund saying 'I'll soon be alright again, anyway, and you won't worry yourself sick . . . ' (p. 42), with Mary responding, 'But, I'm quite alright, dear'.

Act II

The whisky bottle is on the table. Edmund and Jamie defiantly sneak drinks and then add water because Tyrone memorizes the level each time, symbolizing his penurious nature. The sons openly express their concerns about their mother's state. Jamie indicates that he is aware of her difficulties but that when Edmund was younger, it was kept from him. They have noticed their mother's recent peculiar detachment, in her voice and manner. When Mary joins them, the boys scan her closely, trying to figure out what is going on.

The three men have more drink before the meal, Tyrone referring to whisky as being an appetiser, the best of tonics. May is ambivalent or confused about alcohol, in one breath saying that drink will kill Edmund and then retracting, 'one small drink won't hurt Edmund. It might be good for him, if it gives him an appetite' (p. 59). Tyrone meanwhile drinks more as a reaction to his wife's activities. She hits back by complaining about his drinking, 'You will be drunk tonight. Well, it won't be the first time, will it? – or the thousandth?' (p. 60). At this point Tyrone attempts to confront her, but falls short, merely insinuating. Mary feigns ignorance 'I don't know what you are talking about'. Tyrone then buys into this by saying 'Never mind. It's no use now' (p. 60).

Later in the scene, the family as a whole gathers again. More of Mary's grievances surface; how she gave up her beloved father's home to marry Tyrone. She complains that his priorities have been wrong throughout the marriage. As Mary retires upstairs, Jamie, for the first time, makes direct reference to what the mother is doing: putting it bluntly, he exclaims, 'another shot in the arm' (p. 65). Further arguing ensues about whether there is still time to stop her addiction. Jamie is pessimistic, feeling she is already under the drug's influence.

The conversation shifts to Edmund's consumption and his need to go to a sanatorium. The boys plan to go together to the doctor's appointment in the afternoon, but Mary (who has re-entered) is afraid that they will come back drunk. She worries that Tyrone will also become drunk and angry but he repudiates this, denying drink to be an issue: 'I've never missed a performance in my life' (p. 71).

Mary details her family past, the contrast between her idealized father's home and fondly remembered convent schooling and her subsequent isolation after marrying an actor. The history of her morphine use becomes intimately linked with elements of her family history or mythology. She claims she was healthy before Edmund was born, in spite of a life on the roads, living in shabby hotels and so on. The sickness that followed Edmund's birth and the intervention of the cheap hotel doctor at the time had lead to her fateful first use of morphine. There had also been a bereavement; before this, there had been another child (Eugene) who had died as a result of exposure to Jamie's measles. Another central complaint emerges: that Tyrone had insisted that she had another baby to take Eugene's place in order to get over the bereavement. 'I was afraid all the time I carried Edmund . . . I wasn't worthy . . . I never should have borne Edmund' (p. 76).

As Edmund reappears to ask his father for the carfare, he is clearly worried about leaving his mother, and Mary feels guilty about what she has

said to Tyrone about Edmund. The mother–youngest son dynamic inten-
sifies, Edmund knowing about the seriousness of his health but unable to
get it across, while Mary responds with denials and an attempt to baby
him. Edmund voices concern over Mary's relapse, his desperate plea that
she can still stop while she has the will-power. Mary offers a double message, both saying 'I don't know what you're referring to' and in the same
breath suggesting an excuse for her current relapse, 'But that's no excuse!
I'm only trying to explain' (p. 80). Towards the end, Mary is clearly in an
intensely ambivalent state about her children going off, complaining that
she is lonely without them but also wanting to get rid of them. Their contempt and disgust for what she is doing make it difficult for her to stand
them.

Act III

O'Neill uses the metaphor of fog surrounding the house to refer to the
implied addictive state, 'It hides you from the world and the world from
you . . . no one can find or touch you any more' (p. 84). Mary talks to one
of the servants, Kathleen, telling her about her younger self, her once
beautiful hands, her love of playing the piano as a child, which her father
so admired. She expresses two early life dreams: 'To be a nun, that was
the more beautiful one. To become a concert pianist, that was the other'
(p. 89). The present reality intrudes and she looks her hands, which now
symbolize disgust and decay. Like her hands, the beautiful dreams have
withered. Morphine, however, ' kills the pain' (p. 90). She talks about first
meeting Tyrone, her immediate love for him. In her devotion she forgot
all about becoming a nun or a concert pianist.

Edmund and Tyrone return, having been drinking. Mary then offers to
pour more drink. Jamie is still out. The conversation starts to target him
for having dragged Edmund down and disgraced the family. Drink started
to take over Jamie's life. Mary says to Tyrone, 'You brought him up to be
a boozer, since he first opened his eyes he has seen you drinking, always
a bottle on the bureau in the cheap hotel rooms' (p. 96). Tyrone, stung by
this, denies that he is to blame for his son's alcoholism, then blames her
accusations on 'the poison' inside her. The men drink more in order to
rein in the growing acrimony. But Mary continues, complaining that she
would not have married Tyrone if she had known that he drank so much.
Tyrone denies his drinking has ever been a problem. Mary recalls their
marriage and honeymoon and his drunkenness.

Edmund struggles to tell Mary about the doctor's verdict, but she treats
the news with denial and blames the doctor. Edmund insists that he will
have to go to a sanatorium, but Mary blames the doctor for getting it
wrong. She accuses Edmund of being dramatic, like an actor. Edmund

blasts out, in exasperation, 'It's pretty hard to take at times, having a dope fiend for a mother!' (p. 105). Mary goes upstairs again and perhaps internalizes the shame by saying, ' I hope, sometime, without meaning it, I will take an overdose' (p. 105).

Later, Mary's real fear that Edmund will die finally leaks through and she breaks down. Tyrone is angry and says that he will be cured, that he will not die. Tyrone turns on her, blaming her for taking more of that 'God-damned poison'. Mary counterattacks, 'You say much mean, bitter things when you've drunk too much. You are as bad as Jamie or Edmund', and the scene ends (p. 107).

Act IV

By midnight Tyrone and Edmund are drunk and there is a brewing row between them. There is a familiar rhythm to their rows, which reach a crescendo followed by attempts to placate or to change the subject. The desire to forget difficulties is strong for both parties. They can hear Mary moving around upstairs, knowing that by now she will be a 'ghostly presence', through the effects of morphine.

Tyrone counsels Edmund regarding how he should understand his mother's version of her family past, and cautions, '. . . you must take her memories with a grain of salt' (p. 118). He de-idealizes her picture and brings in the fact that her own father was an alcoholic; 'she condemns my drinking but she forgets his' and that it 'finished him quick – that and the consumption' (p. 119). He blames the nuns for cultivating unrealistic dreams in Mary.

Tyrone and Edmund share despair about Mary, how she creates a 'blank wall' around herself, like a 'bank of fog in which she hides and loses herself' (p. 120). At this Edmund agrees, keen not to blame his mother, but then shifts the blame on to his father's stinginess, the implication being that had she had a decent doctor at childbirth she might never have used morphine. Tyrone is enraged by this and defends himself. Edmund duplicates his mother's grievances by accusing his father of having dragged Mary around the country. Tyrone is incensed, but also evidently stirred to guilt. Tyrone, goaded by Edmund into the ultimate vindictiveness, plays the trump card; quoting his wife's, '. . . if you hadn't been born she'd never ...' (p. 123) and stops ashamed. There is a temporary cooling down.

The anger that has been visited cannot be contained, and resurfaces. They talk about the visit to the doctor. Will Tyrone be miserly, or will he pay for a good sanatorium? At this point, Tyrone counterattacks, bringing in his own family past and poverty. At 10 his father deserted his mother and, returning to Ireland, died there. His mother was then a stranger in a strange land, with four children to survive somehow. The little Tyrone had known real suffering and had to be the man of the house. This is the reason why he is sensitive to money and will not be called miserly. His mother's fear was that she would get sick and old and die in a poorhouse, and this is why Tyrone is also afraid of ending up in poverty. He adds that perhaps his early life overdid the lesson for him and that his potential career as a 'fine actor' was blighted by the mistake of getting stuck in a role in one particular, 'God-damned' play. Tyrone continues, exalting his former acting abilities, how he might have been a great Shakespearean actor. There is a tone of grandiosity, of how he 'had life where he wanted it' (p. 131).

During the course of this Jamie arrives home, intoxicated and noisy. The boys find themselves together for a while. Jamie talks about his night on the town, ending up in a brothel. He identifies with 'the other bums', their degeneracy, and luxuriates in his abject state: 'That's where I've got – nowhere' (p. 141). Momentarily, he insults his mother and Edmund hits him, bringing Jamie quickly to his senses. He admits to feeling 'so damned sunk' (p. 142) and that through wishful thinking he had erroneously believed that his mother had kicked her habit. Coming close to recognizing their respective addictions (i.e. alcohol and drugs), he admits, 'I'd began to hope, if she'd beaten the game, I could, too' (p. 143) and then begins to sob.

An important shift occurs at this point in the conversation between the boys, with Jamie beginning to warn Edmund about his own baleful influence over him and the sense that the family has divided over the degenerate son (Jamie) and the exalted one, the family 'white hope' (Edmund). Jamie steels himself and, with bleary-eyed affection starts to tell Edmund things he would not to able to if sober. He begins with, 'Want to warn you – against me. Mama and Papa are right. I've been a rotten influence' (p. 145). Jamie admits to how he twisted values, glamorizing alcohol and whorehouses, of how he did not want Edmund to succeed and thus make himself seem even worse. He holds Edmund's arrival responsible for his mother's addiction. With deadly conviction he talks about a jealous, revengeful side of himself and wanting to damage Edmund: 'The dead part of me hopes you won't get well' (p. 146). Although Edmund hears all this as so much crazy, drunken talk, Jamie strongly advises him to get him out of his life. As Tyrone re-enters, he pours scorn over Jamie: 'A wreck, a drunken hulk . . . ' (p. 148).

Finally, Mary joins the rest of the family. She carries her wedding gown and expresses a regressive fantasy: 'I'm going to be a nun . . . ' (p. 152). She is searching for 'something', but does not know what, appearing lost in a semi-delusional world. In the final speech, as the men drink, Mary continues to bring in elements of her girlhood past. She falters and says, 'Yes, I remember. I fell in love with James Tyrone and was so happy for a time' (p. 156). Here, the play ends.

Brief discussion

The play richly details repeating family mechanisms, involving grievance and blame and the open or secret use of substances. Perhaps the two sons mirror problems of the parents, since all share some difficulties in pro- gressing in life. Can Jamie ever transcend his abject state? Will Edmund separate from him and realize some of the family hopes placed in him? Is Tyrone stuck in replaying the story and fears of his family past? And can Mary, the injured spouse and disappointed mother, envisage a way through the fog? The substances both block and facilitate communications, with a pattern of drawing back and mutual reassuring following bouts of acrimony and fear. In spite of the blame and hurt, one is struck by the homeostatic patterns – patterns gluing vulnerable individuals together.

Dynamic processes

The role of shame

An association of addiction and shame has often been noted. The link to shame in a family system is well illustrated by O'Neill, particularly centred around Mary's morphine habit. She knows this and indeed internalizes the shame, both trying to explicate her desperate position by reference to past experiences (childbirth, the difficult circumstances of married life, etc.) and through self-rejection (a sense of ugliness localized in her hands, passive overdose wishes and so on). Feelings of shame have a universal dimension but can be difficult to distinguish from other emotions, such as guilt, even anger. For example, in the play, is Tyrone guilty about his role as father and husband or does he feel, underneath the self-righteous anger, some shame about how he has conducted himself? Is Jamie guilty for having been a bad influence on his brother, or is it to do with shame about being degenerate, in an abandoned state? And the latter comes out only in the context of drunkenness, which had the added effect of rein- forcing the problem he is complaining of in himself. Perhaps there is a mixing of the two emotions. Shame, however, involves a sense of the *self* being bad or defective in some way, whereas guilt refers to *actions* by the self, or omissions. Flores (1997) writes, 'To feel shame implies feeling exposed and having to allow others to have seen one's imperfections' (p. 237), as in the case of Mary who knows her behaviour is being observed. Anger or narcissistic rage can be a response to exposure, to the implosion caused by shame; again, we see examples of this in Tyrone's enraged response to criticism.

One of the possible sources or prompts to shame is a situation in which something or someone is out of control. For the addict, that an exogenous substance (the drugs) has taken hold of their lives, and for the affected relative that they are unable to avert or influence the course of its influence. Bean-Bayog (1981) talks about the narcissistic injury caused by this simple admission that life has become out of control in some way; in such circumstances a person can simply refuse to admit that something has got out of hand, or angrily attempt to re-assert control. In the fictional example, we have an evocative description of Mary's relapse and how the menfolk know and dread what might be happening, desperately hoping that she might pull back before it is too late. Is control still possible? With respect to how families might defend themselves against shame, I recall an anecdote (quoted by Brown 1985) of relevance to the paradoxical rules that children and partners acquire in response to alcoholism (although this could apply to other forms of family dysfunction, such as violence): 'there were two rules in our family: the first was, "there are no problems here" and the second, "don't tell anyone"' (p. 238).

With respect to the real world of clinical experience with concerned others, I have noticed that powerful feelings of shame can be evoked at the start of engagement. When a concerned other is invited to talk about what brings them for help, there is often a temporary breaking-down, linked to having to admit that a loved one is addicted or that a domestic situation has become unmanageable. It is as if the act of naming a problem brings home the painfulness of reality, so that the person is flooded with helplessness. This is true in individual appointments, but also in group, where there are fellow witnesses, as it were. Often, especially for newcomers, there is an additional source of shame, this being the feeling that they are *responsible* or implicated at some level. We have usually administered a questionnaire to newcomers (see Appendix), which taps into particular patterns of behaviour and response that may have built up over long periods of time. It can also tap into certain beliefs the relative or spouse holds about the other person's addiction, and it is here that shame might enter the picture: a feeling that the addiction reflects their *own* inadequacy or that if only *they* had been different people the addiction or the latest relapse might not have taken place, and so on. Problems that may be associated with substance misuse, such as violence or abusive threats, are equally shielded from view at first. When they are admitted to, however, shame can surface, shame in the fact that a family situation has effectively broken down, that a once loving relationship has deteriorated, that not enough aversive action was taken earlier on, that the children were not adequately protected. The list is a long one, and relatives or concerned others require help in beginning to articulate such experiences, which had been shielded from the outside world and, indeed, also from the individual. Gorman and Rooney's (1979) interesting research on Al-Anon members talks about the long periods of delay (an average of seven years) after the first occurrence of problem drinking before finally seeking help. They suggest that the spouse simply takes this amount of time to come to terms with or to define the 'problems' sufficiently. Shame can be a factor in understanding this delay.

Other relatives, although not holding themselves responsible for another person's addiction, nevertheless experience the impact and sometimes the responsibility for that person's recovery. In some families, addiction may bring shame on the parents or the family as a whole. One instance of this is that of some Asian families, where family honour is strongly affected. The idea, as I have encountered it with several families, is something like: 'your drug using reflects badly on us as a family and others will judge us by this'. But then being judged, regardless of culture of origin, is a bedfellow of shame: others (neighbours, elders, other relatives, etc.) will disapprove of *my* role or association with this problem.

The blame dynamic

One of the easiest methods for disposing of feelings of helplessness and shame is that of blame. Lansky (1987) argues that this mechanism is appealing because 'Emotional equilibrium is restored, at least while the act of blaming is in process and the blamer feels competent, masterful and in control – not helpless, empty and disorganized' (p. 194). Combatants in family systems blame each other, but the fact that relationships can and do endure in spite of such blaming suggests its collusive nature. Elsewhere, Lansky (1994, p. 47) writes '. . . it is a hallmark of pathology in family systems that people who are counted on to be supportive persons traumatize or re-traumatize vulnerable and fragile persons. . . ' and that one of the methods is by '. . . maneuvers that turn the tables and return the shame to the other . . . '.

In the case of the Tyrones, these blaming mechanisms are all too clear, between father and sons, husband and wife, sons and mother. Although facing common problems, they know each other's weaknesses all too well and often use this knowledge to hurt. Perhaps the play could be likened to a circle of hell, with moments of real emotional violence between the participants, yet at other times clear affection or concern. Increasingly, the drinking facilitates expression of these feelings. This tendency to put down and induce shame in others is well described by Mary, when she describes Jamie's methods: '. . . he's always sneering at someone else, always looking for the worst weakness in everyone' (p. 52). Mechanisms of reversal can easily come into play in such fraught situations, so that the *other* is made to feel vulnerability or guilt. Mary adds, either by way of explanation or excuse, that such processes become natural since they are the product of life experience: 'They're done before you realize it. . . '.

Clinical example of blame

When I met the Smiths, the drinker (the father) was considering residential rehabilitation, though not without misgivings. In a family meeting, I asked the family members (and the drinker) to describe what life was like during periods of intoxication and periods of sobriety. The spouse singled out unpleasant arguing and verbal abusiveness during intoxication and 'treading on eggshells' during periods of sobriety. When drunk, the drinking father would also put down his son, using derogatory expressions to undermine him. I noticed the words used in these attacks (I asked for examples) and wondered about the father's need to attack his son's masculinity and development as a young man. Immediately, I thought of a link between this and his own unsatisfactory family history at the hand of *his* father and an effort to relocate shameful feelings. In other words, something like: 'I want to make *you* feel worthless and humiliated, rather than *me*'. He was apologetic and contrite towards his son in the meeting. In another meeting with the Smiths, although the father was able to acknowledge the impact his drinking had had on the family, he sounded angry and blameful. For example, he brought up numerous grievances against his wife for the ways in which he felt she had let him down. These had been woven into the fabric of their marriage and constituted regular flashpoints during rows. At one point he then questioned her version of how much he drank over the years, that she was exaggerating. There was a deal of bitterness on both sides and I wondered how much the Smith couple would be able to transcend anger and blame or what room there might be in the future for some measure of forgiveness, on both sides.

Relatives or concerned others often report that their concerns have been met by repudiation, that they are accused of exaggerations, as I saw with the Smiths. Many will, as a result, start to doubt their own judgement. There can be a similar tendency to downplay the experience of abuse or violence – perhaps *others* have had it worse, I am making too much of it, perhaps it will stop, and so on. The relative can end up feeling the blame and experience shame for either *seeing* problems or *saying* something about them.

Splitting

Families in conflict and dysfunction often resort to splitting in order to simplify reality. If someone can be regarded as 'all bad' and perhaps someone else seen as the victim or as 'all good', then the world becomes more manageable. Elsewhere (Weegmann 2002b), I have written about how such splitting can become reinforced and constitute a form of (mal-)adaptation by children growing up with addiction in parent(s). In such circumstances, it is easy to see how families invest in particular solutions, clinging to the belief that 'if only such and such happens' then all will be right. Desperation sets in, the spouse implores the drinker to stop or seek treatment. The relative demands that their loved one be 'taken away' for a while, taken off their hands. Likewise, the user promises that 'this time', they *will* change. For children, experiencing family problems caused by addiction, similar feelings or pleas can arise. In a family interview, a young child drew a picture of the family huddled in a corner, with the explanatory caption, 'our family is unhappy because my dad drinks'.

Splitting: good/bad children; male/female; drugs/alcohol

There are several instances of splitting in the O'Neill play. For example, Jamie is painted as the degenerate who has squandered his life away. He also portrays himself in this way, warning his brother. Edmund, by contrast, still represents family hope. Although the family sees him, or likes to regard him, still as the baby and as the fragile one, he is seen as having been corrupted by Jamie's malign influence.

Then, there is a male/female dynamic, so that it is more shameful for Mary to be a user of substances than for the menfolk. This doubles up with a further split between the different substances: drink is acceptable and rationalized, but drugs are regarded with horror. Mary is ashamed and is made to feel ashamed of what she is doing (a public secret between them), whereas the boys and their father drink because it is normal or because they are entitled. A feminist perspective could be useful here (e.g. Van Den Berg 1992), insofar as the play conjures up a macho atmosphere around male drinking and the denial of it being a problem ('I can hold it', and so on), which means an avoidance of weakness. Mary, on the other hand, is more subject to an external locus of control, with an emphasis on how her addiction takes her over (unlike men and their drinking). In O'Connor et al.'s (1994) study of different affect states in recovering individuals, women scored higher on ratings of shame and depression, whereas men were significantly higher on detachment. Perhaps in general, women can be reproached more readily, as being unfeminine, morally weak, increasing the need to hide (rather than flout) the addiction. The addiction is a stigma, and because of this Mary ends up feeling invalidated; indeed, by the end she is breaking down and desperately or delusionally holding on to fragments of the past to salvage coherence. Mary is torn, hating the drinking and its effects, voicing protest around the men becoming intoxicated. She expresses concern at the effect of drink on Edmund's frail health. Yet, she also encourages them to drink at different junctures. There may be a cultural aspect here, with different values accorded to different substances; Goodwin (1988) comments on the Irish-Catholic influences in O'Neill's life and work, which may explain the values such as those around male drinking, for instance.

Clinical example of splitting

I have seen members of many Asian families, both users and relatives, where the son(s) were heroin users but there was a significant current or past issue of alcohol misuse or dependence by a parent (the father). Drug use and relapses were regarded with horror because of the association with shame, whereas the effects of the drinking was ignored or side-tracked. In one case of therapy with a heroin user, I was curious about his father's past alcoholism (he was now sober) and particularly in helping my client to think through the reality of this. However, he found it hard to relate to or to describe this, as though the drinking had simply been part of the normal reality of family life and therefore 'unnoticed'. The metaphor of the fog used in the play is an apposite one, since serious problems continue over time and become incorporated into expectation, outlook and a sense of 'this is how things are' (see Weegmann 2003b). My client similarly seemed lost in a fog he could not see.

The family seemed either to have protected itself or suppressed know-ledge of the father's alcoholism, while being preoccupied by the heroin use. In other families, children with drug problems may be encouraged to take up drinking (even as part of a 'recovery' strategy), because this is seen as socially acceptable, although tragically we know of the elevated rates of alcohol problems among primary drug users.

Psychotherapeutic groups for relatives

The Relative Service was established within a substance misuse service in west London during the mid-1990s. The service has been led by a clinical nurse specialist and the author, a consultant clinical psychologist, taking referrals direct and from colleagues in both the alcohol and drug teams. The main objectives in setting up the service, were (a) to create a formal response and opportunities for anyone who was affected by someone else's addiction, (b) to be proactive, thereby to legitimize the needs of concerned others and, most importantly, (c) to enable relatives to be seen in their own right (or 'unilaterally'), even if their loved ones were not in treatment.

The groups

We offer individual interventions, but the main clinical intervention has been that of the meeting and, nowadays, the long-term group. Originally, we recruited relatives into blocks of four groups over one month, with one follow-up meeting. We tried these for some years, and the main theme in feedback discussions was a desire for an ongoing group as people did not like that fact that the blocks of groups came to an end; they felt abandoned. As a result, we moved towards a weekly psychotherapeutic group, accommodating core members (currently seven), who might attend over several years and newcomers, who could join at any stage. The service is predominantly female (around 90 per cent), with a majority of spouses or partners, but we have also worked with parents, siblings, and some adult children of alcoholics. A small number have been in recovery from drug and alcohol problems of their own. The following vignette is a composite from one of the block groups.

Clinical illustration

Following introductions, Gina spoke of leaving her husband and keeping in regular touch with him, since he 'seemed more serious this time'. She conveyed both determination – 'he's got to swim in his own mess now '– and helplessness, doubts about her ability to cope without him and hence needing to keep a link. Others were sympathetic, picking up on the tendency to leave 'loopholes' with their partners, leaving the 'door open', and giving 'last chances'. A mother described her anguish about seeing her alcoholic son living on the streets, her disgust and at the same time being riddled by guilt and unable to 'let go' as advised by the rest of the family. Another mother agreed with this and concentrated on the 'failure', as she saw it, of services to help and of having to risk her own health as a result. As conductors, we listened actively and promoted links between group members and their respective concerns. We wondered, but did not articulate it at this stage, whether they had a fear that we might criticize them, admonish them for 'collusion' and not appreciate how torn they were. We were alerted to criticism from the mother's comment about services – perhaps we were being blamed as well for not doing enough.

Another voice emerged, that of Annie, who told us of the support she had received through Al-Anon and one of her mottos, 'tough love'. Debate followed, around the need for 'detachment', but the difficulty of this in practice. We took up the theme of powerful ambivalence, being hurt by their loved ones, feeling responsible.

Joan felt angry after living with 15 years of drink abuse. She felt she was moving from pity to anger, which she announced as progress. But why did she leave it so long? She expressed anguish at the damage that her children might have suffered. We took up the theme of damage as a result of addiction, including unnoticed damage as a result of habituation to difficult relationships. We also spoke of the impact on children, living with uncertainty and divided loyalties. Several of the group were brought up with alcoholism in their families.

Terry spoke of her own 'mad behaviour' as a result of provocation and frustration. It had made her ill. Peter identified with this and how sick he had become about his brother's addiction. Peter was trying to 'keep his distance' and attend to his own needs. We looked at guilt and unconscious expiation and the chronic impact of being blamed by others. Jeykell and Hyde behaviour was compared in partners, but do relatives start to mirror the highs and lows of the user as well? Towards the end there was discussion about those who did and those do did not have prior group or meeting experience, with encouragement for newcomers.

Comment

In this vignette, we can glimpse the nature of the suffering caused by addiction in relationships and family members. Both acute situations and chronic one were discussed. We also see the element of shame (e.g. the 'failing mother') and self-blame (e.g. the person riddled by guilt), as well as anger directed at the user. There is clearly a good degree of identification and resonance, with members supporting each other and sharing examples of what might have helped.

Conclusion

I hope that the description and discussion of O'Neill's play, *Long Day's Journey into Night*, illustrates something of the complex and repeating patterns of a family locked into despair, as well as providing some insight into the micro-responses around a particular person's (Mary's) resumption of drugs. I have built upon themes in the play to explore shame, blame and splitting in particular. As the 'family secret' of addiction unfolds, emotional resources can become depleted, and responses to it polarized. When and if a user enters recovery, considerable readjustment and rebuilding might need to take place, by the whole family system. Finally, I briefly described the service we offer to family members and relatives. How do relatives or concerned others address their own needs – with or without the user – and thereby construct their own path of recovery? And what happens when the relative begins to look at their own situation in its own light?

Appendix

The following questionnaire was devised by the author and Nuala Quinn, clinical nurse specialist.

Does this apply to you?

You may be a partner, a husband or wife, a relative or a parent of someone who is abusing either alcohol or some kind of drug(s).

If so, consider the following questions:

Part A

Have you ever:

1 Lent the other person money to supply their drink/drugs?
2 Bailed them out when they have got into legal or other troubles?
3 Been consumed with worry about them?
4 Neglected your own life or needs for them?
5 Made excuses to cover up a practical problem they have created?
6 Tidied up a practical or emotional mess they have created?
7 Obtained drugs/drink on their behalf?
8 Found yourself going along with, or adding to, their denial of the problem?
9 Acted as a 'memory' or 'organizer' for the other person?
10 Put important activities of your own at risk, e.g. family commitments, job, holidays, etc.?
11 Felt desperate and alone in your suffering?
12 Lost out on your own leisure or social activities?
13 Felt ashamed of your situation or embarrassed for his/her behaviour?
14 Been afraid of upsetting the other person?
15 Felt you were responsible for causing their drug/alcohol use – or their relapse?
16 Found yourself doing more and more for the other person; feeling responsible for their welfare?
17 Found that your commitments or involvement with the other people deteriorated significantly?

Part B

The following are example or different beliefs that partners, relatives, or parents may hold. Do any of these ring true for you?

1 I am a bad wife/husband/parent, and that is why they have resorted to drink/drugs.

2 I have caused him/her to have the problems in the first place, without which they would never had misused drink/drugs

3 If only I hadn't done or said such and such, he/she would not have used substances or had a relapse.

4 I have to protect him/her and look after them as much as I can.

5 I have got to be by him/her all the time, just in case.

6 I have to try my best to control his drink/drug use.

7 I deserve some of the treatment I have had.

8 I feel guilty for causing them difficulty in some way of another.

9 Did you ever feel his/her hopes depended on you?

If some of these questions or beliefs apply to you, you may want to think about getting help. We have a service for relatives and partners, where you can be seen individually or in a weekly group. Please ask for details.

CHAPTER 11

Working with gay men in an alcohol support group

COLIN MACRAE

The aim of this chapter is to highlight some of the issues to be considered when facilitating a support group for gay men who use alcohol. The first part of the chapter provides a review of the literature concerning the use of alcohol by gay men, in order to heighten awareness of the limited amount of research on this topic. In addition, the literature review provides an opportunity to consider a theoretical perspective on the use of alcohol by gay men. The second part of the chapter is very different in style and content. It describes my experience of establishing and co-facilitating a support group for gay men who use alcohol. Drawing from that experience, issues such as developing a working alliance, agreeing group rules, deciding on the aims and purpose, common themes emerging, and common challenges encountered are all highlighted.

The terms 'gay' and 'homosexual' are used interchangeably in this chapter. This does not detract from the idea that the self-label 'gay' may say more about lifestyle and politics than its colder counterpart 'homosexual', which may be more representative of sexual orientation. However, using the words interchangeably is more reflective of the conflict in the existing literature, some of which is now quite dated.

The term 'coming out' refers to the process of identity formation of sexual orientation.

Alcohol misuse as a particular issue for gay people

Unfortunately, there is not a great deal of research that focuses on gay people's alcohol use. Nardi (1982) found only 42 references to homosexuality in the *Journal of Studies on Alcohol* between 1951 and 1980. This is despite some indication of high estimated rates of alcohol problems amongst gay populations (Fifield 1975, Lohrenz et al. 1978, Saghir and Robins 1973).

In the study by Saghir and Robins (1973), 35 per cent of the 57 lesbians reported excessive alcohol use or alcohol dependence, compared to only 5 per cent of the 43 heterosexual women in the control. Of the 89 gay men studies, 30 per cent reported excessive use or alcohol dependence, compared to only 20 per cent of the 35 men in the heterosexual control. Saghir and Robins used one-to-one interviews lasting 3–4 hours, and questions on alcohol were only a small part of a larger study of lifestyle.

Lohrenz et al. (1978) conducted a study of 145 gay men, selected from two Kansas universities; 29 per cent of the sample were categorized as alcoholic. A further study was conducted by Fifield (1975). Gathering self-reporting data from 200 gay bar users, 98 bartenders, 53 'recovering alcoholics', and 132 gay service centre users in Los Angeles, Fifield concluded that problem drinking rates among the gay populations were probably three times higher than in the general population. However, comparing gay people with general populations might not provide a true picture, particularly if declines in alcohol use are associated with age in the general population. For example, this might be due to the stability and responsibility of raising children, so an analysis that compares those with children and those without might offer a more complex understanding of the differences.

Nevertheless, most recent research exploring gay people's alcohol use continues to compare the differences between the gay and the heterosexual populations. Startling findings continue to be suggested. Bloomfield (1993) conducted a study of lesbian alcohol use and found patterns of higher incidence of problem drinking. In comparison to a study of the US general population, where 8 per cent of the women in the study reported problem drinking (Clark and Midanik 1982), Bloomfield found this figure to be as high as 35 per cent of the lesbian study. In the 1982 study, 16 per cent of men reported problem alcohol use; Bloomfield estimates the figure for gay male populations to be as high as 30 per cent.

Other recent studies have found similar high rates of problem alcohol use amongst the gay population. McKirnan and Peterson (1989) conducted a study of 3400 gay men and lesbians (the sample was 22 per cent female, 78 per cent male) and then compared findings with a general heterosexual control sample. They found that substantially higher proportions of the gay sample used alcohol, cannabis, and cocaine than was the case in the general population. Further, the gay group showed higher rates of alcohol problems. Additionally, while substance use declines with age in the general population, this was not the case with the gay sample.

However, although such studies represent a shift in the focus of research from that of causal relationships, caution is still needed in interpreting the results. Falco (1991) points out that, 'most studies lack a representation of a cross-section of gays and rely upon self-reporting'

(p. 149). Kowszun and Malley (1996) pick up on this point and highlight that most of the studies focused on white, middle class, North American gay men in their mid-30s.

Additionally, these US studies are hard to compare with those from other countries, such as the UK, and there has therefore been a recent call for further UK-based studies (Kowszun and Malley 1996).

Accepting that there may well be higher incidences of problem alcohol use among gay people, as suggested in the studies above, we still have no understanding of such a relationship. Many reasons for the differences in incidence of alcohol use have been suggested. Recent theories tend to fall between sociocultural and learning theories. However, this is a relatively new understanding. For many decades, followers of Freudian thought have sought to explain alcoholism simply in terms of latent homosexuality. Somewhere between these early psychoanalytical ideas and the current sociocultural views lies a vast chasm of misguided research, theories, and unanswered questions. Nardi (1982) provides an overview of these, and the next section of this chapter focuses on these theoretical relationships between alcohol and homosexuality.

Theoretical perspectives of alcohol problems and homosexuality

Psychoanalytical theories

The relationship between problem alcohol use and the psychoanalytical theories has been made explicit since the 1900s. 'Classic psychoanalytical theory emphasizes orality and homosexuality as the genesis of alcoholism' (Buss 1966, p. 445). Alcoholics are seen to be fixated in either the oral or the anal stage, to be anxious about masculine inadequacy and incompleteness, to have emotionally absent fathers and overindulgent mothers, to have experienced traumatic weaning, or to display penis envy (Roebuck and Kessler 1972, Small and Leach 1977). These same phrases have also been used by psychiatrists to describe the aetiology of homosexuality (Bieber et al. 1962, Socarides 1968; both cited in Nardi 1982).

Although modern psychoanalytical theory does not hold the same basic assumptions, it still emphasizes that homosexual urges are controlled by drinking. Central to the assumption of the psychoanalytical approach is the belief that if an individual can learn to overcome their homosexuality, this will in turn 'cure' the alcohol problems (Nardi 1982). Viewing both alcohol problems and homosexuality as disease concepts allows for them to be treated by similar techniques – psychoanalysis and aversion therapy – and only by medical experts (Nardi 1982).

However, the psychoanalytical approach is criticized for ignoring the range of sexual practices and many dimensions of emotions of same-sex relationships; for not accounting for lesbians; for not accounting for homosexuals who remain 'in the closet' but do not report alcohol problems; or for 'out' gay people who do not report alcohol problems (Small and Leach 1977). No attention is given to issues such as homophobia or heterosexism in society, which may well contribute to the reasons why some gay people may not come out. Furthermore, the psychoanalytical approach attempts to study homosexuality in people with alcohol problems, rather than alcohol problems in gay people, hence not recognizing diversities of sexuality or lifestyle.

In summary so far, the psychoanalytical approach has been a major source of false assumptions about the relationships between problem alcohol use and homosexuality. Furthermore, the research that has been conducted has used oppressive and sexist concepts and ideologies (Nardi 1982).

Biogenetic theories

Some have searched for a biological aetiology of alcoholism, such as metabolic abnormalities, tissue chemistry, allergies, enzyme defects, or genetic transmission (Kessel and Walton 1965, cited in Nardi 1982; Goodwin 1976). Although genetic or biological explanations cannot be ruled out entirely, no there is no conclusive evidence for a dominant biological or genetic trait for alcoholism.

Similarly, some have presented biological or genetic abnormalities to explain homosexuality (Lang 1940, Kallman 1952, Wilson 1978,). However, again, no substantial evidence has been forthcoming to support these biological or genetic explanations of homosexuality (West 1967, cited in Nardi 1982). More recently, LeVay (1991) has claimed that by examining the anterior hypothalamus of gay men who had died of AIDS-related illnesses and comparing the results with a control group, differences could be found in the size of a group of neurones thought to be responsible for male sexual activity. However, the control group had not died of AIDS-related illnesses and therefore the possibility that the AIDS-related illness itself had caused the changes to the group of neurones cannot be ruled out.

Nonetheless, as a gay man himself, LeVay's interest in locating a biological aetiology of homosexuality is to provide a positive moral alternative to the interpretation that homosexuality is a choice. Although the findings might well contribute to the overall understanding of problem alcohol use and homosexuality, their use as a single-theory explanation is potentially damaging to the people the research should be serving. By locating the source of the behaviour in genetics or biological factors, oppressive social conditions may be absolved or overlooked.

Learning theories

From this perspective, alcohol use is a learned response resulting from reinforcement of pleasurable experiences or avoidance of negative ones. Tension reduction, relaxation, peer approval, and feelings of power have all been associated with alcohol use (Schuckit and Haglund 1977). Negative reinforcement occurs when anxiety is reduced and positive reinforcement occurs, when social groups reward drinking behaviour, or when pleasurable effects are experienced. As problem alcohol use has been learned, learning theorists believe it can be unlearned by using similar systems of reinforcement. An example of this is when nausea-inducing medication such as disulfiram (Antabuse) is offered to help people remain abstinent from alcohol.

Parallel theories have been used to explain homosexuality, with similar beliefs that homosexuality can be unlearned. The use of shock therapy for this purpose is well documented (Davies and Neal 1996). Others view homosexuality as a gradual process of reinforcement. Inhibitions towards homosexuality decrease as positive rewards are gained from homosexual experiences. This continues through the coming-out process and into the gay bars, where social rewards are maximized and anxiety about being different is minimized (Akers 1973, cited in Nardi 1982).

However, Nardi (1982) points to a different explanation of gay people's heavy drinking, which is still based on learning theories. He argues that gay people may drink heavily to join in with something rather than to escape negative feelings. This is based on the idea that gay bars emphasize leisure-time dimensions of gay identity by providing some protection from the homophobic dominant world, and permit sexual contacts to be made with relative safety and respectability (Achilles 1967, cited in Nardi 1982). Therefore, reinforcement might come in the rewards associated with being part of a gay community, where heavy drinking may be perceived as the norm. Nonetheless, it is also pointed out by Nardi (1982) that the extent to which this is a realistic theory requires further systematic exploration.

Kus (1988) rejects the idea that gay bars are central to the development of alcohol problems. Using a grounded theory approach and theoretical sampling of 20 'recovering gay alcoholics', Kus concludes that 'the belief that gay bar ethnotheory explains the etiology or incidence of alcoholism is a myth' (Kus 1988, p. 31). All of the 20 men that Kus interviewed stated that they began heavy drinking before ever entering a gay bar. However, all of them stated that they believed the gay bar scene to be related to the high incidence of alcohol problems among gay people.

Kus (1988) provides a further theory from his research, which relates to what he terms the 'critical link'. That is, that non-acceptance of gay self as a positive attribute, during the coming-out process, is related to the development of alcohol problems.

In summary, learning theories, despite their early association with 'unlearning' homosexuality, may provide several avenues of research for analysing problem drinking amongst gay people at various stages in their identity formation.

Sociocultural theories

Kessel and Walton (1965, cited in Nardi 1982) offer a sociocultural explanation of alcohol problems by emphasizing incitements, such as money, leisure time, and advertising; and opportunity, such as number of bars available in the area, occupation, or social class; and example, such as peers and parents.

Others have argued that drinking behaviour is related to definitions emerging from social interaction, emphasizing the power of labels and socially constructed meanings. McAndrew and Edgerton (1969; cited in Nardi 1982) observed that social behaviour while drunk is highly variable and situationally defined. Their observations of Urubu Indians of Brazil, for example, highlight that alcohol can transform a machete-wielding group of head-hunters into singing and dancing peacemakers with their neighbouring enemies. As with any psychoactive drug, the kinds of social behaviour and subjective feelings that occur when drinking reflect the interaction of personality characteristics, experience with alcohol, mood, social expectations, and the social setting (Hills 1980).

Conrad and Schneider (1992) argue that those with the power to make and enforce rules impose definitions of problem drinking. The emergence of the temperance movement is an example of this, where the consumption of alcohol amongst the working classes was labelled, socially defined, and controlled by the Quakers in the early nineteenth century (McMurran 1994).

A sociocultural analysis of homosexuality has also been developed, focusing on society's definitions, norms and attitudes towards it. Nardi (1982) suggests that by studying the social context within which people develop their sexual identity, a clearer understanding can emerge of how the identity has been acquired and what society does with it. Hills (1980) suggests that stigma, oppression, anxiety, and individual rage are seen to be created by society and cannot be fully understood apart from the dominant culture's beliefs and values. Conrad and Schneider (1992) add that the fact that homosexuality has been seen as a sin, a crime, a moral issue, and a lifestyle illustrates the importance of social definitions in relation to how gay people are treated and how they perceive themselves. Therefore, the meanings constructed both by gay people and by those in power become a potential focus of study. By focusing on the social context in which gay people find themselves, how they define reality and perceive their situation, and what symbols and values they hold with respect to alcohol use, a more complex and less reductionist picture of the relationship between alcohol and homosexuality emerges (Nardi 1982).

Summary

In summary, it appears that gay men may well use alcohol at levels above that of the general population and may, as a result, experience higher rates of alcohol-related problems. However, the search for a relationship between homosexuality and alcohol use has so far been relatively confusing. Beginning with the early psychoanalytical theories, much misguided research and many limiting, negative assumptions have been made about both alcohol problems and homosexuality. This has not been to the benefit of gay men, not least of all because of the view that homosexuality itself is a 'condition'. Biogenetic theories may provide some thought-provoking suggestions, but in the absence of any conclusive evidence they remain only as valid as other theories. Some have argued for the benefits of finding a biological cause, but there is still a danger of overlooking the oppressive social conditions facing gay men in the UK in the early twenty-first century. It should be noted that Section 28 of the Local Government Act 1988, which prevents the promotion of homosexuality as an alternative family, was abolished only in late 2003. Additionally, antidiscriminatory legislation for the workplace was implemented only in December 2003. Although 'Civil Partnership' may equalize issues related to legal recognition of partners, such as tax and pension benefits, this has still to be implemented (scheduled for October 2005). Lastly, whilst a review of the sexual offences legislation is currently underway with a commitment to equalization, this has proven to be a thorny issue with much debate and, as yet, not many decisions made. Learning theories, despite their early association with unlearning homosexuality, have provided some interesting areas of possible research, particularly those related to learning to fit into a lifestyle. However, if oppression of homosexuality is apparent in society today, then it may be argued that it is necessary to be aware of how such oppression affects gay men before considering the facilitation of a group for gay men who experience problematic alcohol use.

The group

This part of the chapter focuses on my experience of a weekly group for gay men who identify as having alcohol problems. Issues related to the establishment of the group and the co-facilitation of the group are discussed and topics specific to the group highlighted. Case examples of group members are used to highlight some of the common matters arising in the group. Pseudonyms have used to protect identity, and additionally all the men attending the group gave written consent for information to be presented in such a way. This section of the chapter is written in a descriptive style, as the aim is to share my experiences of the group that I was involved with.

Background of the group

The opportunity to consider a group for gay men who use alcohol followed my appointment to a busy alcohol treatment service. The service, which was statutorily funded, was situated in the heart of the commercial gay scene of a large UK metropolis. Such a venue seemed an appropriate place to consider a specific group, as the area already acted as a safe place for gay men to congregate, socialize, and make use of a range of commercial services including pubs, clubs, coffee shops, restaurants, doctors, dentists, housing agencies, etc. On the one hand this venue appeared ideal, for the reason given, but there was an alternative consideration. As the commercial gay scene centres around the use of alcohol, with an abundance of pubs and clubs used as meeting places, we wondered if being in the area would act as an increased high-risk situation for men trying to control or abstain from alcohol use. Nonetheless, as the area also offered some alcohol-free spaces such as coffee shops and cafés, we considered that this was an improved situation, as many gay commercial scenes do not offer such a choice. Furthermore, when the initial group members were asked about the venue, they confirmed the perception that as the area was already a safe gay space, it was the area where a group for gay men should happen.

From my previous experience of considering gay men's health needs in relation to substance misuse, it was clear to me that alcohol use was by far the biggest issue, although recent initiatives had been concerned with drug use. However, there was a lack of services for gay men who use alcohol. One agency in the metropolitan area provided a specific service to gay men who use alcohol, albeit as an adjunct to a larger service. This service, funded by charity monies, had an identified gay male worker, who was keen to expand the service provision and to consider a group facilitated in a central area.

Nature of the group, its aims and purpose

When considering the nature of the group, several options were explored including open and closed groups. In the end, we decided on a semi-closed group. The group was closed in the sense that not anyone could attend, as criteria had to be met. On the other hand, the group was not totally closed in the sense that not all members joined the group at the same time, or stayed in the group for the same length of time. However, rather than have a continual influx of new members joining at any point, a decision was made that new members would be invited to join only once a month. This decision arose from existing members who claimed that it was disruptive to have new people join the group every week who might stay for only one week, decide it was not for them, and then not return.

The criteria used for selection to the group were agreed as follows:

- is an existing client of either service involved in the partnership
- identifies as gay or bisexual man
- identifies having an alcohol problem
- is willing to commit to group work.

The aims of the group were agreed after discussion about the criteria for selection and assessment. In particular, a great deal of discussion focused around the stage of change that potential group members might be at, i.e. pre-contemplative, (drinking), contemplative, (drinking), or action and maintenance (not drinking). Concerns were expressed by both facilitators about having a group of men, some of whom had stopped drinking, some of whom had no intention of doing so, and some who were unsure. We were worried that there might be jealousy from the men who felt that they had no other choice but to stop. However, when we explored other service provision and came across Gay AA, with its abstinence-based philosophy, we decided that it would be useful to provide something different from that. Therefore, we decided on an inclusion criterion rather than exclusion. Inevitably, such flexibility did not suit everyone's needs. Some men attending the group did not like the fact that some other members were still drinking, whereas some members who were still drinking gained a great deal from hearing from those who had chosen to attempt abstinence. The following two examples highlight this difference.

Tom

Tom was 43 years old when he joined the group. He referred himself to the gay-specific voluntary service, after discussing his concerns about his drinking with his GP. Recently, Tom felt that his drinking had escalated and he was worried about becoming dependent. He had been drinking up to two bottles of wine per evening, every day for the past couple of years. Tom was diagnosed HIV-positive 12 years ago, and although currently on a medication holiday, was being treated for secondary problems associated with HIV. He was known to alcohol treatment services, and had a brief period of treatment 12 years ago when first diagnosed HIV-positive. Tom had been unemployed for some years since his diagnosis. He was single and had not been in a relationship for many years.

On joining the group, Tom appeared ambivalent about his drinking and associated problems. He was unsure what to do, and whether or not he wanted to do anything. However, after many weeks of attending the group and engaging with other group members who had made changes to their drinking, Tom set himself a goal of a trial period of abstinence. Tom became abstinent following a self-detoxification over a number of weeks. Tom remained abstinent for 12 months before leaving the group, having successfully gained meaningful employment.

Matthew

Matthew was 36 years old when he joined the group. He had referred him-self to the gay-specific voluntary service, following a community alcohol detoxification. Matthew wished to increase his support systems to help him remain abstinent. He was in a long-term gay relationship with an alcohol-using partner, who was also attempting abstinence. Matthew also attended both Gay AA and AA on a regular basis, and subscribed to the disease concept model.

Matthew found the group difficult as not all of the members shared his beliefs about the nature of alcohol problems. Additionally, he found it dif-ficult to be in a room with others who had no desire to stop drinking but were instead attempting to control their use. He focused on these other members and tried to convince them that they were mistaken to try con-trolled use. After only eight group sessions, Matthew decided to leave the group and continue with AA and Gay AA alone.

On the whole, Matthew's decision did not cause enough difficulties for us to consider reviewing the criteria. What all group members agreed to, was a commitment to find a way of addressing their perceived alcohol problems.

The aims of the group were established as follows:

- to allow group members to explore and resolve ambivalence about their alcohol problems,
- to allow group members space to freely discuss issues of importance to them as holistic individuals including dimensions of their sexuality such as relationships, casual sex, risk taking, etc., without fear of dis-crimination or judgement,
- to provide abstinence support to those members who had chosen abstinence,
- for all of the above to occur in a weekly space that was non-alcohol-based and was gay-identifiable,

Logistics of the group

It was decided that the group would run weekly, at the same time every week, and be held in a suitable group room on the premises of the statutory service. The group would last for 90 minutes with a 10-minute break in the middle. An agreement was reached that we would have a maximum of eight clients, four from either organization at any one time, and that the respective worker would assess the respective clients.

The assessment for membership of the group is an extremely important first contact. In addition to assessing suitability, it also provides an opportunity to disseminate information about the group's purpose and clear up any misconceptions about it. This was particularly necessary, given the gay-specific nature of the group. Some men interested in the group held the view that the group would be a good venue to find a new partner, especially as there might be a sense of shared identity with others who are gay and have alcohol problems. As there are not many non-alcohol-related meeting spaces for gay men, this view was understandable. All potential group members were explicitly informed at the assessment stage that his was not the purpose of the group.

Generally, the assessment contained all of the common elements of group assessment, including previous experience of groups, ability to be with others, ability to offer commitment to attend the group, difficulties in travelling to the group, etc. As the group was for alcohol users, clients referred had to be at a stage where they could be alcohol-free while attending the group and preferably for the night before. This altered the membership profile and excluded those who were severely alcohol dependent, for whom it might be unsafe to expect them not to drink for a whole day without considering their withdrawal states. The rule of being alcohol free is important in providing a space that is physically safe and risk-free for those attempting abstinence from alcohol. As will be outlined later, this was a rule that was tested on more than one occasion.

Negotiating the group rules

Most groups benefit from having some simple rules that all members and facilitators are expected to agree to and adhere to. In addition to setting out what is expected and what is acceptable, the rules also make the group a safer space for vulnerable people to attend, such as those attending for the first time. Although both of us were clear that there needed to be some basic rules, we were also keen to offer space for the original members to be involved in the setting of the rules. If the group members are involved in the process of establishing the rules, there is a higher likelihood of gaining agreement and adherence. As highlighted earlier, the group has to be a safe place for those attempting to abstain from alcohol, so it had to be established as a rule that there should be no evidence of alcohol during the group. Also, we acknowledged that some group members, even although informed of the group's purpose and what the group was not, might still develop their relationship to the point where it might become sexual. This was offered to the original group members for problem-solving. The agreement that was reached was that if two or more men in the group developed a sexual relationship, then one or more had to leave the group. This expression of this rule had to be balanced to accept that there would be nothing wrong with developing a sexual relationship but that it would alter the dynamics of the group and therefore members had to take responsibility for this. The members negotiating this rule handled the agreeing of the boundary very well and very quickly without too much debate, but did want the wording to reflect that gay sexual relationships were acceptable outside membership of the group.

Other rules established were pragmatic in nature and common to most groups: start and stop times, expected behaviour within the group (i.e. no violent behaviour or language), and how to contact if unable to attend on the day.

Lastly, the standard rule of confidentiality was explored in great depth when discussing the group rules. Although all members agreed that the issues discussed in the group should remain confidential other than under specific circumstances, the matter of identification outside the group required further clarification. Although the group was for gay and bisexual men who had already identified themselves as such, assumptions could not be made that group members were 'out' in all aspects of their life, for example to distant relatives or indeed in the workplace. Therefore, a rule had to be agreed that there would be no recognition of group members when outside the group, unless the members previously stated they would be comfortable with such contact. This provided the additional safety of avoiding situations where members had to explain how they knew someone who had just said 'hi' to them.

Issues arising in the group

A diversity of themes emerged during the 2½ years of facilitating the group. These included childhood sexual abuse, domestic violence, sexual risk-taking, casual sexual encounters, sexual health, and depression. However, there were also a number of issues that recurred among different group members. These were experience of homophobia, either external or internal, and experience of loss. Symptoms of internalized homophobia include low self-esteem, chronic anxiety, inability to concentrate, treating other gay men/women poorly, viewing gay life as distasteful, continual striving for high achievement, physical illness, and inability to engage in same-sex encounters without the use of alcohol or drugs (Kus 1995).

Understanding the social conditions in which many gay men find themselves is an important factor when considering gay-specific services. Linked to this is the way in which gay men form their identity, or come out. The following example illustrates a group member whose drinking and therefore needs from the group, were related to issues of internalized homophobia.

Jamie

Jamie was 32 years old when he joined the group. He referred himself to the gay-specific voluntary service after his arrest for drunk and disorderly behaviour. He had never been in trouble before with the criminal justice system. Jamie was abstinent when he joined the group and wished to have abstinence support and to discuss being gay.

Jamie had been diagnosed as experiencing obsessive–compulsive disorder (OCD) and was being treated regularly by a psychiatrist and also saw a psychotherapist weekly. He did not feel that either of these support systems allowed him to be 'true' to himself. Indeed the diagnosis of OCD, for which he was prescribed medication, was centred around Jamie's self-reports of his sexual risk-taking behaviour and preoccupation, at times, with casual sex in a public environment such as parks and public toilets.

Jamie displayed high levels of symptoms of internalized homophobia, including low mood, anxiety, a desire to be successful, engaging in same-sexual encounters only when intoxicated, and unexpressed anger. However, he had no knowledge of internalized homophobia or its implications. he did acknowledge that he was in a difficult situation, living at home with his parents who did not accept his sexual orientation.

Jamie attended the group consistently for the 2½ years that I facilitated the group. The group provided a space for him to learn more about the nature of gay life, the nature of public sex environments, the nature of gay relationships, and a way of connecting with others with whom he identified. He had previously used the commercial gay scene for all of the above purposes, but in his early attempts to achieve abstinence he wished to stay away from pubs and clubs, as he felt unable to use commercial alcohol-based facilities without drinking large amounts of alcohol to gain confidence and feel he fitted in. During the course of his attendance, Jamie began to question his own assumptions and moral beliefs about himself and his sexual desires. He benefited from hearing of the beliefs of other gay men who seemed more content with their sexuality.

Loss is commonly associated with problem drinking. Sometimes this is related to the loss of the use of alcohol when attempting abstinence. At other times it relates to the loss of a loved one or role as a precipitating factor in developing alcohol problems. Loss was a common feature in the group, as the following two examples illustrate.

George

George was 52 years old when he joined the group. He was referred to the alcohol service following an in-patient alcohol detoxification. His key worker offered him a referral to the gay men's group.

A school teacher, he had recently found himself at the end of a 20-year same-sex relationship. Although George described that he had always drunk heavily, he reported that his most recent dependent drinking was a direct result of the break-up of his relationship, which was against his wishes.

Charlie

Charlie was 72 years old when he first joined the group. He was referred to the alcohol service by his GP, who was concerned about Charlie's recent alcohol use. He was drinking up to half a bottle of spirits most evenings.

Charlie had a long history of depression and was currently prescribed antidepressants, which he did not believe were working well. He was aware of the effects of alcohol as a depressant drug, but was unable to consider life without alcohol as his only 'real little helper'.

He had been in a long-term same-sex relationship for the past seven years. His partner did use alcohol, but not on a daily basis. Charlie had a previous long-term same-sex relationship, which lasted 40 years before his partner died. Charlie referred to this relationship fondly and with sadness.

Charlie was diagnosed with prostate cancer two years before joining the group. He refused surgical treatment, for fear of the impact on his sex life.

Charlie valued life and living, as evidenced by his current relationship and his desire to have a healthy sex life, but often expressed ideas of being fed up and tired with life. He was unsure what to do about his drinking. His focus during his time in the group was not changing his alcohol use, but changing his mood and experience of depression.

Common problems experienced within the group

In addition to themes emerging from the group members, such as loss and internalized homophobia, common problems related to the facilitation of the group also arose. Specifically, these difficulties related to the agreement that all members were concerned enough about their drinking to want to explore ways of addressing their difficulties. Appearing on more than one occasion was the experience of the group member who, after a substantial number of sessions, made no changes, or indeed increased his drinking, while gaining approval from the other group members. The following example highlights this and how it was dealt with.

Robert

Robert set himself a goal of controlled use during his attendance at the group. However, his intake seemed to be increasing rather than decreasing during his attendance. He would often turn up at the group when visibly in a state of mild withdrawal. When he was approached by the facilitators about this, Robert became quite hostile and suggested that he was not wanted in the group. He seemed really stuck with his alcohol problems, which on the one hand gave him the confidence he felt he needed to engage in gay sex and on the other acted as an emotional blunter when he felt ashamed of his behaviour. He was unable to contemplate life without alcohol, yet it was becoming clearer every week that his level of physical dependence was increasing. Robert had been attending the group regularly for three months.

After a concerned discussion between the facilitators, Robert was offered a 4-week contract with the group. He was provided with details of an alcohol detoxification service and referred back to his key worker to discuss this further. If he decided to undergo detoxification, then he could continue his membership in the group. One the other hand, if he refused, then he would be asked to leave the group on the grounds that it was becoming unsafe for him to not drink during the day without experiencing increasing withdrawal effects.

After four months of attendance in the group, Robert decided that the group was unable to support him and he chose to leave, after two consecutive non-attendances and an angry letter to the facilitators.

A similar problem that arose on more than one occasion was the group member who attended the group intoxicated. This challenged the safety of the group, and was in opposition to the agreed group rules. The following example highlights this scenario and how it was dealt with.

Sam

Sam was 35 years old when he first joined the group. He had referred himself to the voluntary sector gay-specific service and in turn was assessed and invited to the gay men's group. Sam's drinking was associated with his pay day, when he would buy vodka which he would drink until he had spent most of his money. He therefore had many days of not drinking. However, Sam was concerned that when he entered one of his binges, he also engaged in risk-taking behaviour. During several groups, Sam recounted his experiences of waking up outdoors somewhere with no trousers on and his wallet stolen, for example. Although this sounded like a very frightening experience to other group members, Sam was rarely able to express this fear verbally. He discussed such 'adventures' in a rather excited way.

Sam had been in a long-term relationship for five years, but this was in the process of breaking up. He was clear that the end of his relationship upset him greatly, and he worried about who would look after him, if his partner no longer wished to be in the relationship.

After attending several groups, Sam turned up to one group intoxicated. Unfortunately, this was not noted until he was already in the group. The facilitators addressed the issue with Sam in the group before preceding any further. Ultimately it was suggested that Sam leave the group for the day and attend next week without having had a drink. After his departure, other group members were invited to discuss how they were feeling in relation to Sam's behaviour. A great deal of anger was expressed to the facilitators, and the view was expressed that the group had not been understanding enough to Sam who was clearly struggling to deal with his alcohol problems. Only two group members felt that not having Sam in the group on this occasion was the right thing to do.

The following week, Sam turned up at the beginning of the group. He was again intoxicated and when approached by the facilitators Sam quickly offered, 'I'm not coming in today, cos I've been on the piss'. Instead he was happy to tell of his most recent alcohol adventure to the other group members as they congregated before attending the group.

The issue was discussed between the facilitators, and we decided to devote a great deal of time in that group exploring with members how this behaviour might affect the group. On this occasion, almost all group members felt that it was not helpful to the group or Sam for him to turn up intoxicated and agree not to come in but instead have his 'own group' as one member expressed it, before the group started. When the group had finished, Sam was again waiting for the other group members.

The following week, Sam was not present. One of the group members explained that Sam had requested that some members go drinking with him last week. The members who had been asked had refused, and suggested that Sam not bother them with invitations of drinking. The group members who had taken such action were left wondering where Sam was and how he was doing. He was not seen in the group again for three months. After his return there was no repeat of his intoxicated behaviour, or his discussion of the glory of his adventures. Other group members made clear to Sam what they expected of him if he was to return.

Conclusion

This chapter has highlighted some of the issues to consider when planning and facilitating a long-term group for gay men who identify as having alcohol problems. The first part of the chapter has outlined the literature surrounding gay men's alcohol use and explored some the theoretical explanations for gay men's alcohol use. The second part reported on my experience of facilitating a gay men's alcohol support group over a 2½-year period. The following key points have emerged:

- Gay men may well use alcohol at levels above that of the general population, and as a result might experience higher rates of alcohol-related problems.
- The search for a theoretical understanding of gay men's alcohol use has been confusing.
- Psychoanalytical theories, learning theories, and sociocultural theories have been explored, with no overall conclusive claim.
- Multifactorial theories are likely to be the most helpful.
- A gay men's support group might benefit from being facilitated by gay-identified facilitators, but if the group is to be by gay men and for gay men, then consideration has to be given to the amount and usefulness of self-disclosure by the facilitators.
- It is important to consider the background of the facilitators of the group and to find some common ground on which to build.
- Assumptions should not be made that all gay men want to attend a gay men's group, nor that all gay men have the same needs or wants.
- Group purpose and aims need to be considered carefully and be clearly expressed.
- Group rules need to be discussed openly and should consider issues related to confidentiality, including recognition of members outside of the group, and also issues of forming sexual relationships within the group.
- Themes most likely to arise consistently in such a group relate to individual experience of homophobia, either external or internalized, and issues of loss.

CHAPTER 12

Dilemmas and counter-transference considerations in group psychotherapy with adult children of alcoholics

MARSHA VANNICELLI

Many special issues arise for group leaders who are working with adult children of alcoholics (ACOAs) in groups. Since 'family-of-origin issues' are likely to resonate with themes and issues for all group leaders, sensitivity to special counter-transference issues and dilemmas is particularly important. This chapter addresses these issues as they affect all therapists, with special attention to those therapists who may themselves be adult children of alcoholics.

Importance of a continuously self-reflective stance

In group therapy, as in individual therapy, the most effective therapist will be the one who can maintain a continuously self-reflective stance, examining his or her own feelings and attitudes in response to the patient. In the interaction between the patient and therapist it is essential to continuously monitor the dynamic process – what the patient projects, what belongs to the therapist, and what is the interface or interaction between the two. One's own personal therapy experience is an invaluable aid in this task, as is supervision. As Imhof, Hirsch and Terenzi (1983) point out with regard to psychotherapy with substance abusers:

> Given the endemic and epidemic nature of substance abuse in society today, it is no longer unlikely that a member of the therapist's family may have a serious problem with drug abuse, including alcoholism. In such instances, there is an even greater need for heightened awareness of countertransferential and attitudinal derivatives emanating from the therapist's personal life. It is imperative to recognize to what extent, if any, a therapist's own personal issues become intertwined with the separate treatment issues of the patient . . . (pp. 507–508).

179

Clearly, when we are talking about work with ACOAs, we are facing identical problems regarding the likelihood of therapist resonance with patient issues and the likelihood of counter-transferential complications that need to be carefully monitored and attended to. It should be noted that at times the therapist will initially be more aware of the defence *against* counter-transference feelings than of the counter-transference feelings themselves. For example, the therapist may be aware of feeling excessively conciliatory as a defence against counter-transference rage, or of feeling overly concerned about 'helping and caretaking' in the face of an angry, denigrating patient who is accusing the therapist of being 'worthless'. In these instances it takes careful self-reflection and self-scrutiny to understand the counter-transference feeling and its meaning for the patient. It should also be noted that any counter-transference reaction that is not understood impedes the work of the therapy because valuable information about the patient and his or her interactions is lost. On the other hand, counter-transference that is understood – whether subjective or objective, positive or negative – furthers the work of the therapy, by clarifying what is transpiring between the therapist and the patient.

Heightened counter-transference reactions in ACOA therapy groups

Clearly, when we are talking about counter-transference feelings, we are not talking about 'good' or 'bad' reactions on the part of the therapist. Rather, we are talking about the therapist's reactions to and resonance with the patient, and the importance of understanding these reactions in order to maximize therapeutic effectiveness. Although the potential for powerful reactions to the patient and resonance with his or her material exist in individual therapy as well, these feelings are often particularly intense in group therapy. I like to think of this as similar to the infinitely greater number of possibilities for resonance in a large ensemble compared with a single instrument playing the same tune. The more parts or voices, the greater the potential for resonance. The potential for this kind of resonance clearly occurs in all therapy – but it is probably heightened in group therapy, and for many therapists is heightened even more in ACOA therapy groups. The latter, I believe, has to do with the fact that, in one way or another, all therapists are 'adult children' wishing to address something that was dysfunctional in their own families of origin. Thus, the powerful family dynamics in ACOA therapy groups are likely to pull for even greater counter-transference reactions on the part of group leaders.

The leader who is an ACOA

An unusual characteristic of those who treat ACOAs is that many are, themselves, adult children of alcoholics. It is particularly important that these ACOA therapists be reflective about their motives in choosing to work with this population and the feelings that are stirred up in the course of their work with ACOA clients.

The extent to which the ACOA group leader resonates with the clinical material may be his or her greatest treasure in working with ACOA clients. This resonance may, however, also get the therapist into trouble if it is not adequately examined and understood. The ACOA therapist must be aware that counter-transference is part of life as a therapist and that certain buttons may be especially likely to be pushed when they are related to issues that recapitulate the family drama. In this regard, the ACOA therapist's interest in doing group psychotherapy with ACOA patients is both an asset and a potential liability. Familiarity with the issues is helpful, as long as distance and perspective are not lost.

In one group that I supervise, a particularly clear instance of leader resonance with a group theme occurred.

During the first weeks of its formation this group struggled to identify the 'most problematic patient'. The ACOA leader found herself, by the end of the first session, colluding with the group – feeling, with them, that a particular 'problem patient' did not 'fit', and allowed the group to persuade this member that he did not belong. When the patient did not return the following week, the leader expressed relief, stating in supervision, 'the group will be better off without this patient; he really is too sick'. The leader's own wish to 'save the family' by 'ridding it of its troubled member' – a dynamic that she was all too familiar with – blinded her to the realization of what the group (and she) was re-enacting. Instead, she colluded with them and helped this 'unfit' patient leave the group, thus recapitulating the family fantasy that everything would be fine if only the problem member was removed. A few weeks later the group took up the same cause again, searching anew for a problem patient to eliminate. At this point, the leader, understanding her own earlier collusion, was able to intervene more effectively and this time helped the group retain, and work with, the new problem patient that it had identified.

It is important to consider the possibility (pointed out by Alan Surkis at the 1989 International Group Psychology Association meeting in

Amsterdam) that the therapist's level of development and integration may impose a ceiling on the level of development and integration that will be reached by the group as a whole or by individual patients within it. As is often the case in families when offspring surpass the accomplishments of their parents, anxiety is produced in the group members when an individual member or the group as a whole moves beyond the level of development of the leader. Even if the group has the potential to move ahead, and actually begins to do so, regression is ultimately likely.

Although there is always the possibility that the therapist can grow along with the group, it is the therapist's responsibility to take care of his or her own growth in another arena (i.e. in the therapist's own psychotherapy). The example above illustrates the way in which the leader's own resistance can hold back the group.

The assumption of sameness

The assumption of sameness among group members (or between members and a leader who is known to be an ACOA) may at times be used as a defence against exploring issues in greater depth and against tolerating differences and conflict. Thus, at times of stress in the group, members may attempt to abort further exploration with comments such as 'This is a typical ACOA issue'. However, assumptions about 'shared understanding' and sameness may create a 'you know how it is' mentality in the group about 'typical ACOAs', leading to tunnel vision and a reluctance to explore 'the obvious'. Because the assumption of sameness may prevent the group from moving from one stage of group life to the next, it is important that leaders challenge this assumption when it emerges. An ACOA label should not be accepted as an adequate summary or explanation of what is going on, but should rather be understood as the patient's attempt to temporarily close the door on painful issues. Thus, when group members summarize what is going on as, 'This is a typical ACOA issue', or 'That was a typical ACOA reaction', leaders should ask 'How so?'. The leaders should also inquire further about what specifically was going on for the patient involved and what additional kinds of feelings or reactions others in the group might have (thus furthering differentiation rather than supporting the defence of sameness).

While applying a label or behaviour can be helpful in providing a mechanism for conceptualization, premature or inexact labelling may be seen as the kind of defensive soothing that occurs when rationalization is used. Thus labelling such as 'That's my ACOA behaviour' provides a simple surface 'explanation' without, in fact, really addressing what is going on. As Bader (1988) points out,

Labels and catchphrases substitute for real understanding and analysis. A patient will say, 'That's my ACA stuff', and invite the therapist to collude under the reassuring pretense that this phrase explains something important, when in actuality it reflects the patient's desire *not* to analyze what s/he is really feeling. [And] short-term relief is purchased at the cost of long-term cure and insight (p. 98).

Because it is important that labelling not be confused with explaining, when a patient says, 'That's my old ACOA behaviour', the therapist should ask for more information by inquiring, 'What do you mean?' and the following up with, 'What do you make of it?' or 'How do you understand your doing this particular thing?'. Too often, particularly in groups, the process seems to stop once the label has been applied. It is important that group leaders go beyond the naming to find out more about the real phenomenon.

ACOA labelling can cause problems in yet another way, namely, when a member of a long-term generic therapy group decides that in order to 'work on my ACOA issues', some alternative treatment is indicated. Often, the group leader is baffled (if not hurt and outraged). The generic group is working well – with family-of-origin issues, as might be expected in any well-functioning psychodynamic group, part of the life and heart of the group. The leader's initial reaction may be to wonder whether he or she is doing something wrong, or missing something. When this comes up it may be helpful for leaders to ask the wavering member, 'What issues do you feel you would deal with in an ACOA group that you are unable to deal with here?'. If the patient mentions some particular issues, the leader might enquire about why the patient feels that those issues would not be appropriate for *this* group;. The therapist might also explore whether, in fact, such issues had been dealt with in that group already and wonder about the patient's current feelings that *somewhere else* would be a more appropriate place to deal with them. It should be noted, that sometimes a wish to leave the group in order to 'move on to an ACOA group' may reflect not eagerness to explore these issues in greater depth, but the opposite. When a patient joins a new group, frequently the momentum gained in the previous group is slowed down and the move to another group can aid resistance – helping the patient to avoid doing what he or she may fear (while, of course, on the surface giving lip service to the opposite).

Additional issues for the ACOA therapist

Wood (1987) describes, with particular clarity, some additional dilemmas of the ACOA therapist. She points out that many ACOAs have sacrificed 'a substantial portion of their selfhood in order to minister to the physical and psychic needs of their parents' – a sacrifice motivated by love and compassion for their parents, fear of losing them, and intense longing for a satisfying, sustaining relationship (p. 144). Understandably, the role of strong helper is preferable to the vulnerable role of the dependent, fearful child. Thus,

> A sizeable number of these instinctive helpers choose to specialize in the treatment of chemically dependent individuals and families. They often bring to their work an extraordinary capacity for empathy, and their will to restore . . . can become the basis for the very qualities of hope, courage, and dogged perseverance that are indispensable to success in this field (pp. 144–145).

However, as Wood also points out, this 'will to restore' can become a 'destructive force' when accompanied by 'an impatient "rush to recovery" by the therapist' whose own sense of emotional safety and self-esteem are dependent on the patient's progress in therapy (p. 145).

ACOA therapists may also, at times, have a propensity to block or dampen patients' expressions of painful feelings, since, 'in the heroic therapist's family of origin, emotionality and conflict never came to a good end' (Wood 1987, p. 146). Through Wood's discussion, we come to understand how the ACOA therapist may hinder the work of patients by employing the same blocking manoeuvres that were once used to 'restore the false harmony' of his or her own alcoholic family (p. 154). Since, however, the goal of therapy is not to eliminate painful feelings but to help the patient experience them in a safe context in which they can become reintegrated, the ACOA therapist needs to stay on top of his or her own reactions when strong feelings emerge.

In clarifying the forces at work in the ACOA therapist, Wood (1984) brings to bear the concept of 'fate neurosis' (Deutsch 1930, Wurmser 1981). She thus explains the ACOA hero's 'indomitable and sometimes self-destructive will to restore the alcoholic parent' by citing Wurmser's (1981) lucid comments:

> The aim [is] not to find the good parent, the idealized one; it [is] to find the severely damaged and disappointing parent, toward whom all anger and pain [are] still raging and to repair and restore him, to wipe out his peculiar damage, to undo his specific disappointments – and the greater his shortcomings, the more exciting the hope of his restoration (cited in Wood 1984, p. 6).

Through this mechanism the therapist operates under the unconscious belief that finally healing the impaired loved one will also heal his or her own damaged self – eventually allowing victory over past suffering.

Pull towards the self-help model

Another potential hazard for therapists who are themselves ACOAs is that they may find themselves pulled toward the self-help model, with con-comitant pressures toward self-disclosure and sharing of personal experiences (as one might do in the role of an AA or Al-Anon sponsor). ACOA therapists who are in Al-Anon may, at times, be confused about how the role of therapist differs from or converges upon that of sponsor. It is essential to recognize that the two roles are quite different. A sponsor continues to help him- or herself while also helping the other. As thera-pists we also continue to grow in the course of our work, but our growth is never the focus of the therapeutic relationship; it is always the patient's growth that comes first. We need to be clear that the interventions we make are responsive to the patients' needs, rather than meeting needs of our own. In this regard, being effective as an ACOA therapist is quite dif-ferent from functioning effectively as an Al-Anon/ACOA sponsor.

Other issues regarding therapist transparency and self-disclosure

Most therapists at times feel pressured by patients' questions and concerns about personal aspects of the therapists' lives – on the surface, requests for 'facts' about the therapist. Those requests that seem to have the most legit-imacy (and the ones that the therapists often feel the most pressured to respond to) are generally those that bear directly on the presenting issues: for example, in an ACOA group, the question of whether the therapist is an ACOA; in a recovery group, whether the therapist is a recovering alco-holic; in a couples' group, whether the therapist is married or has a partner. Yet, other questions are often equally important to the patient – for example, how experienced the therapist is. It is important to recognize that simple 'straightforward' answers may not, in fact, be responsive to the concerns being raised by such questions. Generally being raised is a wish for reassurance that the therapist will have the appropriate credentials to help the patient with his or her areas of concern.

Let us examine, for example, the question to the couples' therapist, 'Are you married?'. Though not stated, what is generally of interest is not simply whether or not the therapist if married but whether his or her per-sonal experience has been adequate to deal effectively with the relationship problems that the patient presents. (A successful marriage might well be a credential – but would 10 years of strained, impoverished relating, even if one were still with the same partner?). Since in most instances what the patient is requesting is reassurance that the therapist will be able to help, what is most important in handling these questions is not the precise answer that is given – or even whether or not a specific answer is given – but how the question is handled. In general, in my experience, when therapists are uncomfortable with a question (often because the patient's doubts resonate with their own), they either rush in too quickly to answer the question or in some way convey defensiveness. These responses are motivated by resonating counter-transference feelings – that is, the therapist's own concerns about his or her level of expertise, credentials and ability, ultimately, to help.

A brief clinical vignette will help illustrate what I am getting at.

Not long ago, a new group leader in our clinic, who had just graduated from social work school, was 'initiated' by her group, on the night that she entered, with the question, 'Are you still a trainee?'. The new young leader, vastly relieved to be past her training responded, 'No, I finished my training in June'. Although to group members the young therapist's response may not have felt quite as reassuring as she had hoped, what was more important was that she had shown her lack of experience by hastily answering the question, without doing anything to process its underlying meaning. The group members, by this time quite sophisticated about the workings of a group, responded by informing her, 'Our therapists don't usually answer questions like that'.

As this example illustrates, patients often need reassurance about the therapist's skill and ability to handle problems in areas that are also conflictual for the therapist. Understanding what the questions trigger in the therapist is essential to adequate handling of the patient's concerns.

In an ACOA group, 'curiosity' about whether the leader is an ACOA is also fairly common. The question relates, in part, to patients' concerns about whether the therapist had had the same kind of unpredictable parenting that they have had – and whether, in turn, the therapist will replicate that erratic parenting in the group, as some members find themselves doing in relationship to their own children. Even the positive, initially good therapist (the idealized leader) may come to be viewed with suspicion. Group members may feel, 'You've been good tonight, active, responsive, done things the way we like – but will you stay this way beyond the first few sessions?'. It is as if members are communicating that they do not want to count on something that will disappear. Their own concerns about inconsistent parenting are thus projected onto the leader, with the particular concern that the leader may be as inept as their own parents (and as they may be with their own children). For the ACOA who has experienced inconsistency in parenting, the question may periodically resurface regarding how consistent the leader will be – since even good things often turn bad.

Concerns about consistency and predictability of the leader can be addressed, in part, by the general demeanour of the leader with regard to consistency, limit setting, clear boundaries, and so forth. Many leaders may also be tempted to answer questions about their ACOA status directly. However, whether one answers or not, it is essential, here too, to take up the underlying concern that is being expressed about the therapist's ability to understand and to help.

A simple 'straightforward' response may convince patients that they cannot get the kind of help that they need. For example, if the leader says, 'I'm not an ACOA', patients may feel, 'How can you possibly understand what I've been through when you have no idea what it is like to live with an alcoholic parent'. But the response, 'I too am an ACOA', may be a double-edged sword. For some patients this may initially seem like the only acceptable answer, but for others it may signal that the therapist is 'no better off than we are' and 'not equipped to care for us'.

In all likelihood, the reason that this question is frequently handled as if there were nothing more to it than simple curiosity is that many therapists are persuaded by the success of the many alcohol-related self-help groups available (AA, Al-Anon and Al-Anon/ACOA groups), where, indeed, all help *is* provided by others with similar problems. Thus, the therapist who would ordinarily explore or interpret similar questions from other patients (e.g. from a mother who wants to know if the therapist has trouble with his or her adolescent children) may neglect to explore requests from ACOA patients regarding the therapist's family of origin. However, it is essential to interpret for the ACOA, as it would be in the parallel instance for the non-ACOA, the concerns underlying these questions about the therapist.

Other personal issues in the life of the therapist

It is likely that the therapist's personal life experiences and conflicts may resonate in a number of ways with those of the patients. As Kanfer and Schefft (1988) point out, it is important for the therapist to be aware of sensitive or unsettled personal areas and to pay special attention when working with patients who are struggling with similar issues. For example, a therapist who is recently divorced or separated may need to exercise special caution in treating patients whose central presenting issues involve marital discord. Similarly, an ACOA therapist who has recently succeeded in getting an alcoholic father into treatment may need to pay special attention to his or her reactions to a patient whose alcoholic parents are still abusing drinking. 'Significant life experiences that have strong emotional valences make the therapist particularly vulnerable to reacting on the basis of her own needs rather than those of the client' (p. 374).

When working with patients whose issues resonate with the therapist's, blurring of boundaries is more likely. It is important that the therapist be clear about the ground rules and, when one of them is about to be broken, make a conscious and thoughtful decision that such a modification is in the patient's best interest. When rules are broken without any active decision on the part of the therapist, we can usually infer that counter-transference issues are being stirred up (and that the therapist's behaviour may not, in fact, be in the patient's best interest). As Langs (1975) succinctly states,

> Many deviations and techniques are not undertaken primarily because of the patient's needs, but are rationalizations of the extensive counter-transference gratifications they offer the psychotherapist. In so doing, therapists neglect the ego-strengthening factors . . . inherent in the firm maintenance of proper and clearcut boundaries and ground rules . . . and [the] disruptive aspects inherent in the therapist's failure to maintain these much-needed boundaries (p. 117).

In addition to paying special attention to the operating ground rules and modification that may be introduced, the therapist concerned about the impact of personal issues on his or her clinical work may need to seek additional support or consultation (through personal therapy or supervision). If complications remain and the therapist continues to feel that his or her own reactions are getting in the way of a particular patient's therapeutic growth, referral to another therapist should be considered.

On counter-transference goodness and availability

As therapists it is important to be aware of how we have come into the work that we do and what we expect of ourselves. As Searles (1979) points out, 'We originally entered this profession in an unconscious effort to assuage our guilt . . . over having failed to cure our parents' (p. 28). Many therapists, and perhaps especially those who are themselves ACOAs, believe that they should always be able to 'stretch themselves a little bit further' – extending themselves yet a little bit more. How often we hear of patients who call at late hours of the night or on weekends and who get extra time between sessions as a sort of 'unofficial therapy'. Clearly, these *outside* sessions are just as important as the 'official' sessions that the patient has planned and paid for. (Therapists who do not think so should ask themselves why not.) The therapist should consider setting up contracts with patients about such contacts that occur outside the usual hour: (1) charging for these extra sessions; (2) putting limits on them; and (3) offering additional planned sessions when it appears that the usual frequency is not adequate.

As one ACOA therapist that I supervised put it, 'I feel that I am making a living as a therapist during the hours that I see patients in their official appointments. However, it feels more like 'doing God's work' [Does this need to be free?] by being infinitely able to pick up the pieces at odd hours of the day or night or on weekends'. For this therapist the 'real test' was to be able to soothe her patients at times of unpredictability and chaos. However, as Searles (1979) points out,

> [W]e see that kind of therapist devotion characteristic of such . . . situations is a genuinely 'selfless devotion, but selfless in a sense that is, in the long run, precisely anti-therapeutic. . . . Such 'devotion', . . . inevitably must be revealed, one day, as a lie. This disillusioning discovery, now, that the therapist after all is a separate person with a self of his own and self-interest of his own, after the patient has been led for so long to assume otherwise, will repeat, for the patient, his bitter childhood experience that . . . people are only interested in themselves (pp. 86–87).

The therapist who reacts to a needy and demanding patient by feeling the need to 'give just a little bit more' may fail to set adequate boundaries around private time. Doing so does not help patients learn how to contain out-of-control feelings. Moreover, endless gratification of the patient's demands may communicate to the patient that even excessive needs can be met and that no change in behaviour is required to meet the demands of reality (Chu 1988). Worse yet, patients who continue to barrage the therapist during off hours and the small hours of the night frequently become frightened about the damaging potential of their neediness and rage. That is, such patients come to fear that they may 'use up' or 'drive away' the therapist, thereby destroying the safe 'frame' that they long for and which could contain them (if the therapist helped with this). It is thus important to give our patients the message, 'I'm not going to let you use me up'. Patients need boundaries to feel safe, even though they may need to test the boundaries occasionally by pushing up against them.

The message must be clearly communicated that impulses can be contained and talked about in the therapy session, and that the therapist will provide a predictable structure to do this. It needs to be *safe* for the patient to bring a crisis to the therapy group. A nice example recently came to my attention of a therapist who helped to bind or 'contain' her patient's rageful impulses between sessions in a manner that also protected the boundaries of the therapy relationship.

The therapist was treating an ACOA with self-destructive impulses that took the form of self-mutilation with the matte-cutting knives used in her photography studio. The therapist instructed her patient, when these impulses came upon her, to gather up all the knives and put them in a cardboard box that she should then tape around the edges, wrap with brown paper, and, finally, retape and tie. The bound box containing the destructive implements was then to be brought to the next group therapy session, where the impulses would be discussed.

What this therapist was very cleverly helping her patient to do was to concretely 'contain' her impulses by wrapping up the dangerous implements. The therapist thereby conveyed that the dangerous impulses could be safely talked about in the next therapy session, where they would no longer pose a danger to the patient. The therapist was also, appropriately, expecting the patient to assume some of the responsibility for her treatment and for her own safety.

In addition to the benefits (for both the patient and the therapist) of clear limit-setting by the therapist, there is an extra bonus, both for the patient directly involved and also for the other members of the group. For patients who find it impossible to consider their own needs and to say 'no' to others, the therapist can serve as a valuable role model by declining the role of omnipotent provider. The opposite is, of course, also true, and, consequently, when we extend ourselves beyond our own reasonable limits, we need to be aware of the message that this gives to our overgiving patients.

Often related to our overextending ourselves are feelings that we have about looking fair, nice, kind or generous. Although, to some extent, such feelings are common to all of us, we may want to explore them further if they assume excessive importance. Are we motivated by the wish to give a reparative experience, or perhaps the desire to feel good about ourselves? While neither of these motives is necessarily inappropriate in our work as therapists, they are also rarely sufficient.

It is clear that we cannot afford to be unselfconscious and unreflective about our behaviours. We need to be responsive to our guts and at the same time guided by our heads. This is not to be understood as encouragement to act on 'gut reactions', but rather for therapists to pay attention to their own feelings as a mechanism for *understanding* what is going on and responding thoughtfully and therapeutically.

Avoiding non-therapeutic encounters

Because of powerful wishes 'to help better' and 'to do more', the therapist may at times feel pulled to do more than is, in fact, appropriate. And so, in closing, a few words are in order about what *not* to do when patients tug for more.

The limits of the therapeutic relationship have been articulately discussed, with considerable overlap in points of view, by therapists from the cognitive-behavioural tradition (Kanfer and Schefft 1988) as well as by those from the more traditional psychodynamic orientation (Wood 1987, Cooper 1988). Cooper discusses this from the standpoint of 'therapeutic neutrality'. He states,

> The neutral stance, combined with our constant efforts to remain empathically attuned, keeps us very involved with our patients, but as a psychotherapist rather than as a friend or parent or lover. . . . [As such,] over time patients come to appreciate that we are involved with them in a different enterprise from that to which they are accustomed, and that it is our interest in them and our respect for their autonomy which leads us to remain neutral (p. 8).

Kanfer and Scheft (1988) similarly warn that the therapist needs to 'guard against the expectation by the client that an intense emotional involvement will develop between them' – in particular, 'the client's expectations of extending the relationship to one in which the therapist assumes the role of the parent or lover' (p. 103). These authors reinforce the boundaries of the therapy relationship and the limits on the therapist's behaviour by clearly articulating the distinction between social and therapeutic interactions.

Wood (1987), addressing this same issue, also warns against the therapist's temptation to exceed the limits of the therapy relationship – particularly when feeling pressured by the patient's wish to be 'held'. Citing Guntrip (1969) and Winnicott (1954/1975), she indicates that 'the therapist can adequately satisfy the longing that is being expressed by accepting and understanding the patient's need' (p. 85). That this issue is addressed so frequently in the literature is an indication, perhaps, of the tremendous pull that therapists often experience to extend the boundaries of the therapy relationship.

These struggles often intensify as patients criticize the therapist's 'coldness' and demand more 'closeness'. In my experience, patient's protestations regarding closeness with the therapist often speak one message in terms of the overt content, while another message is covertly being played out in the patient's behaviour. Thus, while simultaneously criticizing the therapist (and perhaps other group members) for not being close enough, giving enough, and so forth, the demand quality of the protestations serves to push them further away. If the therapist listens to the overt message, he or she may hear that the therapist has disappointed the patient by being too cold and distant. Yet, what may be missed by such interactions is that such protests often follow closely upon the heels of an incident in which the patient (or group members) have come too close. The protest covers the very real anxiety about the closeness.

For example, in one group a young woman, following an empathic response by her group leader, began complaining about the *content* of therapist's intervention. Touched by the empathic intent of the therapist, but discomforted by the intensity of her own yearnings to be close (as well as the feelings of actual closeness that emerged), she handled her discomfort by protesting that she did not like the *words* the therapist had chosen and proceeded to struggle with her (thereby creating distance for the next several weeks). The therapist, confused and not understanding what it was that she had done, tried to clarify her *words* – missing the point that the patient's discomfort was *not* related to the *content* but to the *process* and to the patient's fears regarding their emerging closeness.

In another group a young woman used her protests about the therapist's failure to hug her – as a way of creating distance after a particularly intense group session in which she shared her tremendous love for the therapist – sputtering out through tears, 'I . . . only wish . . . if only my real . . . mother . . . could have been . . . like you'. The therapist, also very moved, made an empathic comment indicating how hard she knew it was for the patient to share this and how important it was that she was able to, and the session ended. The next session the patient returned, ragefully protesting that she did not know how the therapist felt about her, that she 'would have expected a hug – or at least to have the therapist touch her arm or shoulder or something' – adding that now she was *sure* that the therapist 'didn't care at all about her'. Again, the patient's words, while suggesting that she wanted even more closeness, were contradicted by the rageful demanding nature of her request, and the entire communication served in keeping with the unconscious intention, to re-establish a more comfortable distance.

Conclusion and comment

In conclusion, this chapter has addressed important issues that affect our work with all clients but may be heightened at times when working with ACOAs (in particular if the therapist is also an adult child or, like most of us, resonates with the issues).

Because of the potential hazards for group leaders who are themselves ACOAs (over-identification with the population, assumptions of sameness, etc.), there may be some advantage to a co-therapy team that combines one group leader who is an ACOA and one who is not. Although this is probably the ideal combination (particularly when one is male and one is female), it may not always be possible. To some extent, tunnel vision will be reduced by the use of *any* co-leader (even if the second is also an ACOA) since, for the most part, two leaders are less likely to get caught up in the same places and will be able to provide some distance and perspective for one another. Another alternative is the use of a non-ACOA supervisor who can help the ACOA group leader process the group material and who will tend to be less caught up in the dysfunctional family that the leader may be resonating with while in the group. Finally, counter-transference supervision groups may be helpful in which several ACOA group leaders come together in a group format to process and deal with counter-transference issues raised when working with this population.

CHAPTER 13

Addressing substance-related offending

MARY MCMURRAN AND PHILIP PRIESTLEY

These days, the principles of 'what works' guide offending behaviour programmes. These are founded upon a number of meta-analyses of studies that help answer the question 'what treatments work best with what kinds of people under what conditions?' McGuire and Priestley (1995) summarize the key features of programmes that are effective in reducing crime. Effective programmes:

- focus on 'criminogenic needs' (thoughts, feelings, or behaviours that are linked with crime)
- have a strong theoretical foundation
- are multimodal, skills-based, and cognitive-behavioural (non-directive approaches and punishment do not work in reducing offending)
- suit participants' learning styles, in that they are structured, active, and participatory
- match risk of reoffending and programme intensity; that is, those who are high risk get intensive programmes, those who are medium risk get less intensive programmes, and those who are low risk usually get little formal intervention
- are delivered with integrity; that is, those delivering programmes are well trained, adhere to treatment manuals, and receive supervision and support; furthermore, programmes are well resourced and prioritized by managers so that they are not casually cancelled or otherwise disrupted
- are delivered in the community, which means at least that programmes started in prison should have a through-care element to assist the programme graduate in generalizing change to community settings.

These principles of what works in correctional treatment have significantly influenced practice in many countries worldwide. In the UK, they form the basis of guidelines for accreditation of correctional services (the term used to refer to prison, probation, and youth justice services collectively) programmes in England and Wales (Home Office 1999), the Scottish Prison Service (Scottish Prison Service 1998), and the newly established Community Panel in Scotland. To become accredited, programmes must satisfy a panel of experts that they accord with the 'what works' principles. Programme designers must document their programmes comprehensively and submit their manuals to the panel. Not only are programmes examined, but so are the sites that run the programmes. These must have the resources and procedures adequate for the good running of programmes.

Among the range of programmes fully or provisionally accredited in England and Wales are those that target substance use. The focus here is on one particular programme – Addressing Substance-Related Offending (ASRO; McMurran and Priestley 2001). ASRO was written by us on request for the National Probation Service for England and Wales, and was later adapted for use in HM Prison Service.

ASRO has a sister programme called Programme for Reducing Individual Substance Misuse (PRISM; Priestley and McMurran 2001), a 21-session, manualized programme for one-to-one delivery. Since group interventions are the focus of this text, PRISM is not described at length here, save to say that it is currently being used in two probation areas in England and Wales, and at eight sites – prisons and probation offices – in Sweden. It has the same theoretical basis as ASRO, and uses many of the same methods, but it is structured into a personalized sequence of assessment, goal setting, and skill training, followed by applications and relapse prevention sessions.

Key principles of the ASRO programme

ASRO, a group treatment programme, is described in relation to the ideals of the seven 'what works' principles.

Criminogenic need

A considerable amount of effort worldwide is spent on the development, implementation, and evaluation of treatment programmes that address substance misuse in offending populations. That substance misuse is a cause for concern in correctional services is unsurprising. First, drug use is in itself a crime and so is a legitimate target for change. Second, the use of some substances, alcohol in particular, can affect behaviour in ways that increase the likelihood of crime, and people who behave antisocially after drug or alcohol consumption may be appropriate for education or treatment. Third, dependence on drugs and alcohol creates a need that is expensive to satisfy and increases the likelihood of crimes of economic necessity, such as theft, fraud, and prostitution. Finally, as substance use and crime become an entrenched part of life, so the person becomes trapped in an antisocial lifestyle that is hard to escape. For all of these reasons, drug and alcohol use are seen as important treatment targets in reducing the likelihood of crime amongst prisoners and probationers.

ASRO is designed for users of any type of drug or alcohol. Groups of users of any specific drug may be constituted by selection (e.g. a group of heroin users). ASRO is for people subject to supervision by the Probation Service, that is, who are currently at liberty to use drugs and alcohol. P-ASRO, the prison version of ASRO, is only for drug users, since the current prison strategy separates drug and alcohol resources. ASRO and P-ASRO aim to reduce crime by targeting substance use as one important criminogenic variable.

Theoretical foundation

ASRO is based on a developmental risk factor model of the relationship between substance use and crime. This model begins with an acceptance of individual differences evident from very early on in life, which are inherited personality traits with a biological basis. A person's nature affects the way other people react, and others' reactions in turn affect how a person behaves and how they grow up to see the world in relation to themselves. A developmental risk factor model explains everyone's behaviour in the same terms, but, since each person's traits and experiences are unique, different outcomes are readily understood. The developmental risk factor model for substance use and offending is illustrated in Figure 13.1.

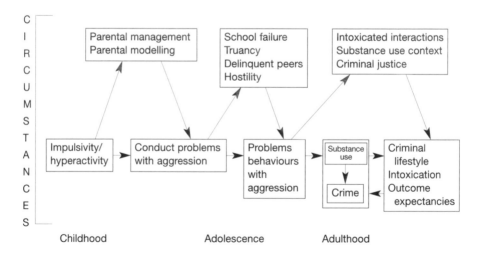

Figure 13.1 Developmental risk factors for substance use and offending.

The ASRO model starts with a first-order trait of impulsiveness, associated with hyperactivity, and traces the unfolding interaction with the physical and social environment. Longitudinal research indicates that impulsivity and hyperactivity are independent risk factors for both substance use and crime (Klinteberg et al. 1993, White et al. 1994). A difficult child causes stress to parents, who may consequently fall into family management styles that are associated with the child's later delinquency and substance use, namely unclear expectations for behaviour, lax monitoring of behaviour, harsh discipline, and few rewards for positive behaviours (Farrington and Hawkins 1991, Hawkins, Catalano and Miller 1992). Under such circumstances, the child is unlikely to learn to control their behaviour, which poses problems at school. Not only is academic achievement poor, which may set the scene for later problems with employment (Le Blanc 1994), but the child is probably unpopular with teachers and peers alike. Being unpopular and treated harshly by parents and teachers allows for the development of hostile beliefs about the world, which are predictive of violence (Dodge et al. 1990, Serin and Kuriychuk 1994).

Through being scolded and punished, as well as failing in class, the child comes to dislike school, which may lead to truancy. Truants gather with other truants, and peer influence is understood to affect both delinquency and substance use. Longitudinal studies have shown that bonding with delinquent peers predicts later delinquency and drug use in that order, that is, delinquency comes first (Elliott, Huizinga and Ageton 1985). Thus, in the early stages at least, drinking and drug use do not cause crime. Early on, it is easiest for youngsters to become involved in petty crimes, such as vandalism and theft, and, perhaps through having money from theft, the next easiest thing is to buy alcohol, a widely available licit drug. From there, some will go on to illicit drug use.

Substance use affects behaviour, both directly and indirectly. Alcohol consumption, for example, increases aggression in direct relationship to the quantity consumed, especially in people with an aggressive disposition (Taylor and Chermack 1993). There is some evidence that other depressant drugs (e.g. diazepam) have similar effects (Taylor and Chermack 1993). Cocaine, particularly crack cocaine, is also associated with violence (Boles and Miotto 2003). A large proportion of acquisitive crime is committed to sustain habits of drug use, with one recent study estimating that a drug-using individual may spend as much as £21,000 a year on drugs, this often being financed through shoplifting, burglary, and selling drugs (Turnbull et al. 1999).

Involvement in conventional society, i.e. commitment to the family, school, work, and non-offending peers, protects against the development of delinquency (Farrington and Hawkins 1991). As delinquency and drug use emerge, however, opportunities for involvement in conventional society decrease and a lifestyle of substance use and crime develops (Walters 1994). Lifestyles of crime and substance use lead people into social contexts which breed further crime and substance use, and the individual becomes trapped in an antisocial way of life. Crime and substance use make relationships difficult to sustain, job prospects diminish, and alternative lifestyles seem impossible. People rationalize their behaviour, developing and strengthening beliefs that crime is a reasonable way to live, and that substance use is a productive life-choice, e.g. 'I only steal from people who are insured', 'Violence is the only language some people understand', and 'A drug high is the best state to be in'.

The developmental pathway as described above allows for the identification of a number of risk factors for substance-related crime, as presented in Table 13.1. These risk factors may be historical and so cannot be changed, but others are changeable and these are targeted in ASRO.

Table 13.1 Risk factors for substance-related crime

Impulsiveness and hyperactivity
Poor family management
Parental models of substance use
Poor academic achievement
Hostile beliefs
Association with delinquent peers
Substance use
Economic hardship
Criminal lifestyle
Antisocial rationalizations

Multimodal, skills-based, and cognitive-behavioural

The developmental risk factor model reveals aspects that are open to change, and aspects that are not. It is important to convey to participants that efforts to change should be directed at what *can* be changed and that what cannot be changed should be accommodated. A person's upbringing, for example, may have left something to be desired, but there is little to be gained from lamenting the past; far better to get on with making the most of what life can offer in the present. The developmental risk factor model suggests that, for adults, substance use and crime are broad lifestyle issues that should be addressed in the present. Thus, ASRO deals primarily with identifying and altering the current triggers for substance use.

ASRO begins with a motivational enhancement module, devoted to enhancing participants' motivation to change as described by Miller and

Rollnick (1991). ASRO then goes on to teach methods of self-control by bringing automatic substance use back into conscious processing so that changes can be made. This is called being a 'personal scientist' (Mahoney and Thoresen 1974). 'Personal scientists' learn to monitor their urges and cravings as well as their substance use, identify what triggers these cravings and behaviours, set goals for change, make changes to behaviour, and generate incentives for maintaining change (Miller 1992).

The third part moves on to address relapse prevention through teaching participants first to identify high-risk situations (e.g. interpersonal conflict, emotional distress, cravings). ASRO focuses heavily on cravings and coping with cravings. This is expedient when working with people who may already be abstinent from substances but who may nonetheless wish to consolidate control skills, and for people who may feel cautious about telling a probation officer about substance use per se, which is, after all, illegal. Coping with urges and cravings follows Marlatt and Gordon's (1985) procedure of decision review, positive self-statements, enduring the feelings until they subside, and engaging in distracting activities.

Within relapse prevention is a social problem-solving component called 'Stop and Think!' (McMurran et al. 2001). This is based on the work of D'Zurilla and colleagues (D'Zurilla and Goldfried 1971, D'Zurilla and Nezu 1999), and aims to teach people a strategy for solving problems independently. This component is considered important in equipping people to deal with the inevitable emotional and social problems consequent on quitting substance use and substance user networks.

Finally, broader lifestyle changes are encouraged so that improvements can be maintained. Lifestyle modification is a holistic approach facilitating the development of a reinforcing non-drug, non-criminal lifestyle. Walters (1998) suggests the following process:

- Identify what is being met by the antisocial lifestyle, i.e. what will the client miss if they stop drinking, drug use, and crime?
- Select substitute activities that will satisfy these needs through work, relationships, and leisure activities.
- Encourage commitment to a new lifestyle by reviewing the decision to change, enhancing social support, and abandoning the 'addict' or 'criminal' identity.

Since lifestyle changes cannot be made instantly, we recommend that the individual's case worker support the goals in this section outside ASRO sessions. Often, the best way forward is to put people in touch with specialist local agencies and services (e.g. NACRO, JobClub, sports associations).

The core treatment components are outlined in Table 13.2, and these may be seen to follow the process of change described by Prochaska, DiClemente, and Norcross (1992) in their stages of change model. That is, change is a *process*, not an event, and people move from contemplation, through action, into maintenance and eventual termination.

Table 13.2 ASRO core components and stages of change

Enhancing motivation to change	Contemplation
The Personal Scientist – increasing self-control	Action
Relapse prevention	Maintenance
Lifestyle modification	Termination

Structured, active, and participatory

ASRO is designed to suit the learning styles of clients in criminal justice settings. We know from meta-analyses that unstructured programmes do not work in reducing reoffending, therefore ASRO is a structured programme, where each session follows a plan that targets the identified needs in ways that are supported by research evidence. Although facilitators do listen to participants' narratives and current concerns, unstructured talking about problems for long periods of time is avoided. People who offend are not typically academic, and many have had a bad experience of education in their schooldays. Sessions are, therefore, designed to engage participants in the learning process by using active and innovative methods, many of which were creatively generated by probation officers in the early field trials. Role plays, learning exercises, and written work are all interspersed through the programme. The materials used are graphically presented, and plain English is used to the best of our abilities. Completion of assignments, including self-monitoring, self-reflection, and problem-solving is expected between sessions. Throughout ASRO, group facilitators adopt a motivational style and use Socratic teaching methods, where they draw learning points from the participants rather than tell them what to think. The lessons of the programme are repeated over sessions and in end-of-session summaries to maximize the chances of the participants learning and remembering.

Risk of re-offending and programme intensity

There are four selection criteria for ASRO, namely that the candidate is:

- at medium-to-high risk of reoffending
- a user of one or more substances

- someone whose substance use increases the likelihood of crime
- sufficiently literate to understand written materials.

Risk of offending is measured using the Offender Group Reconviction Scale (OGRS), a research-based formula for calculating the risk of reconviction (Copas and Marshall 1998). For participation in ASRO, participants should be at least medium risk, i.e. have an OGRS reconviction likelihood of 50 per cent or more. Individuals with a high OGRS score, i.e. 70 per cent or more, are likely to have a wider range of criminogenic needs than can be met by ASRO alone, and such people should be referred to additional accredited programmes, such as one of the suite of cognitive skills programmes — 'Think First' (McGuire 2000), 'Enhanced Thinking Skills' (Clark 2000), and 'Reasoning and Rehabilitation' (Ross, Fabiano, and Ross 1986).

ASRO is a 20-session programme, with each session lasting 2–2½ hours. The total ASRO programme therefore takes 40 to 50 hours, to which may be added the extra time that participants spend on homework assignments. This programme duration is at the *lower* end of the spectrum for today's accredited prison and probation service treatment programmes. Those who are high risk of reoffending are deemed to require programmes of many hours' duration, over many months or even years.

Programme integrity

Programme integrity is the extent to which the programme implementation matches the programme design. ASRO and P-ASRO manuals contain detailed accounts of the theory behind the programme, a compendium of instruments for assessment and evaluation, and a comprehensive guide for running each session. In addition to this, the National Probation Directorate and the Prison Service have produced manuals for treatment managers, specifying how the operation of the programme should be organized and monitored. This documentation ensures clarity about what is expected of all those involved in ASRO or P-ASRO, and permits audit of practices according to set standards.

Mechanistic recitals of programme content, delivered without understanding, without skill, without proper supervision and monitoring of standards, is a recipe for failure. It is also the case that worker effects can be positive as well as negative – skill, knowledge, experience, warmth, and empathy yield dividends at the personal as well as the programme level. Consequently, staff are carefully selected for training to run programmes. A comprehensive training programme to prepare people to run ASRO has been prepared by Steve Delight (2001), a professional trainer. This teaches the theoretical foundation of ASRO and the detail of the content, as well as training staff in the practical skills for delivery. The training programme is meticulously documented, and so new trainers can be trained, all using the same material.

Integrity is further promoted by openness in working. Programmes are facilitated jointly, allowing for peer support both informally and through post-session debriefing. All programmes in prisons and probation settings in England and Wales are now routinely videotaped, and tapes are submitted to independent scrutiny to ensure that treatment is being provided as specified. In probation, the responsibility for maintaining programme integrity is increasingly undertaken by treatment managers who typically deliver the programme part-time, and who also support, monitor, and supervise other delivery staff. Treatment managers are beginning to receive dedicated training for their role. Delivery sites are also the subject of management audits to ensure that programmes are supported at institutional level, for example by having enough adequately trained staff, ensuring that their work timetables permit them to attend fully to programmes, and resourcing the programmes well in terms of facilities.

Community and prison

Meta-analyses of correctional treatments show that they are more effective when conducted in the community rather than in prisons. McIvor (2001) suggests that the reasons for prison treatments being less effective are that behaviour changes that are adaptive in prisons may not be adaptive in the community, or because the environment to which the prisoner returns after release exerts a powerful influence that causes changes to decay and disappear. Treatment in a community setting may be more effective because the person is at liberty to practise new skills and experience their effects, and also to develop and maintain supportive networks (McIvor 2001).

ASRO was originally commissioned for use by the Probation Service in community settings. Although evidence supports the greater effectiveness of community- rather than prison-based programmes, there are two realities that confront these findings. The first is that many of those who are the most seriously addicted and who commit disproportionate amounts of crime in the pursuit of drugs or under their influence are currently to be found in prisons, often serving very long sentences. It makes sense therefore, to address their substance use while they are locked up. In fact, people with serious substance use problems present almost insuperable difficulties to staff in probation and community-based services who try to engage them in systematic programmes, since the problem of substance use goes hand in hand with fluctuating motivation, crises, and unreliability. Working with substance users when they are in prison can actually mean that regular contact is easier.

Therefore, the fact that the community is the better place for treatment should not mean that prisoners are neglected during their period of incarceration. Indeed, one way of making prison-based treatments more effective is to ensure that there is through-care between prison and community so that treatment needs can be addressed at key transition points.

To become accredited, all prison programmes must address through-care matters, and P-ASRO is no exception. Indeed, in both ASRO and P-ASRO the final module, lifestyle modification, aims to connect people with other sources of help and support after the conclusion of the programme. Participation in a 20-session programme is not all that is required to effect long-term change. Whether in prison or in the community, maintenance of change must be planned by considering work, leisure, accommodation, and relationship issues.

The preceding sections describe ASRO and P-ASRO in relation to the principles of good practice. We shall now consider how they translate into practice.

ASRO in practice

The implementation of ASRO is directed from the National Probation Directorate headquarters by a programme development manager. In ASRO's formative days, Claire Wiggins held this post. Evaluation of ASRO, part of a wider programme of evaluation, was commissioned by the Home Office Research, Development, and Statistics Directorate from independent evaluators (Hollin et al. 2002). Starting in May 2000, ASRO was piloted in four Probation Service areas: Gloucestershire, Inner London, Lancashire, and South East London. These pilots allowed Probation Service staff to check what worked and what did not, and feed back their experiences and suggestions to the authors. Changes were made to the programme, and then ASRO was rolled out to other areas during 2002, a process that is continuing.

In some of these areas the programme is integrated into Drug Treatment and Testing Orders (DTTOs), which are specific sentences of the courts; in others, the programme is administered as a condition of probation; and in others attendance is voluntary. It is administered by probation officers, probation service officers, or DTTO personnel who may be seconded health or drugs workers who have received a standardized 9-day training.

ASRO staff report favourably on their experience of using the ASRO programme materials and find them useful for the target groups, who respond positively to the programme experience. Typical comments are:

> 'I enjoy it all. The changes you are working with are so massive. If you get them at the right time they are really motivated.'

> 'The atmosphere in the last session was electric. One man's mother came – the most significant person in his life – and spoke about the changes he had made in his life – and of course she cried. Everybody cried.'

> 'I like the structure. Personal Scientist has gone really well; it's them telling us where they're at; they are in control doing their assignments. It puts the shape in the programme.'

Participants too – those who survive to the last session – speak of what they have learned:

> 'Stop and Think; self-monitoring; positive self-talk; recognizing situations and not letting yourself be drawn into them; the ability to say no to people.'

> 'Found the cravings sheets useful, and the action plans – coming back to say what you had done.'

> 'The Personal Scientist was good.'

> 'I've been on drink and drugs for 25 years or so – it is an extremely big change – but this has helped me.'

> 'I was sick to death of drugs – I just needed this extra push.'

> 'We joke about it – but what are we going to do on Tuesdays and Thursdays?'

The earliest part of the evaluation focused on implementation issues, and it is this information that we have to date. ASRO participants have mainly been white men aged 18–30. ASRO was seen as directed mainly at white men, and the view was that materials would need to be modified to suit women and people from different ethnic groups. Group size was between four and 13 members, with eight being considered optimum.

From interviews with staff, Hollin et al. (2002) noted that ASRO was well received, not only because it was a relevant and 'expertly designed' programme, but also because of the attendant evaluation. Programme implementers were keen to benefit from the knowledge about effectiveness that the research would provide. The programme content was generally found to be acceptable, but there were also some criticisms. The early sessions were rather slow, the literacy levels required were quite high, and it was sometimes hard to get participants to comply with self-monitoring.

Another difficulty was the focus on 'cravings', which means different things to different people (and nothing at all to some!). Cravings, rather than actual substance use, were a deliberate focus of programme design for a number of reasons. First, looking at cravings was considered a prudent proxy for drug use which is, of course, illegal. Second, focusing on cravings permits work with those who are currently abstinent, along with current users. Finally, it is useful to teach substance users to focus on feelings and thoughts that occur before substance use and are warning signs.

The biggest issue in the management of ASRO in the community, however, is that of group member attrition. This is most marked in the period between sentence and first group meeting, which can be a period of months in some areas with low numbers of probation orders (i.e. there is a long wait until enough people have been assembled to form a group), and low numbers of trained staff. In one area, 149 orders were made during a 12-month period specifying attendance at an ASRO programme. Of these, 38 people made it to the first meeting of ASRO, and only 10 completed the programme. So, 74 per cent of the sentenced individuals were lost to the programme before it began, and only 7 per cent of them completed it. Of those who started ASRO, 74 per cent failed to complete it. Fortunately, other areas have done better than this.

Overall completion rates appear to be rising in response to a number of measures. For example, a holding group in one area helps maintain contact during the waiting period for the next ASRO programme to start. In another area, as an experiment, strenuous efforts were made to maintain participant attendance at one group, through written and telephone reminders of meetings, help with transport, visits, and the use of volunteers. This resulted in a very high rate of compliance, but the effort was deemed unsustainable in terms of staff time and other resources, given the other pressures on the service. Some anecdotal evidence suggests that participation in a DTTO programme, which entails daily attendance and a varied menu of services and activities, raises completion rates compared to stand-alone ASRO conditions in ordinary probation orders, but this is not always the case.

Attrition rates are an immediate and direct reflection of the difficulties of working systematically with individuals at liberty in the community where continuing active involvement in the drugs and crime scene is virtually inevitable. Nor are these problems particular to ASRO – general offending, violence, and drink-driving programmes experience similar problems, if not quite to the same degree. In one area, the advent of ASRO raised completion rates for other programmes by removing from them unreliable participants with severe substance habits. Every probation area is currently required to have an attrition action plan in place. Some ASRO groups meet in the evening or at weekends to accommodate employed participants and individuals engaged in other daytime activities. Staff awareness sessions are being improved, case management is tightening up, and treatment managers are providing more support.

Overall programme completion rates are likely to rise towards some maximum achievable level under current levels of provision, but substance programmes are always likely to prove an unpromising area for improvement. There is some evidence from North America to suggest that reward schemes, using vouchers, tokens, or cash, can substantially improve substance programme attendance, compliance, and completion: *'Give them presents and they will come.'* Practitioners in the UK respond to news of these procedures with raised eyebrows, and references to the tabloid headlines that would inevitably follow their adoption here: 'Drug fiends get treats on the taxpayer', for example.

Staff were positive about the training they received to deliver ASRO, although there was a view that group work skills should be added to the training along with the specifics of ASRO. Furthermore, it was suggested that follow-up sessions should be held to clarify implementation issues. Such meetings are now held under the auspices of the National Probation Directorate's (2002) *Change Control Strategy*. This permits the systematic identification of design and implementation problems, followed by planned and approved change, thus being sensibly flexible but at the same time maintaining programme integrity.

Other live issues for ASRO in the community, as for other programmes, include the quality of support and supervision for front-line delivery staff, ongoing staff training and professional development, and strengthening the role of case managers in the supervision and provision of parallel services to individual participants.

The independent evaluators will, in time, collect information about the processes of change from psychometric measures that are included in the ASRO programme. These include assessments of stages of change (McConnaughy, Prochaska and Velicer 1983, McConnaughy et al. 1989), locus of control (Levenson 1975), and social problem-solving (D'Zurilla, Nezu and Maydeu-Olivares 2002). Reconviction studies after ASRO, when participants have been at liberty long enough, will tell us whether ASRO has reduced reoffending. Demographic data that are being collected will tell us who does best in ASRO – younger or older, users of what kind of drug, and under what conditions treatment was provided. Collecting information on individuals after contact with correctional services has concluded is costly, and so what might be untestable is how ASRO impacts on substance use per se: Do ASRO graduates stop, reduce, or change their substance use?

Prison ASRO

P-ASRO is HM Prison Service's adaptation of ASRO, which is now in use in several prisons in England and Wales. It was initiated with staff training in mid-2002 and is now running in 11 establishments in different parts of England and Wales, with the plan to expand this to at least 20 sites. The participating prisons have completed between two and seven programmes each. An early evaluation of implementation was commissioned by HM Prison Service and was conducted by MORI (2003). They focused on three prisons, where they interviewed prisoners, P-ASRO facilitators, P-ASRO managers, and other prison staff about their experiences. MORI identified many positive views of P-ASRO.

The programme itself was commended for being well structured, focusing on skills for change, improving participants' self-confidence, allowing a degree of creativity in its delivery, and taking a holistic approach. From an organizational point of view, there was appreciation of P-ASRO's accredited status, which brings with it resources and commitment, and also of the support received from HM Prison Service's central Drug Strategy Unit.

Comments from staff were:

'Overwhelmed at the impact the programme has made – and the thank you letters and cards we have received.'

'Feedback from officers regarding the change witnessed in certain individuals is rewarding.'

'P-ASRO has sold itself by word of mouth – we are filling programmes months ahead.'

'People are using Stop and Think! [social problem-solving] on an everyday wing basis – actively working at trying to change the way they cope with personal pressures. It's fantastic to see a real pay-off from the work.'

P-ASRO participants appear to appreciate engaging constructively with a major problem in their lives, learning specific techniques that they can use with drugs and other issues, and, significantly in view of the cognitive-behavioural basis of the programme, the opportunity to re-think their habit and the possibilities of change:

'I have done drugs programmes many times before – this is the first time I've "got it".'

'I've never thought about it like this in my life.'

'And then on Session Eight – I got it. I realized I needed to change the way I was thinking; I was still thinking like a 'smack-head.' It was all I could talk about at work, and I was having sleepless nights.'

'I now believe that change can happen.'

'It changed me – people who know me say they can see the change.'

'Changed the way I think about everything.'

'I've even stopped swearing at the servery.'

'It's helped me loads here as drugs are easy to find and I've been strong enough to say no.'

'It's a thinking process.'

'I think things through more carefully – I don't act on impulse.'

'I don't just want to survive – I want to live.'

There were, of course, aspects of the programme that were viewed less positively. There was in prison, as in the community, lively debate about the definition of 'cravings', and whether it was the most appropriate term to use, especially for men who had been incarcerated *and* abstinent for a period of years. Also, despite a recognition that feeling states are important in triggering substance use, some people did not feel comfortable with either the words or the need to talk about feelings in the group sessions.

One graduate thought P-ASRO was *'a shallow, very obvious, ordinary way of looking at a very serious problem – there was a lot of repetition.'* Repetition of material is recommended in the programme accreditation criteria, where there is the statement that 'there should be an adequate level of repetition and practice to reinforce learning across sessions' (Correctional Services Accreditation Panel 1999, item 7). Repetition is, therefore, one of the keystones of the ASRO/P-ASRO programme architecture, and it is based on sound learning principles. Although this criticism was not repeated by many other participants, further thought as to how it is put into practice without boring participants is clearly required.

Some felt that the content of P-ASRO was aimed at too low an intellectual level. Authors are instructed by the Accreditation Panel to keep the content and the language simple. Although it is often worth reminding authors to avoid abstruse terms and jargon, it may be the case that language and concepts can be simplified to the point of seeming patronizing. It is interesting to compare this criticism of P-ASRO with that of ASRO, where required literacy levels were considered too high.

Other problems in prison related to working with other agencies. Prisons employ CARATS workers (Counselling, Assessment, Referral, Advice and Through-care Services) who refer to P-ASRO, and it was thought that referral criteria needed to be specified more clearly. Through-care was thought to be good in principle, but in practice it was limited by the low availability of services. P-ASRO staff also report grappling with ongoing implementation issues – access to suitable premises; shortage of staff time to do as many programmes as they would like, and to do the ones they do to a high standard; and the transfer of prisoners without regard to their programme status.

Prisoners and prison staff suggested a number of ways of improving P-ASRO, including introducing booster sessions, using programme graduates as mentors for programme starters, and having group activities outside P-ASRO sessions to enhance bonding. Group bonding, and perhaps the success of P-ASRO, may be best where there is a dedicated residential wing or unit for P-ASRO participants. This was the arrangement in one prison, where two P-ASRO groups ran simultaneously, and prisoners were resident on the unit for the duration of their programme participation. Unfortunately, prisons often need maximum flexibility to use spaces as population needs dictate, and the residential P-ASRO unit is under threat.

Common issues

In both the community and in prison, there are some common issues that arise in relation to the programme content. The definition and use of the idea and the word 'cravings' is an example. Some participants deny that they have cravings – sometimes because they have been abstinent for a long period, in prison, or in the community, and their need to use has diminished or vanished; or sometimes because they 'wake up craving' – it is simply the condition of being alive and awake that they feel the need to use on a constant basis. There can also be problems in groups with a membership that includes abstainers and people in stable maintenance of non-use together with active users and relapsers.

Structured programmes for substance misusers: future developments

ASRO is not the only structured cognitive-behavioural treatment programme for substance users operating in UK corrections services, and the plan is to introduce others. Nor are structured cognitive-behavioural programmes the only types of programme operating in UK correctional services. Therapeutic communities, based on the 12-step approach, are well established (e.g. Martin and Player 2000). This is as it should be; a variety of programmes needs to be available to maximize the chances of success, whether this be by finding the 'best' programme or by having a range of programmes that suit the needs of different criminal justice clients.

What is certain is that drug treatment programmes in correctional services in the UK are already reaching large numbers, and that number will grow over the coming years. The Government's Crime Reduction programme funds diverse evidence-based approaches to the reduction of crime, including programmes in prison and probation services in England and Wales. One of the national targets of the Crime Reduction Programme when it was set up in 1999 was to reduce the levels of repeat offending by drug users by 25 per cent by 2005 and by 50 per cent by 2008. This target is to be achieved partly by increasing participation in drug treatment programmes. Recent research identified that 73 per cent of a sample of prisoners had taken an illicit drug in the 12 months before their imprisonment, with 47 per cent having used heroin, crack, or cocaine, and 55 per cent of drug users admitting a connection between their substance use and crime (Liriano and Ramsay 2003). With a prison population approaching 70 000, the numbers who might be eligible for treatment in prison alone are substantial.

In principle, treatment approaches in correctional services may not differ markedly from those available to substance misusers in health services or voluntary agencies, in that cognitive-behavioural and therapeutic community approaches are used. The differences lie in:

- their duration, with many treatments being longer in correctional than in health settings
- their documentation, with a greater degree of manualization in correctional services
- the closeness of scrutiny, with a greater degree of monitoring and audit evident in correctional services.

These differences may narrow in the coming years with the Government's recently established National Treatment Agency, whose remit is to increase the availability, capacity, and effectiveness of treatment for drug misusers (National Treatment Agency 2003). Whether treatment works to reduce reoffending is a question for researchers, and it is laudable that both the Crime Reduction Programme and the National Treatment Agency include research within their remits.

CHAPTER 14

Work discussion groups for professionals*

MARTIN WEEGMANN

Substance misuse professionals (hereafter SMPs) often manage complex, multifaceted roles, in a climate of increasing regulation. The role of the NHS psychiatric nurse, as one example, often combines overall care management or 'key working', the management of short-term or longer-term detoxification or maintenance regimes (for problem drinkers and problem drug users respectively), a monitoring role, and acting as counsellor and/or group therapist. As a key worker, the nurse is called upon to maintain a brokering role, attending to the client's immediate needs but also establishing links and negotiating referral with other agencies or professionals (e.g. day centres, hospital facilities, GP surgeries, social workers). Increasing legislation and regulation mean that within this the nurse has to be cognizant of risk and meet a variety of clinical and administrative requirements. A frequent complaint is of not having enough time to think, due to having constantly to meet these external pressures. At its worst this creates much anxiety – e.g. 'what if something goes wrong?' or 'will my work be criticized?' and the danger of becoming ritualistic, going through the motions to satisfy these external conditions.

Keeping such role complexities in mind, I shall first attend to some of the emotions and interactional pressures to which SMPs are exposed during the normal course of their work. This might put us in a better position to understand how the work discussion group can assist.

The daily unconscious

SMPs are called upon to contain the complex needs of substance misusers (hereafter SMs) from first assessment, through the early stages of treatment, and frequently on a continuing basis thereafter. As we have

---

* This chapter is adapted from a paper published in *Drug and Alcohol Professional* (2003: 3(1)).

described, the SMP may function in direct, co-ordinating, and monitoring roles in order to respond optimally to these needs. Khantzian (1988) talks cogently about, 'meeting the needs of substance-dependent patients for safety, stabilisation, control, and comfort' (p. 544). However, the pressures of what I shall term the *daily* or *everyday unconscious* is continual, and we may underestimate the personal and emotional strains inherent in such a situation. For example, a user who is seriously out of control can threaten the stability and abilities of the professional, who might then also start to feel that he or she is out of control. The SMP has to deal with individuals in considerable difficulty and distress but who have also caused great distress to others within their network of close relationships. The SMP may, as result of the latter, have to deal with the worry caused to relatives and spouses, for whom the behaviour of the substance misuser may have generated distressing feelings of impotence or resulted in thwarted attempts to control them; relatives may expect the SMP to produce the results that they have failed to achieve, and feel disappointed when we are unable so to do. In other words, there are individual pressures coming from the user, who seeks relief, and systemic pressures from, say, family members who seek relief from the consequences of the addiction. In addition, we naturally wish to be able to meet our own internal expectations of efficacy and the expectations of our colleagues (e.g. the referrers) who turn to us. A highly experienced alcohol nurse once shared with me the fact that she felt well able to contain most pressures coming from service users and their relatives, but felt defensive (feared criticism) in relation to referring GPs. They seemed to represent powerful adults in her mind, potentially exposing of her inadequate efforts.

The substance misuser presents us with a range of states of mind, concomitant or coexisting with the use of drugs and alcohol. They want us to act in various ways, to take away the distress, to provide relief. As a result of this pressure, we may be expected to act unconsciously as a replacement drug, able to take away mental or physical pain. Depending on the nature of the treatment establishment (e.g. rehabilitation, day centre, prescribing service), certain client expectations will follow, including, in some settings, the request for actual drugs. Khantzian (1988) argues, 'Addicts and alcoholics suffer not only because they lose control of their substance use. They suffer as much because of longstanding problems with regulating their emotions, self-esteem, relationships, and behaviour' (p. 166). It is not surprising, therefore, that there is some consistency between how we are treated and how other, significant people in the substance misuser's life are treated. Just as there is the use and abuse of the drug, so there can be the use and abuse of treatment, which brings in the importance of clear values and supportive structures surrounding the worker. Without the latter, a worker can be quickly isolated.

At assessment, the client may vividly convey their plight in a powerful way, verbally and non-verbally, giving the worker a condensed experience of the desperation or the dilemmas with which they struggle much of the time. Elsewhere (Weegmann 2002c), I have written about the possible dynamics and pressures of the 'first meeting' and how the individual shows us their suffering, inviting us to know something of what life is like in their shoes. At the same time, we may see only a glimpse of a person's vulnerability since the suffering is walled off, with considerable defensive resources drawn upon to 'protect the drugs', as it were. A drinker told me appreciatively, after two years of abstinence-based group therapy, that he had initially disliked me because I threatened to 'spoil an affair' with alcohol; it was only when he embraced the need for change that he could experience me as an ally. I am reminded of Bill W.'s (1967) description, in his characteristic plain language, of how individuals bind themselves to their liabilities and want to remain in control: 'If his arrangements would only stay put, if only people would do as he wished, the show would be great' (p. 320). In other words, the status quo is threatened along with all that might be invested in this state.

It is a considerable challenge, then, to make real contact or to reach the suffering part of the user. How do we make our assessments therapeutic, helping the user to *own* their own need for help? Assessment could be seen in terms of such facilitation, creating 'therapeutic space' and not simply being drawn into action or remedy without understanding. Bronstein and Flanders (1998) write, "Therapeutic space" suggests a relationship which enables and promotes inquiry and a desire to know about oneself through being able to tolerate the psychic pain involved in exploring and learning about one's psychic reality, without having recourse to omnipotence . . . ' (p. 12). One the other hand, understanding alone is seldom sufficient with our clients, where the worker has also to construct a plan of care or a response to managing an active addiction. The capacity for such empathic contact, clearing space for thinking, is, however, a complex skill, involving cognitive and emotional abilities to identify with the patient 'from within', as well as maintaining some professional distance so as to be able to reflect on one's acquired understanding. It can be hard to create a reasonable 'three dimensionality' in a situation of immediate pressure or crisis, and much depends on the skill and subtlety of the worker. Miller and Rollnick (1991) rightfully underline that empathic skills are not the same as any simple 'technique', but involve a cultivated human ability or capacity. Workers certainly need opportunities to build up and to maintain such skills, and need to be receptive to exploring their own prejudices and interpersonal style. Cartwright (1980) researched the importance of an overall positive/accepting attitude towards this group of patients and the influence of factors in professionals such as experience, training, and self-esteem. Clinics and treatment agencies that attend to their ethos, self-purpose, and training needs, perhaps stand a greater chance of caring and being able to support the individual SMP. In this argument, workers who feel that the agency has good empathy and support for their position may thus be able to sustain greater empathy with, and commitment to, their clients. Validation is increased.

Loss of control or the inability by the user to continue to use alcohol and drugs without problems, confront the individual with uncomfortable feelings of dissonance and a potential state of defeat. The addicted person in pre-contemplation may fight this off, attempting to play for time and or resisting the need to change. In fact many, if not most people who present, do so at a time not of their own choosing, having faced overwhelming physical obstacles, legal troubles, relationship ultimatums, and so on. Orford (1985) spoke of the importance of factors like 'livers and lovers' in motivating individuals to seek change. Complex defences come into play, such as disavowal of the consequences of the addiction, postures of self-sufficiency, and denial of the need for assistance from others (see Weegmann 2002a). SMPs have to tread a line between helping the person to stay with the seriousness of their situation, while maintaining a message of optimism that problems can be addressed. As I have suggested, the worker attempts to reach the client's vulnerabilities, but in so doing faces those first-line defences that have formed a protective shield around the addiction. Very often the professionals are fought against, actively or passively, since they represents change: metaphorically we find ourselves in a three-object situation, illustrated in Figure 14.1.

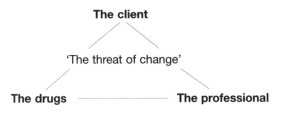

Figure 14.1 A three-object situation.

As well as helping the individual at the first point of contact, the SMP has to provide, or become, a reliable resource during the treatment that might ensue. Robert Hale (2002) talks about the addict's search for a reliable container, when reliance on the drug of choice has broken down. So not only are we there at the beginning, when the person first brings their story, but we continue to act in varying capacities as psychosocial agents whose job it is to manage or negotiate change. In my supervisory experience with key workers (in their roles as counsellors and group therapists), seeing patients over a long period of time, I am aware of the importance of qualities such as patience, maintaining thoughtfulness, and regarding treatment as continual assessment. We have to act as good diplomats, able to take and to tolerate great degrees of ambivalence in our patients about embarking upon change.

Part of the deal for SMPs is the management of chronicity: dealing with multiple episodes of care, responding to reversals, relapses, or break-down in efforts to sustain recovery. Not everyone likes the term 'relapse', but in spite of various efforts to change the term, there seems no getting away from the prefix 're-'! (see Gossop 1989). This is not to imply pessimism, since we know that in an overall sense many treatment strategies do work and that we need flexible, differential ways of conceptualizing client progress (see Miller 1992). Yet, we also know that many individuals will not respond to treatment initially, or even after time, and that a significant proportion of our clients will deteriorate. In a recent well-designed, large scale study around 28 per cent of clients were either non-responsive (18 per cent) or became worse (Moos, Moos and Finney 2001). This is compatible with other estimates (e.g. Shaw *et al.* 1990), with alcoholic patients). Although we may statistically accept this likelihood with little surprise, its human impact for the individual concerned and the professional who sees them is another matter. Frequently, we have to find a way of 'holding' our patients, hoping that we can help prevent a worsening state or total abandonment to drugs. A man I once assessed put it bluntly: 'look man, I don't know you from Adam, but I'm asking you to save me – my life is going down the pan fast'. Another patient, Sam, reflected on the fact that before embarking on psychotherapy he had not expected that he would have survived heroin addiction and that he had been 'holding on to life with a thin thread'; I had shared a similar foreboding at the time. Before treatment, Sam had been a worrying example of the deterioration we often see before our eyes, which is distressing to witness, yet he was also a testimony to healing and recovery. We all need to see some recovery to counterbalance the difficulties.

The worker has to keep a long-term view in mind, accepting the chronicity but not the inevitability of addiction. The 'harm reduction' approach and philosophy has clearly been one of the responses by services to the difficulty of managing addiction, but the approach is not a new one, and contains no simple solutions either (see Velleman 1994). I have heard contrasting views and conflicts with workers based in treatment agencies with different clients or philosophies, e.g.:

> *'I find it demoralizing in this clinic, since all we ever do is put sticking plaster on the clients. We seem, as a matter of principle, to expect so little from our clients'* (harm reduction drug service).

'It is unrealistic here and therefore stressful – we seem to want everyone to stop using overnight and to conform to our ideas of "good change"' (abstinence-based drug service).

'I'd hate it working on the drug side, offering people substitutes instead of helping them to face reality' (alcohol worker).

Perhaps such examples merely point to the importance of reasonable compatibility between the worker and the setting and/or philosophy of the service in which they work, but also the need to maintain a critical mind, so that questions of practice can be posed. The 'stepped care' approach in addiction – helping our patients to attain different things at different stages – is one remedy for the stress posed by more global expectations of change (see Wanigaratne 2003).

The professional unconscious

The professional has defences also, of a different kind, to protect them from being overwhelmed by the work or hurt by the more difficult experiences. Perhaps we all require our own damage limitation strategies, especially at the level of feelings and self-esteem. Sources of professional stress are numerous (as these brief examples highlight) and serious difficulties arise where there is an interaction between professional strain and areas of personal vulnerability, combining to form a malignant cycle. In one example, Sally, a drug worker, was experiencing depression arising from her personal life, and for a period was particularly susceptible to clients who devalued her. In fact, one particular client was so critical by nature that he became, for Sally, a persecutory object and she dreaded sessions with him. Since the professional also has an unconscious mental life, I would argue that the SMP needs to develop awareness of their preferred defences and interpersonal style and be willing to examine the contribution these might make to any ongoing difficulties with a client. We can be quick to describe some of our patients as 'difficult', but forget that they can equally identify our difficult traits.

Several writers have commented on the complex counter-transference difficulties that arise in this domain of work (e.g. Imhoff, Hirsch and Terenzi 1983, Kaufman 1996, Rodriguez de la Sierra 2002, Weegmann 2002c). Among these, unidentified negative counter-transferences (e.g. blaming the client, retreating into postures of cynicism, over-identifying with the client) can play a role in the creation of treatment obstacles and impasses. Here, however, I shall simply single out one example, that of the worker's need for experiences of *efficacy*. This concerns, 'a person's need to experience the self as an effective agent . . . the associated *efficacy pleasure* appears to be derived from the enhanced awareness of the self having been strengthened through the experience of efficacy' (Wolf 1988, p. 181). We need to have experiences with our clients that confirm our ability to promote change and facilitate movement. Of course, the substance misusers also need such experiences to feel that they can also take action, achieve goals, build up abilities to resist drugs, negative peers and so on. Indeed, the relapse prevention approach (Marlatt and Gordon 1985) draws considerably on self-efficacy theory and social learning perspectives.

During a training exercise with a drug team, I invited them to explore more unconscious feelings towards different clients in their caseloads, by imagining a line-up of their clients whose treatment they were asked to rate on a scale from the most negative to the most positive. They were then encouraged to share their reasons for so doing. Not surprisingly, the reports of the most positive relationships with clients invariably involved a worker's sense of being able to help a client to take measures towards their own recovery or progress, and that this could be independent of severity of psychopathology. The important thing was the client's wish to struggle on and their receptiveness to being assisted, no matter how modest the treatment objective.

Those with the lowest ratings were viewed as difficult in the sense of 'frustrating', 'passive', 'avoidant' 'unmotivated' – unreceptive, it appeared, to being helped. Lack of efficacy can become a source of burnout amongst professionals, because of the discouragement involved; in the example of supervisory work with Sally, her critical patient evoked powerful feelings of ineffectiveness and self-criticism, to which she was already prone. The client made her feel useless.

Supporting the helpers

Support for workers can take place in different ways. Clearly, in a healthy service, appropriate management and supervisory frameworks enable professionals to know that their position is understood and that help is at hand. A well-functioning team contains many informal elements of support, such as informal advice and catharsis, referral between different professional groups, and so on. I am suggesting that in trying to contain damaging and self-defeating states of mind, the helper needs to be kept in mind and that reparative experiences are essential in our work. We need to see some progress to offset the damage that we witness. Margaret Tonnesmann's (1979) discussion of stress in professionals, draws creatively on ideas of 'holding' and 'containment' derived from Winnicott (e.g. 1971). It is a truism in psychotherapy that the client can go only as far as the therapist can go. Rifkind (1995, p. 211), writing from her experience of consultative work, states

> It is therefore one of the essential tasks of the staff support group to be able to create an environment where the vulnerable parts of ourselves which have been shielded by our defences can be responded to and understood.

In the remainder of the chapter, I single out one particular format within which this support can take place, that of the 'work discussion group'. Since the focus is primarily on work-related experiences, these are not the same as a traditional staff support group, where, amongst other things, difficult feelings between workers might arise. Some of the other forms of staff support and the differences between them are usefully clarified by Haigh (2000).

Work discussion groups

I believe work discussion groups can play an important part in the overall framework of supervision and are compatible with clinical governance. Audits can evaluate visible manifestations of the work (such as recording, files, response rates and so on), but the work discussion group can attend to those essential, but less visible aspects of quality: the worker's therapeutic capacities, empathic skills, awareness of interpersonal processes and pressures. How often, one might ask, are we asked to describe what we do, how we conduct or comport ourselves during our sessions, in any depth?

Historically, work or case discussion groups had their origin in the pioneering work of Michael Balint working at the Tavistock Clinic during the postwar period (see Stewart 1996). The work started with groups of interested GPs, but later spread to discussion seminars amongst other professional groups. Balint's efforts were throughout based on the passionate conviction that the unconscious mind played a contributing part in all professional relationships and that some exploration of the work was essential for good practice. Gosling (1996), an early colleague of Balint, has written:

> The subject for discussion was always a case-history that one of the GP members had on his mind, one that oppressed him, challenged him or amused him: it was one that in some way got under his skin, whether painfully or otherwise. (p. 90).

The focus was on the doctor–patient relationship: 'to clarify what the doctor was doing to the patient in terms of emotional life and what the patient was doing to the doctor' (p. 90). Describing the qualities which

Balint brought to bear, Gosling continues

> he offered a model of someone who listened. He listened to everything that
> went on – to the preamble, to the story as it unfolded without interruption,
> to the asides, to the unconsidered remarks and to the jokes . . . he also took
> in everything that went on in the here-and-now of the session . . . and tried
> to make some sense of it all. (p. 94)

Consistent with the spirit of Balint's approach, the work discussion groups I conduct in substance misuse settings (a community alcohol team, a community drug team, and an in-patient detoxification ward) are similarly aimed at clarifying the relationship between clinician and patient, or the relationship between patient and the service. Dynamic understanding is explored as an aide to overall case management, helping staff to develop skills of observation, empathy, imagination. The workers themselves use different models, such as relapse prevention, cognitive therapy, health promotion and so on.

The following are some of the guidelines or framework I use, which have evolved over time.

- The groups are divided according to different teams (alcohol, drug and in-patient) and consist of up to eight members. Clearly, not all can attend each session due to shifts, leave, courses, and so on.
- Attendance has become mandatory, which means that such groups need the active support and sanction of a manager and team leaders. Membership has been predominantly, but not exclusively nursing – medical colleagues have tended to have their own, separate support systems. The role of other therapies, such as psychology and occupational therapy, has helped with the mix.
- All the members work together in the same team and I have not allowed students or observers in.
- In terms of who presents, I have left it to the respective groups to decide this in advance, although when this does not happen (frequently) there is inherent value in allowing something spontaneous to emerge. I do not confine presentations to individual cases, although these predominate, but encourage workers also to present groups sessions or more general issues in the work – e.g. bereavement, endings, counselling v. case management.
- While not banning case notes (which sometimes serve a symbolic, reassuring role for the presenter as well as a practical aide memoire), I encourage the worker to rely in the first instance on memory and reflection and to give an illustration of interactions from a recent session. Examples of what was said and how it was said, by both patient and worker, is particularly useful in bringing the clinical material to life. Such presentation skills also have to be learned.

- Standard rules for group work apply, such as confidentiality, honesty, ownership of the group, chairs arranged in a circle. The groups are also ongoing, allowing time for members to get to know each other and to feel safe to present difficult work and difficult feelings elicited by the patient.

Clinical examples from work discussion groups

'Wanting and not-wanting to know'

A member of an experienced alcohol team described a referral from a psychiatric team, who had been informally labelled an 'alcoholic personality disorder'. Discussion was generated around the role of negative attitudes or 'dumping' amongst generic psychiatric teams and, in this instance, a case no one wanted to know. However, one of the nurses made the important point that it is always easier to identify 'dumping' and contributions to splitting in other teams or professionals and that it was important to be able to identify prejudice within oneself.

Immediate impressions of the client were described, a harrowing account of her history, including multiple rejections. It seemed that the patient could not process mental pain and the way she spoke was rather like a discharge consistent with a characteristic acting-out of her problems. Issues around the worker being supported in her continuing assessment of this client came up, and some thought about why it might not have been possible for the other team to have a more validating attitude towards this complex individual; the risk existed of both acting-out a rejecting attitude and thus falling into the patient's history as well as being propelled to the idea of being able to offer the special intervention that others had failed to provide hitherto.

Discussion

In many ways this particular discussion ran spontaneously, reflecting the experienced nature of the team. I noted the immediate resonance of disapproval between members concerning issues of labelling and dumping stemming from the other team. However, someone perceptively tried to own the process, seeing the 'other team' as partly an issue within the alcohol team; one person, for example, could understand the pressures that generic teams might be under and the counter-temptation within the addiction teams of not wanting to take on 'psychiatric cases'. Integrated thinking was difficult. I suggested a link between wanting and not-wanting complex new cases and a difficulty the patient may have in being able to process, tolerate and contain her own mental states. Substance misusers often present with a desire for action and difficulties in being able to mentalize their problems. The mode in which the professional had presented the case – a succession of shocking clinical facts – seemed to mirror the patient's effort to discharge her feelings. Perhaps this patient's dramatic presentation was like an acting-out, rather than a reflection upon, her history.

Towards the end of the group, there was a more reflective atmosphere and a number of constructive ideas emerged about how the worker could be supported with the client in question. Discussions within this team usually focused on personality disordered patients, who created a degree of confusion and chaos within the worker or the team.

'Establishing a culture'

Two members of a discussion group arrived late, referring to 'having to deal with a client' as the reason. There was some delay in deciding who was to present, with a couple of people quietly saying that they did have someone to discuss instead if no one else wanted to. A case was then presented with an emphasis on the difficulty in operating boundaries – lateness, failures to attend, and backtracking on agreements all featured in the description.

Discussion

An issue of boundaries was manifest in the discussion group itself, insofar as there was a pattern of lateness in starting. It seemed that not uncommon complaints around having to manage prescriptions and client lateness had created an incursion into the group time, with two members being temporarily detained. There was an acknowledgement of the real pressure in dealing with such matters, but how, as a result, an opportunity for the staff to have their own space and time had been compromised.

Following this, there was some exploration around the anxiety of presenting, and I commented on the apparent diffidence of the people involved, both indicating that they had difficult situations in mind but finding it hard to assert themselves and claim the time for themselves. I began to wonder if there was a link between learning some assertiveness in the discussion group and handling the prescription and other issues that were reported, which had delayed the start of the group.

I decided on this occasion to concentrate less on the content of the presentation, but more on the process of how the group had proceeded. Clearly, the work discussion group is not intended to be a therapy group, but attending to some of the dynamic aspects of how the group itself operates might be important periodically. In retrospect, I recognized that I had been active in facilitation and reflection with this group, which had only recently been established. Not everyone was familiar with the culture of such discussion groups and this attempt to create a mini-'culture of inquiry' (see Main 1989) in the clinic: talking in a more personal and reflective manner about intimate work experiences. However, there were other members who had known similar groups before and they helped newer people to understand how things could work. The task is also about building an ethos, to counter the tendency to simply react to or distance from patients through a variety of professional defences. It is also about helping professionals be more thoughtful about what the person is communicating through and beyond their addiction.

'Worn down, embattled'

During a discussion group on an in-patient detoxification ward, nurses described a particularly stressful period, with some difficult clients and the demanding situations that they had needed to manage – one member singled out frustrations with a subgroup of relatively older men, well known to the ward; another felt that a group of opiate addicts had been troublesome. Different metaphors were used, such as feeling under fire, besieged, or worn down. One person summarized a relapse prevention group and how resistant and disruptive the meeting had been – one of the conductors that felt 'this high' (making a finger gesture to express being belittled) after the group, and the other conductor felt embarrassed by the attitude of some of the male clients towards her.

Discussion

During this group, I found myself simply listening for at least half an hour. I then wondered if the group needed catharsis, so I said something like 'it seems important today for you to give me a really good taste of what you, as a nursing group, have had to deal with in the past week or so – challenged from all directions, undermined as well. I can understand your need to discharge some of the accumulated stress. But what else do you think you might need from letting me know all this?'. The tone changed from one of straight frustration to more reflection: what must it be like for people undergoing detoxification? How might older (male) clients feel with predominantly much younger staff? And younger opiate addicts with the reality and rules of the ward environment and professional authority? Finally, the difficulties in running client groups such as the relapse prevention group was explored, and some ideas emerged about devoting some training time to concentrate on building up group-work skills. Staff in an in-patient setting (detoxification) can be particularly susceptible to burnout and demoralization, partly because boundaries have to be continually thought about and implemented, and there is an inherent element of repetition in some of the tasks involved.

Conclusion

I hope to have conveyed something of the aims, the workings and the spirit of work discussion groups with SMPs. Although many of the ideas I draw on are influenced by psychoanalytic ideas and group-analytic principles, I think it essential to be able to adapt understanding to whatever approach the worker may be using. Without this adaptation, workers can feel that their work is being criticized for not conforming to the standards of formal psychotherapy. Workers may often be using models influenced by, say, relapse prevention or motivational interviewing approaches and may be bound by a host of agency requirements, such as urine monitoring, the completing of assessment and outcome forms, and so on. The facilitator, like any good supervisor, has to be able to identify with the workers' situation.

As has been argued, the basic idea of these groups is to provide a resource for the team, a space for thinking (see Mollon 1989). We can all find ways of reducing the impact of what we see, keeping the patient at a distance. Faced with 'mindless' activities and self-defeating patterns, workers can sometimes unwittingly mirror the same problems by becoming over-routine or unreflective in response. In recognizing these tendencies, the group can play a part in helping the worker help the client to be able to have more of a 'mind', as it were (see Hinshelwood 2003). Hopefully, such groups do play an important supportive role, enabling the professional to learn and grow alongside the client, to reduce the pressures of the 'daily unconscious' and thereby to increase 'three dimensionality' (the capacity to think and consider) in the work. Sometimes it is simply about sharing the struggle or the task with others, like a co-struggle. A staff member commented on the groups that, 'we rarely get the chance to have in-depth discussion of our work and the other meetings serve quite a different purpose. With all the everyday business, we need this time to recover our thinking.'

References

Achilles N (1967) The development of the homosexual bar as an institution (in Nardi, 1982).

Adamson E (1984) Art as Healing. Coventure, London.

Ainsworth MDS (1989) Attachment beyond infancy. American Psychologist 44: 709–16.

Akers R (1973) Deviant Behavior: a social learning approach. Wadsworth, California.

Albert-Puleo N (1980) Modern psychoanalytic art therapy and its application to drug abuse. The Arts in Psychotherapy 7(1): 43–52.

Allen JP, Kadden RM (1995) Matching clients to alcohol treatments. In: Hester RK, Miller WR (ed) Handbook of Alcoholism Treatment Approaches. Effective Alternatives, 2nd Ed. Allyn & Bacon, Boston, Mass, pp 278–291.

Allsop S, Saunders B, Phillips M, Carr A (1997) A trial of relapse prevention with severely dependent male problem drinkers. Addiction 92(1): 61–73.

Annis H, Graham J, Davis C (1987) Inventory of Drinking Situations (IDS): user's guide. Addiction Research Foundation, Toronto.

Arensberg F (1998) A consideration of Kohut's views on group psychotherapy. In: Harwood NH, Pines M (ed) Self experience in group. Jessica Kingsley, London, pp 19–23.

Babor TF, Hofman M, Delboca FK, et al. (1992) Types of alcoholics, I, Evidence for an empirically derived typology based in indicators of vulnerability and severity. Archives of General Psychiatry 49: 599–608.

Bacal HA (1985) Optimal responsiveness and the therapeutic process. In. In: Goldberg A (ed) Progress in Self Psychology. Guilford Press, New York.

Bach R (1977) Illusions: The adventures of a reluctant Messiah. Pan Books, London.

Bader MJ (1988) Looking for addictions in all the wrong places. Tikkun 3(6): 13–16.

Bakhtin MM (1986) Speech genres and other late essays. Emerson C, Holquist M (eds.), VW McGee (trans.). University of Texas Press, Austin, Tex.

Bakhtin MM (1990) Art and Answerability. University of Texas Press, Austin, Tex.

Balint E (1972) Fair shares and mutual concerns. International Journal of Psychoanalysis 53: 61–65.

Ball SA, Legow NE (1996) Attachment theory as a working model for the therapist transitioning from early to later recovery from substance abuse treatment. American Journal of Drug Abuse 22(4): 533–547.

Bandura A (1977) Self-efficacy: toward a unifying theory of behavioral change. Psychological Review 84: 191–215.

Bean-Bayog M (1981) Psychopathology produced by alcoholism. In: Bean-Bayog M, Zinberg N (eds) Dynamic Approaches to the Understanding and Treatment of Alcoholism. Free Press, New York.

Beasley R (1998) An existential analysis of the twelve step approach to chemical dependency. Journal of the Society for Existential Analysis 9(1).

Beletsis SG, Brown S (1981) A developmental framework for understanding the adult children of alcoholics. Journal of Addictions and Health 2(4): 2–33.

Betensky M (1987) Phenomenology of therapeutic art expression and art therapy. In: Rubin J (ed) Approaches to Art Therapy. Brunner Mazel, New York, pp 149–166.

Beutler LF (2000) David and Goliath: when empirical and clinical standards of practice meet. American Psychologist 55: 997–1007.

Bieber I, Dain H, Dince P, Drellich M, Grand H, Gundlach R, Kremer M, Rifkin A, Wilbur C, Bieber T (1962) Homosexuality: a psychoanalytical study. Basic Books, New York.

Bill W (1949) The Society of Alcoholics Anonymous. American Journal of Psychiatry 106: 5.

Bill W (1957) Alcoholics Anonymous Comes of Age. Harper, New York.

Bill W (1967) As Bill Sees it: the AA way of life. Alcoholics Anonymous, World Services Inc., New York.

Bion WR (1961) Experiences in Groups. Basic Books, New York.

Bloomfield K (1993) A comparison of alcohol consumption between lesbians and heterosexual women in an urban population. Drug and Alcohol Dependence 33: 257–269.

Blumberg L (1977) The ideology of a therapeutic social movement: Alcoholics Anonymous. Journal of Studies on Alcohol 38(11): 2122–2143.

Boles SM, Miotto K (2003) Substance abuse and violence: A review of the literature. Aggression and Violent Behavior 8: 155–174.

Bowlby J (1979) The Making and Breaking of Affectional Bonds. Routledge, London.

Bowlby J (1980) Loss: Sadness and Depression. Basic Books, New York.

Bowlby J (1988a) A Secure Base: parent–child attachment and healthy development. Basic Books, New York.

Bowlby J (1988b) A Secure Base: clinical applications of attachment theory. Routledge, London.

Brandsma J, Pattison EM (1985) The outcome of group psychotherapy in alcoholics: an empirical review. American Journal of Drug and Alcohol Abuse 11: 151–162.

Bronstein C, Flanders S (1998) The development of a therapeutic space in a first contact with adolescents. Journal of Child Psychotherapy 24(1): 5–35.

Brown S (1985) Treating the Alcoholic: a developmental model of recovery. Wiley, New York.

Brown S (1993) Therapeutic processes in Alcoholics Anonymous. In: Mc Crady B, Miller W (eds) Research on Alcoholics Anonymous. Centre of Alcohol Studies, Rutgers, NJ.

Brown S (1998) Play as an organising principle: clinical evidence and personal observations. In: Berkoff M, Byers JA (eds) Animal Play: evolutionary, comparative, and ecological perspectives. Cambridge University Press, Cambridge.

Brown S, Beletsis S (1986) The development of family transference in groups for the adult children of alcoholics. International Journal of Group Psychotherapy 36(1): 97–114.

Brown S, Yalom ID (1977) Interactional group therapy with alcoholics. Journal of Studies on Alcohol 38: 426–456.

Bryant-Jefferies R (2001) Counselling the Person beyond the Alcohol Problem. Jessica Kingsley, London.

Buss A (1966) Psychopathology. Wiley, New York.

Caldwell PE, Cutter HSG (1998) Alcoholics Anonymous affiliation during early recovery. Journal of Substance Abuse Treatment 15(3): 221–228.

Cantopher T (1999) The place of psychotherapy in drug treatment. In: Waller D, Mahony J (eds) Treatment of Addiction. Routledge, London.

Carroll KM (1998) A Cognitive-Behavioral Approach: treating cocaine addiction. National Institute on Drug Abuse Therapy Manuals for Drug Addiction, Manual 1. National Institutes of Health, Rockville, Md.

Cartwright A (1980) The attitudes of helping agents towards the alcoholic patient: the influence of experience, support, training and self-esteem. British Journal of Addiction 75: 413–431.

Cartwright A (1987) A therapeutic day unit for alcohol abusers. In: Stockwell T, Clement S (eds) Helping the Problem Drinker: new initiatives in community care. Croom Helm, London.

Cartwright A, Hyams G, Spratley T (1996) Is the interviewer's therapeutic commitment an important factor determining whether alcoholic clients engage in treatment? Addiction Research 4(3): 215–230.

Casement P (1985) On Learning from the Patient. Routledge, London.

Chafetz M, Demone H (1962) Alcoholism and Society. Oxford University Press, New York.

Cheyne JA, Tarulli D (1999) Dialogue, difference, and the 'third voice' in the zone of proximal development. Theory and Psychology 9: 5–28.

Christo G, Sutton S (1994) Anxiety and self-esteem as a function of abstinence time among recovering addicts attending Narcotics Anonymous. British Journal of Clinical Psychology 33(2): 198–200.

Chu JA (1988) Ten traps for therapists in the treatment of trauma victims. Paper presented at McLean Hospital, Belmont, MA.

Clark D (2000) Theory Manual for Enhanced Thinking Skills. Home Office, London.

Clark WB, Midanik L (1982) Alcohol use and alcohol problems among US adults: results of the 1979 national survey. In: National Institute of Alcohol Abuse and Alcoholism (ed) Alcohol and Health: alcohol consumption and related problems. National Institute of Alcohol Abuse and Alcoholism, Washington DC.

Clayton GM (1992) Enhancing Life Relationships: a role training manual. YCA Press, Victoria, Australia.

Coehlo P (1993) The Alchemist. Thorsons, London.

Conrad P, Schneider J (1992) Deviance and Medicalization: from badness to sickness. Temple University Press, Philadelphia.

Cooney NL, Kadden RM, Litt MD, Getter H (1991) Matching alcoholics to coping skills or interactional therapies: two-year follow-up results. Journal of Consulting and Clinical Psychology 59(4): 598–601.

Cooper DE (1988) Role requirements of the group psychotherapist: Empathy and Neutrality. Paper presented at the annual meeting of the American Group Psychotherapy Association, New York.

Copas JB, Marshall P (1998) The Offender Group Reconviction Scale: The statistical reconviction score for use by probation officers. Applied Statistics: Journal of the Royal Statistical Society C 47: 159–171.

Correctional Services Accreditation Panel (1999) Programme accreditation criteria. Home Office, London.

Dargert G (2000) The illusion of power in the counsellor's role. Counselling 11(3): 151–153.

Davidson R (1996) Motivational issues in the treatment of addictive behaviours. In: Edwards G, Dare C (eds) Psychotherapy, Psychological Treatments and the Addictions. Cambridge University Press, Cambridge.

Davies D, Neal C (1996) An historical overview of homosexuality and therapy. In: Davies D, Neal C (ed) Pink Therapy: a guide for counsellors and therapists working with gay, lesbian and bisexual clients. Open University Press, Buckingham.

de Shazer S (1985) Keys to Solutions in Brief Therapy. W.W. Norton, New York.

Delight S (2001) Addressing Substance-Related Offending (ASRO): Training Manuals. National Probation Directorate, London.

Denzin N (1987) The Alcoholic Self. Sage Publications, London.

Deutsch H (1930) Ein Fall von hysterischer Schicksalsneurose [A case of an hysterical 'destiny' neurosis]. Psychoanal. Beweg. 2: 273–284.

Diamond N (1996) Can we speak of internal and external reality? Group Analysis 29: 303–316.

Dodge KA, Price JM, Bachorowski J, Newman JP (1990) Hostile attributional bias in severely aggressive adolescents. Journal of Abnormal Psychology 99: 385–392.

Dr Bob (1980) Dr Bob and the Good Oldtimers: a biography. Alcoholics Anonymous World Services, New York.

Dymkowski C (1992) Biographical sketch of Eugene O'Neill. In: O'Neill E (ed) A Moon For the Misbegotten, Nick Hern Books for the Royal National Theatre, London.

D'Zurilla TJ, Goldfried MR (1971) Problem solving and behaviour modification. Journal of Abnormal Psychology 78: 107–126.

D'Zurilla TJ, Nezu AM (1999) Problem Solving Therapy: a social competence approach to clinical intervention. 2nd edition. Springer, New York.

D'Zurilla TJ, Nezu AM, Maydeu-Olivares A (2002) Manual for the Social Problem Solving Inventory – Revised. Multi-Health Systems, Inc, North Tonawanda, NY.

Elliott B (1997) Is the Unconscious really a dirty word? New Directions in the Study of Alcohol 13: 32–39.

Elliott B (2003) Containing the Uncontainable: alcohol misuse and the personal choice community programme. London: Whurr

Elliott DS, Huizinga D, Ageton SS (1985) Explaining Delinquency and Drug Use. Sage Publications, Newbury Park, Calif.

Emrick C (2001) Alcoholics anonymous and other mutual-aid groups. In :Heather N, Peters T, Stockwell T (eds) International Handbook of Alcohol Dependence and Problems. John Wiley, Chichester.

Ezriel H (1973) Psychoanalytic group psychotherapy. In: Wolberg LR, Schwartz EK (eds) Group Therapy. Stratton Intercontinental Medical Books, New York, pp 183–210.

Falco KL (1991) Psychotherapy with Lesbian Clients: theory into practice. Brunner/Mazel, New York.

Farrington DP, Hawkins JD (1991) Predicting participation, early onset, and later persistence in officially recorded offending. Criminal Behaviour and Mental Health 1: 1–33.

Feltham C (1997) Time-Limited Counselling. Sage, London.

Fenichel O (1945) The Psychoanalytic Theory of Neurosis. Norton, New York.

Fifield L (1975) On My Way to Nowhere: alienated, isolated, drunk. Gay Community Services Centre and Department of Health Services, Los Angeles.

Fiorentine R (1999) After drug treatment: are 12-step programs effective in maintaining abstinence? American Journal of Drug and Alcohol Abuse 25(1): 93–116.

Flores PJ (1997) Group Therapy with Addicted Populations – an integration of Twelve-Step and Psychodynamic Theory, 2nd edition. Haworth Press, New York.

Flores PJ (2001) Addiction as an attachment disorder: implications for group therapy. International Journal of Group Psychotherapy 51: 63–81.

Flores PJ (2003) Addiction as an Attachment Disorder. Jason Aronson, Northvale, NJ.

Fonagy P, Steele M, Steele H, et al. (1994) The theory and practice of resilience. Journal of Child Psychology and Psychiatry 35: 231–257.

Forsyth DR (1990) Group Dynamics. Brooks/Cole, Wadsworth, Calif.

Freud S (1921) Group Psychology and the Analysis of the Ego. Standard Edition 18, 67–143.

Garland C (1982) Taking the non-problem seriously. Group Analysis 15(1): 4–14.

Gelb A, Gelb B (1960) O'Neill. Harper and Brothers, New York.

Georgakis A (1995) Clouds House – an evaluation of a residential alcohol and drug dependency treatment centre. Clouds, East Knoyle.

Getter H, Litt MD, Kadden RM, Cooney NL (1992) Measuring treatment process in coping skills and interactional group therapies for alcoholism. International Journal of Group Psychotherapy 42: 419–430.

Glatt M (1998) 'Still with us', by Sarah Shannon. The Oldie, October.

Golden S, Halliday K, Khantzian EJ, McAuliffe WE (1993) Dynamic group therapy for substance abusers: a reconceptualization. In: Alonso A (ed) Group Psychotherapy in Clinical Practice. American Psychiatric Press, Washington, DC, pp 271–287.

Goodwin D (1976) Is Alcoholism Hereditary? Oxford University Press, Oxford.

Goodwin D (1988) Alcohol and the Writer (particularly Chapter 7). Andrews and McMeel, Kansas City.

Gorman R, Rooney J (1979) Delay in seeking help and onset of crisis among Alanon wives. American Journal of Drug and Alcohol Abuse 6(2): 223–233.

Gosling R (1996) The general practitioner training scheme. In: Stewart H (ed) Michael Balint; object relations pure and applied. Routledge, London.

Gossop M (1989) Relapse and Addictive Behaviour. Routledge and Kegan Paul, London.

Groterath A (1999) Psychodrama. In: Waller D, Mahony J (eds) Treatment of Addiction. Routledge, London.

Guntrip H (1969) Schizoid Phenomena, Object Relations and the Self, 7th edn. International Universities Press, New York.

Haigh R (2000) Support systems. 2. Staff sensitivity groups. Advances in Psychiatric Treatment 6: 312–319.

Hale R (2002) In search of a reliable container. In: Weegmann M, Cohen R (eds) Psychodynamics of Addiction. Whurr, London.

Harwood I (1986) The need for optimal, available selfobject caretakers: moving toward extended selfobject experiences. Group Analysis 19: 291–302.

Hawkins JD, Catalano RF, Miller JY (1992) Risk and protective factors for alcohol and other drug problems in adolescence and early adulthood: Implications for substance abuse prevention. Psychological Bulletin 112: 64–105.

Heather N (1992) Addictive disorders are essentially motivational problems. British Journal of Addiction 87: 828–830.

Hills S (1980) Demystifying Social Deviance. McGraw-Hill, London.

Hinshelwood B (2003) Group mentality and 'having a mind'. In: Pines M, Lipgar R (eds) Building on Bion, Volume 1. Jessica Kingsley, London.

Hollin C, McGuire J, Palmer E, et al. (2002) Introducing Pathfinder Programmes into the Probation Service: an interim report. Research Study 247. Home Office, London.

Holmes J (1996) Attachment, Intimacy, Autonomy. Using attachment theory in adult psychotherapy. Jason Aronson, Northdale, NJ.

Home Office (1999) What Works Initiative Crime Reduction Programme: joint prison and probation accreditation criteria. Home Office, London.

Horvath AO (2001) The alliance. Psychotherapy 38: 365–372.

Horvath A, Greenberg L (1994) The Working Alliance. Wiley, New York.

Houston G (1987) The Red Book of Groups. F.C. Barnwell, Aylsham, Norfolk.

Hurvitz N (1974) Peer self-help psychotherapy groups: psychotherapy without psychotherapists. In: Roman P, Trice H (eds) The Sociology of Psychotherapy. Jason Aronson, New York.

Imhoff J, Hirsch R, Terenzi R (1983) Countertransferential and attitudinal considerations in the treatment of drug abuse and addiction. International Journal of Addiction 18(4): 491–510.

Jackson M (1997) The Underground Man. Picador, London.

Jackson P (2000) Remotivate disillusioned carers. Addiction Today 11(63): 14–15.

Jackson P (2001) Relationships: is alcohol your partner? Addiction Today 13(72): 14–15.

Jackson P (2003a) Is it true that people cannot be helped to change unless they really admit that they have a problem? In: Reading B, Jacobs M (eds) Addiction: questions and answers for counsellors and therapists. Whurr, London.

Jackson P (2003b) What can the counsellor do to encourage the client to actually make changes in his or her use of drink or drugs? In: Reading B, Jacobs M (eds) Addiction: questions and answers for counsellors and therapists. Whurr, London.

James W (1907) Pragmatism. Longman, New York.

Jauss HJ (1989) Question and Answer: forms of dialogical understanding. University of Minnesota Press, Minneapolis, Minn.

Kadden RM, Cooney NL, Getter H, Litt MD (1989) Matching alcoholics to coping skills or interactional therapies: posttreatment results. Journal of Consulting and Clinical Psychology 57(6): 698–704.

Kadden RM, Litt MD, Cooney NL, Busher DA (1992) Relationship between role-play measures of coping skills and alcoholism treatment outcome. Addictive Behaviors 17(5): 425–437.

Kallman FJ (1952) Comparative twin study of the genetic aspects of male homosexuality. Journal of Nervous and Mental Disease 115: 283–298.

Kanfer FH, Schefft BK (1988) Guiding the Process of Therapeutic Change. Research Press, Champaign, IL.

Kaplan LJ (1995) Lost Children: separation and loss between children and parents. Harper Collins, London.

Kaskutas LA, Bond J, Humphreys K (2002) Social networks as mediators of the effect of Alcoholics Anonymous. Addiction 97: 891–900.

Kaufman E (1996) Psychotherapy of Addicted Persons. Guilford Press, New York.

Kessel N, Walton H (1965) Alcoholism. Penguin, Baltimore, Md.

Khantzian EJ (1975) Self selection and progression in drug dependence. Psychiatry Digest 10: 19–22.

Khantzian EJ (1985) The self-medication hypothesis of addictive disorders. American Journal of Psychiatry 142: 1259–1264.

Khantzian E (1988) The primary care therapist and patient needs in substance abuse treatment. American Journal of Drug and Alcohol Abuse 14(2): 159–167.

Khantzian EJ (1990) Self-regulation and self-medication factors in alcoholism and the addictions: similarities and differences. In Galanter M (ed) Recent Developments in Alcoholism, Volume 8. Plenum Publishing, New York, pp 225–271.

Khantzian E (1994a) Alcoholics Anonymous – cult or corrective: a case study. Journal of Substance Abuse Treatment 12(3): 157–165.

Khantzian EJ (1994b) How AA works and why it's important for clinicians to understand. Journal of Substance Abuse Treatment 11: 77–92.

Khantzian EJ (1995) Self-regulation vulnerabilities in substance abusers: treatment implications. In: Dowling S (ed) The Psychology and Treatment of Addictive Behavior. International Universities Press, Madison, Conn, pp 17–41.

Khantzian EJ (1997) The self-medication hypothesis of substance use disorders: A reconsideration and recent applications. Harvard Review of Psychiatry 4: 231–244.

Khantzian EJ (1999) Treating Addiction as a Human Process. Jason Aronson, Northvale, NJ.

Khantzian EJ (2001) Reflections on group treatments as corrective experiences for addictive vulnerability. International Journal of Group Psychotherapy 51: 11–20.

Khantzian E (2002) Foreword. In: Weegmann M, Cohen R (ed) Psychodynamics of Addiction. Whurr, London.

Khantzian EJ, Golden SJ, McAuliffe WE (1995) Group therapy for psychoactive substance use disorders. In: Gabbard GO (ed) Treatments of Psychiatric Disorders: the DSM-IV edition. American Psychiatric Press, Washington, DC, pp 832–839.

Khantzian EJ, Halliday KS, McAuliffe WE (1990) Addiction and the Vulnerable Self: modified dynamic group therapy for substance abusers. Guilford Press, New York.

Khantzian E, Mack J (1989) Alcoholics Anonymous and contemporary psychodynamic theory. In: Galanter M (ed) Recent Developments in Alcoholism, vol. 7. Plenum Press, New York.

Khantzian E, Mack J (1994) How AA works and why it is important for clinicians to understand. Journal of Substance Abuse Treatment 11: 77–92.

Khantzian EJ, Treece C (1985) DSM-III psychiatric diagnosis of narcotic addicts: recent findings. Archives of General Psychiatry 42: 1067–1071.

Khantzian EJ, Halliday KS, Golden S, McAuliffe WE (1992) Modified group therapy for substance abusers: a psychodynamic approach to relapse prevention. American Journal on Addictions 1: 67–76.

Klein M (1963) Our Adult World and its Roots in Infancy. Heinemann, London.

Klinteberg BA, Andersson T, Magnusson D, Stattin H (1993) Hyperactive behavior in childhood as related to subsequent alcohol problems and violent offending: A longitudinal study of male subjects. Personality and Individual Differences 15: 381–388.

Kohut H (1977) Preface. In: Blaine JD, Julius AD (ed) Psychodynamics of Drug Dependence. NIDA Publication No. ADM 77–470. U.S. Government Printing Office, Washington, DC.

Kohut H (1978) Creativeness, charisma, group psychotherapy. In: Ornstein P (ed) The Search for the Self, volume 2. International Universities Press, New York.

Kosseff JW (1975) The leader using object-relations theory. In: Liff ZA (ed) The Leader in Group. Jason Aronson, New York, pp 212–242.

Kowszun G, Malley M (1996) Alcohol and substance misuse. In: Davies D, Neal C (ed) Pink Therapy: a guide for counsellors and therapists working with gay, lesbian and bisexual clients. Open University Press, Buckingham, UK.

Krovitz D (1987) Nuts and bolts of recovery: realistic goals for quality support groups. Changes (May–June): 12–15.

Krystal H, Raskin HA (1970) Drug Dependence. Aspects of Ego Functions. Wayne State University Press, Detroit.

Kurtz E (1979) Not God: a history of Alcoholics Anonymous. Hazeldon Educational Services, Centre City, Minn.

Kurtz E (1982) Why AA works; the intellectual significance of Alcoholics Anonymous. Journal of Studies on Alcohol 43(1): 38–80.

Kus R (1988) Alcoholism and non-acceptance of gay self: the critical link. Journal of Homosexuality 13(1): 25–41.

Kus R (1995) Homophobia: the heart of the darkness. In: Kus R (ed) Addiction and Recovery in Gay and Lesbian Persons. Haworth Press, New York.

Lachman-Chapin M (1983) Kohut's theories on narcissism: implications for art therapy. American Journal of Art Therapy 19(October): 3–9.

Lambert MJ, Barley DE (2001) Research summary on the therapeutic relationship and psychotherapy outcome. Psychotherapy 38: 357–364.

Lang T (1940) Studies in the genetic determination of homosexuality. Journal of Nervous and Mental Disorder 92: 55–64.

Langs RJ (1975) The therapeutic relationship and deviations in technique. International Journal of Psychoanalytic Psychotherapy 4: 106–141.

Lansky M (1987) Shame in the family relationships of borderline patients. Chapter 30. In: Grotstein J, Solomon M, Lang J (ed) The Borderline Patient: emerging concepts in diagnosis, psychodynamics and treatment. Analytic Press, Hillsdale, NY.

Lansky M (1994) Commentary on A. Morrison's 'The breadth and boundaries of a self-psychological immersion in shame'. Psychoanalytic Dialogues 4(1): 45–50.

Lavelle T, Hammersley R, Forsyth A (1993) Is the 'addictive personality' merely delinquency? Addiction Research 1(1): 27–37.

Le Blanc M (1994) Family, school, delinquency, and criminality: the predictive power of an elaborated social control theory for males. Criminal Behaviour and Mental Health 4: 101–117.

LeVay S (1991) A difference in hypothalamic structure between heterosexual and homosexual patients. Science 153: 1034–1037.

Leshner AI (1997) Introduction to the special issue: The National Institute on Drug Abuse's (NIDA's) Drug Abuse Treatment Outcome Study (DATOS). Psychology of Addictive Behaviors 4(December): 211–215.

Levenson H (1975) Multidimensional locus of control in prison inmates. Journal of Applied Social Psychology 5: 342–347.

Lewis T, Amini F, Landon R (2000) A General Theory of Love. Random House, New York.

Liebmann M (1986) Art Therapy for Groups. Croom Helm, London.

Liriano S, Ramsay M (2003) Prisoners' drug use before prison and the links with crime. In: Ramsay M (ed) Prisoners' Drug Use and Treatment: seven research studies. Home Office Research Study 267. Home Office, London.

Litman G, Stapleton J, Oppenheim A, Peleg M, Jackson P (1983) Situations related to alcoholism relapse. British Journal of Addiction 78: 381–389.

Litt MD, Babor TF, DelBoca FK, Kadden RM, Cooney NL (1992) Types of alcoholics, II. Application of an empirically derived typology to treatment matching. Archives of General Psychiatry 49: 609–614.

Lohrenz L, Connely J, Coyne L, Spare K (1978) Alcohol problems in several Midwestern homosexual communities. Journal of Studies on Alcohol 39(11): 1959–1963.

Longabaugh R, Wirtz PW (2001) Project MATCH Hypotheses: results and causal chain analyses. Project MATCH Monograph Series, Volume 8. National Institute on Alcohol Abuse and Alcoholism, Bethesda, Md.

Lowenfeld V, Brittain L (1982) Creative and Mental Growth. Macmillan, New York.

Mack J (1981) Alcoholism, AA and governance of the self. In: Bean M, Zinberg N (eds) Dynamic Approaches to the Understanding and Treatment of Alcoholism. Free Press, New York.

Mahoney MJ, Thoresen CE (1974) Self-Control: power to the person. Brookes/Cole, Monterey, Calif.

Main M (1995) Recent studies in attachment: overview with selected implications for clinical work. In: Cassidy J, Shaver PR (ed) Attachment Theory: social, developmental, and clinical perspectives. Guilford, New York, pp 845–887.

Main T (1989) The concept of the therapeutic community. In: Johns J (ed) The Ailment and other Psychoanalytic Essays. Free Association Books, London.

Makela K (1991) Social and cultural preconditions of Alcoholics Anonymous and factors associated with the strength of AA. British Journal of Addiction 86: 1405–1413.

Makela K (1996) Alcoholics Anonymous as a Mutual-Help Movement: a study in eight societies. University of Wisconsin Press, Madison.

Mander G (2000) A Psychodynamic Approach to Brief Therapy. Sage, London.

Marlatt GA, Gordon JR (1985) Relapse Prevention: maintenance strategies in the treatment of addictive behaviors. Guilford Press, New York.

Martin C, Player E (2000) Drug Treatment in Prison: an evaluation of the RAPt treatment programme. Waterside Press, Winchester.

Marziali E, Munroe-Blum M (1994) Interpersonal Group Psychotherapy for Borderline Personality Disorder. Basic Books, New York.

Matano RA, Yalom ID (1991) Approaches to chemical dependency: chemical dependency and interactive group therapy – a synthesis. International Journal of Group Psychotherapy 41: 269–293.

May R (1993) The Art of Counselling. Souvenir Press, London.

McAndrew C, Edgerton R (1969) Drunken Comportment. Aldine, Chicago.

McConnaughy EA, Prochaska JO, Velicer WF (1983) Stages of change in psychotherapy: measurement and sample profiles. Psychotherapy: Theory, Research and Practice 20: 368–375.

McConnaughy EA, DiClemente CC, Prochaska JO, Velicer WF (1989) Stages of change in psychotherapy: a follow-up report. Psychotherapy 26: 494–503.

McGuire J (2000) Think First. National Probation Directorate, London.

McGuire J, Priestley P (1995) What works: reducing reoffending. In: McGuire J (ed) What Works: guidelines from research and practice. Wiley, Chichester.

McIvor G (2001) Treatment in the community. In: Hollin CR (ed) Handbook of Offender Assessment and Treatment. Wiley, Chichester.

McKirnan DJ, Peterson PI (1989) Alcohol and drug use among homosexual men and women: epidemiology and population characteristics. Addictive Behaviours 14(53): 543–553.

McMurran M (1994) The Psychology of Addiction. Taylor & Francis, London.

McMurran M, Priestley P (2001) Addressing Substance-Related Offending (ASRO). National Probation Directorate, London.

McMurran M, Fyffe S, McCarthy L, Duggan C, Latham A (2001) 'Stop & Think!' Social problem-solving therapy with personality disordered offenders. Criminal Behaviour and Mental Health 11: 273–285.

McNeilly G (1983) Directive and non-directive approaches to art therapy. The Arts in Psychotherapy 10: 211–219.

McNeilly G (1987) Further contributions to group analytic art therapy. Inscape Journal of Art Therapy (Summer): 8–11.

McNeilly G (1990) Group analysis and art therapy: a personal perspective. Group Analysis 23: 215–224.

Meares R (1993) The Metaphor of Play. Jason Aronson, Northvale, NJ.

Mearns D, Dryden W (eds) (1990) Experiences of Counselling in Action. Sage, London.

Merry T (2000) Person centred counselling and therapy. In: Feltham C, Horton I (eds) Handbook of Counselling and Psychotherapy. Sage, London.

Miller A (1987) The Drama of Being a Child. Virago, London.

Miller WR (1983) Motivational Interviewing with problem drinkers. Behavioural Psychotherapy 11: 147–172.

Miller W (1992) The effectiveness of treatment for substance abuse; reasons for optimism. Journal of Substance Abuse Treatment 9(2): 93–102.

Miller WR (2002) Spirituality and the treatment of addictions. New Directions in the Study of Alcohol 26: 31–39.

Miller WR, Harris RJ (2000) A simple scale of Gorski's warning signs for relapse. Journal of Studies on Alcohol 61(5): 759–765.

Miller WR, Rollnick S (eds) (1991) Motivational Interviewing. Guilford Press, New York.

Miller WR, Rollnick S (2002) Motivational Interviewing: preparing people for change. Guilford Press, New York.

Miller WR, Wilbourne PL (2002) Mesa Grande: a methodological analysis of clinical trials of treatments for alcohol use disorders. Addiction 97: 265–277.

Mollon P (1989) Anxiety, supervision and a space for thinking; some narcissistic perils for clinical psychologists in learning psychotherapy. British Journal of Medical Psychology 62(2): 113–122.

Montgomery H, Miller W, Tonigan S (1991) Differences among AA groups: implications for research. Journal of Studies in Alcohol 54: 502–504.

Monti PM, Abrams DB, Kadden RM, Cooney NL (1989) Treating Alcohol Dependence: a coping skills training guide. Guilford Press, New York.

Moore RW (1983) Art therapy with substance abusers: a review of the literature. The Arts in Psychotherapy 10: 251–260.

Moos R (1986) Group Environment Scale Manual, 2nd edition. Consulting Psychologists Press, Palo Alto, Calif.

Moos R, Moos B, Finney J (2001) Predictors of deterioration among patients with substance-use disorders. Journal of Clinical Psychology 57(12): 1403–1419.

Moreno JL (1964) The Third Psychiatric Revolution and the scope of psychodrama. Group Psychotherapy 17: 149–171.

Morgenstern J, Longabaugh R (2000) Cognitive-behavioral treatment for alcohol dependence: a review of evidence for its hypothesized mechanisms of action. Addiction 95(10): 1475–1490.

MORI (2003) Evaluating P-ASRO. Unpublished report, HM Prison Service, London.

Mosack H, Dreikers R (1973) Adlerian psychotherapy. In: Corsini S (ed) Current Psychotherapies. Peacock, Ithaca, Ill.

Mosse J, Lysaght M (2002) Group therapy for addiction. In: Cohen R (ed) The Psychodynamics of Addiction. Whurr, London.

Nace EP (1987) The Treatment of Alcoholism. Brunner/Mazel, New York.

Nardi PM (1982) Alcoholism and homosexuality: a theoretical perspective. Journal of Homosexuality 7(4): 9–25.

National Probation Directorate (2002) Change Control Strategy. National Probation Directorate, London.

National Treatment Agency (2003) Business plan 2003/04. National Treatment Agency, London.

Norcross JC (2001) Purposes, processes, and products of the task force on empirically supported therapy relationships. Psychotherapy 38: 345–354.

Nowinski J, Baker S (1992) The 12-Step Facilitation Handbook. Jossey-Bass, San Francisco.

O'Connor L, Berry J, Inaba D, Weiss J, Morrison A (1994) Shame, guilt and depression in men and women in recovery from addiction. Journal of Substance Misuse Treatment 11(6): 503–510.

O'Neill E (1956) Long Day's Journey into Night. Jonathan Cape, London.

Orford J (1985) Excessive Appetites: a psychological view of addictions. Wiley, Chichester.

Parsons OA, Farr SP (1981) The neuropsychology of alcohol and drug use. In: Felskov SB, Boll TJ (ed) Handbook of Clinical Neuropsychology. Wiley, New York, pp 320–365.

Peck MS (1983) The Road Less Travelled: a new psychology of love, traditional values and spiritual growth. Rider Books, London.

Pines M (1998) The self as a group: the group as a self. In: Pines M (ed) Self Experience in Group. Jessica Kingsley, London, pp 24–29.

Priestley P, McMurran M (2001) Programme for Reducing Individual Substance Misuse (PRISM). National Probation Directorate, London.

Prochaska JO, Diclemente CC (1986) Toward a comprehensive model of change. In: Miller WR, Heather N (eds) Treating Addictive Behaviours. Plenum Press, New York.

Prochaska JO, DiClemente CC, Norcross JC (1992) In search of how people change: applications to addictive behaviors. American Psychologist 47: 1102–1114.

Project MATCH Research Group (1997) Matching alcoholism treatments to client heterogeneity: Project MATCH posttreatment drinking outcomes. Journal of Studies on Alcohol 58: 7–29.

Reading B (2001) The application of Bowlby's attachment theory to psychotherapy in the addictions. In: Weegmann M, Cohen E (eds) Psychodynamics of Addiction. Whurr, London.

Reading B, Jacobs M (2002) Addiction: questions and answers for counsellors and therapists. Whurr, London.

Reps P (1971) Zen Flesh, Zen Bones. Penguin, London.

Rice AK (1965) Learning for Leadership. Tavistock, London.

Rifkind G (1995) Containing the containers; the staff consultation group. Group Analysis 28: 209–222.

Ripley H, Jackson J (1959) Therapeutic factors in Alcoholics Anonymous. American Journal of Psychiatry 116: 44–50.

Robinson C (1996) Alcoholics Anonymous as seen from the perspective of self-psychology. Smith College of Studies in Social Work 66(2): 129–145.

Rodriguez de la Sierra L (2002) Countertransference: our difficulties in the treatment of substance misuse. In: Weegmann M, Cohen R (eds) Psychodynamics of Addiction. Whurr, London.

Roebuck J, Kessler R (1972) The Etiology of Alcoholism. Charles Thomas, Springfield, Ill.

Rogers C (1987) Client Centred Therapy. Constable, London.

Ross RR, Fabiano EA, Ross RD (1986) Reasoning and Rehabilitation: a handbook for teaching cognitive skills. University of Ottawa, Canada.

Rudy D, Greil (1987) Taking the pledge: the commitment process in Alcoholics Anonymous. Sociological Focus 20(1): 45–59.

Ryle A (1990) Cognitive Analytic Therapy – active participation in change. Wiley, Chichester.

Ryle A (ed) (1995) Cognitive Analytic Therapy – developments in theory and practice. Wiley, Chichester.

Ryle A (1997) Cognitive Analytic Therapy and Borderline Personality Disorder – the model and the method. Wiley, Chichester.

Ryle A, Kerr I (2002) Introducing Cognitive Analytic Therapy. Wiley, Chichester.

Saghir M, Robins E (1973) Male and Female Homosexuality. Williams & Wilkins, Baltimore, Md.

Sandahl C, Rönnberg S (1990) Brief group psychotherapy in relapse prevention for alcohol dependent patients. International Journal of Group Psychotherapy 40(4): 453–476.

Sandahl C, Lindgren A, Herlitz K (2000) Does the group conductor make a difference? Communication patterns in group analytically and cognitive behaviourally oriented therapy groups. Group Analysis 33(3): 333–351.

Sandahl C, Herlitz K, Ahlin G, Rönnberg S (1998) Time limited group psychotherapy for moderately alcohol dependent patients: a randomized controlled clinical trial. Psychotherapy Research 8(4): 361–378.

Saunders B, Wilkinson C, Allsop S (1991) Motivational interviewing with heroin users attending a methadone clinic. In: Miller WR, Rollnick S (eds) Motivational Interviewing: preparing people to change addictive behaviours. Guilford Press, New York.

Schaffer J, Galinsky M (1974) The theme-centered interaction method, Chapter 12 in Models of Group Therapy and Sensitivity Training. Prentice-Hall, Englewood Cliffs, NJ.

Schuckit M, Haglund R (1977) An Overview of the Etiological Theories of Alcoholism. Mosby, St. Louis, Mo.

Schuckit MA, Li TK, Cloninger CR, Deitrich RA (1985) Genetics of alcoholism. Alcoholism: Clinical and Experimental Research 9: 475–492.

Schuckit MA, Tipp JE, Smith TL, et al. (1995) An evaluation of type A and B alcoholics. Addiction 90: 1189–1203.

Scottish Prison Service (1998) Prisoner Programme Accreditation Services: manual of standards and accompanying documentation for programme and site accreditation. Manual No. 082/98. Scottish Prison Service, Edinburgh.

Searles HF (1979) Counter-transference and Related Subjects. International Universities Press, New York.

Seixas J, Levitan M (1984) A supportive counseling group for adult children of alcoholics. Alcoholism Treatment Quarterly 1(4): 123–132.

Seixas J, Youcha G (1985) Children of Alcoholism: a survivor's manual. Harper & Row, New York.

Seligman M, Marshak LE (1990) Group Psychotherapy – interventions with special populations. Allyn & Bacon, Boston, Mass.

Serin RC, Kuriychuk M (1994) Social and cognitive processing deficits in offenders. International Journal of Law and Society 17: 431–441.

Shaver P, Mikulincer M (2002) Attachment-related psychodynamics. Attachment and Human Development 4: 133–161.

Shaw G, Waller S, McDougal S, MacGarvie J, Dunn G (1990) Alcoholism: a follow-up study of participants in an alcohol treatment programme. British Journal of Psychiatry 157: 190–196.

Simmel E (1948) Alcoholism and addiction. Psychoanalytic Quarterly 17: 6–31.

Skaife S, Huet V (1998) Art Psychotherapy Groups. Routledge, London.

Small E, Leach B (1977) Counselling homosexual alcoholics. Journal of Studies on Alcohol 38(11): 2077–2086.

Socarides C (1968) The Overt Homosexual. Grune & Stratton, New York.

Spinelli E (1994) Demystifying Therapy. Constable, London.

Springham N (1992) Short-term group processes in art therapy for people with substance misuse problems. Inscape (Spring).

Springham N (1994) Research into patients' reactions to art therapy on a drug and alcohol programme. Inscape 2.

Springham N (1998) The magpie's eye. In: Skaife S, Huet V (eds) Art Psychotherapy Groups. Routledge, London.

Springham N (1999) All things very lovely. In: Waller D, Mahony J (eds) Treatment of Addiction. Routledge, London.

Stewart D (1955) The dynamics of fellowship as illustrated in alcoholics anonymous. Quarterly Journal of Studies on Alcohol 16: 251–262.

Stewart H (ed) (1996) Michael Balint: object relations pure and applied. Routledge, London.

Stolorow R, Brandchaft B, Atwood G (1987) Psychoanalytic treatment: an intersubjective approach. Analytic Press, Hillsdale, NJ.

Strupp HH (1980) Success and failure in time-limited psychotherapy further evidence (Comparison 4). Archives of General Psychiatry 37: 947–954.

Strupp HH (1998) The Vanderbilt I study revisited. Psychotherapy Research 8: 335–347.

Strupp HH (1999) Essential ingredients of a helpful therapist. Psychotherapy Bulletin 34: 34–36.

Strupp HH, Hadley SW (1979) Specific versus nonspecific factors in psychotherapy: a controlled study of outcome. Archives of General Psychiatry 36: 1125–1136.

Taylor SP, Chermack ST (1993) Alcohol, drugs and human physical aggression. Journal of Studies on Alcohol (Supplement 11): 78–88.

Thorne B (1989) Person centred therapy. In: Dryden W (ed) Individual Therapy in Britain. Open University Press, Buckingham, UK.

Thune C (1977) Alcoholism and the archetypical past. Journal of Studies on Alcohol 38(1): 75–88.

Tiebout H (1944) Therapeutic mechanisms of Alcoholics Anonymous. American Journal of Psychiatry 100: 468–473.

Tiebout H (1957) Medicine looks at Alcoholics Anonymous. In: Bill W (ed) Alcoholics Anonymous Comes of Age. Harper, New York.

Tiebout H (1959) Alcoholics Anonymous – an experiment of nature. Health Communications, Deerfield Beach, Fla.

Tombourou JW, Hamilton M, U'ren A, Stevens-Jones P, Storey G (2002) Narcotics Anonymous participation and changes in substance use and social support. Journal of Substance Abuse Treatment 23: 61–66.

Tonigan J, Ashcroft F, Miller W (1995) AA group dynamics and 12-step activity. Journal of Studies on Alcohol (November): 616–621.

Tonnesmann M (1979) Containing stress in professional work. Social Work Service 21: 34–41.

Trice H, Staudenmeir W (1989) A sociocultural history of Alcoholics Anonymous. In: Galanter M (ed) Alcoholism, Vol 7. Plenum Press, New York.

Turnbull PJ, Hough M, Webster R, Edmunds M, McSweeney M (1999) Drug Treatment and Testing Orders: interim evaluation report., Drug Prevention Advisory Service Report, prepared by Criminal Policy Research Unit, South Bank University. Home Office, London.

Van Den Berg N (1992) Having bitten the apple: a feminist perspective on addictions. Chapter 1. In: Van Den Berg N (ed) Feminist Perspectives on Addiction. Springer, New York.

Vannicelli M (1982) Group psychotherapy with alcoholics. Journal of Studies on Alcohol 43: 17–37.

Vannicelli M (1992) Removing Roadblocks: group psychotherapy with substance abusers and family members. Guilford Press, New York.

Velasquez MM, Maurer GG, Crouch C, Di Clemente CC (2001) Group Treatment for Substance Misuse; a stages of change manual. Guilford Press, New York.

Velleman R (1994) Harm-minimisation: old wine in new bottles? International Journal on Drug Policy 1(6): 24–27.

Velleman R (2001) Counselling for Alcohol Problems. Sage, London.

Vygotsky LS (1978) Mind in society: the development of higher psychological processes, eds Cole M, John-Steiner V, Scribner S, Souberman E. Harvard University Press, Cambridge, Mass.

Walant KB (1995) Creating the Capacity for Attachment: treating addictions and the alienated self. Jason Aronson, Northvale, NJ.

Wallace J (1985) Working with the preferred defence structure of the recovering alcoholic. In: Zimberg S, Wallace J, Blume SB (eds) Practical approaches to Alcoholism Psychotherapy. Plenum Press, New York.

Waller D (1993) Group Interactive Art Therapy: its uses in training and treatment. Routledge, London.

Waller D (1999) Art psychotherapy. In: Waller D, Mahony J (eds) Treatment of Addiction. Routledge, London.

Waller DE, Gilroy A (1992) Art Therapy: a handbook. Open University Press, Buckingham, UK.

Waller D, Mahony J (1992) Art therapy in the treatment of alcohol and drug abuse. In: Waller D, Gilroy A (eds.) Art Therapy: a handbook. Open University Press, Buckingham.

Waller D, Mahony J (1999) Treatment of Addiction. Routledge, London.

Walsh J (1995) The external space in groupwork. Group Analysis 28: 413–427.

Walters GD (1994) Drugs and Crime in Lifestyle Perspective. Sage, Thousand Oaks, Calif.

Walters GD (1998) Changing Lives of Crime and Drugs. Wiley, Chichester.

Walters ST, Ogle R, Martin JE (2002) Perils and possibilities of group based Motivational Interviewing. In: Miller WR, Rollnick S (ed) Motivational Interviewing: preparing people for change. Guilford Press, New York.

Wanigaratne S (2003) Relapse prevention. The Drug and Alcohol Professional 3(3): 11–18.

Wanigaratne S, Keaney F (2002) Psychodynamic aspects of relapse prevention in the treatment of addictive behaviours. In: Weegman M, Cohen R (ed) The Psychodynamics of Addiction. Whurr, London.

Wanigaratne S, Wallace W, Pullin J, Keaney F, Farmer R (1990) Relapse Prevention for Addictive Behaviours: a manual for therapists. Blackwell Scientific, Oxford.

Weegmann M (2002a) Motivational interviewing and addiction: a psychodynamic appreciation. Psychodynamic Practice 8: 2.

Weegmann M (2002b) Growing up with addiction. In: Weegmann M, Cohen R (eds) The Psychodynamics of Addiction. Whurr, London.

Weegmann M (2002c) Psychodynamic assessment of drug addicts. In: Weegmann M, Cohen R (eds) The Psychodynamics of Addiction. Whurr, London.

Weegmann M (2003a) Alcoholics Anonymous – encouraging greater professional interest. The Drug and Alcohol Professional 3(1): 7–16.

Weegmann M (2003b) Growing up with addiction: can children ever break free? Addiction Today (May/June): 20–21.

Weegmann M (2004) Alcoholics Anonymous – a group analytic view of fellowship organisations. Group Analysis 37(2): 243–258.

Weegmann M, Kavatha E (forthcoming) The continuum of anger in addicted individuals. Submitted to Psychodynamic Practice.

Wegscheider-Cruse S (1985) Choice-making for Co-dependents, Adult Children and Spirituality Seekers. Health Communications, Pompano Beach, Fla.

West DJ (1967) Homosexuality. Aldine, Chicago.

White JL, Moffitt TE, Caspi A, et al. (1994) Measuring impulsivity and examining its relationship to delinquency. Journal of Abnormal Psychology 103: 192–205.

Wilson E (1978) On Human Nature. Bantam Books, New York.

Winnicott DW (1954) Withdrawal and regression. In: Through Paediatrics to Psycho-Analysis. Basic Books, New York, 1975.

Winnicott DW (1965) Maturational Processes and the Facilitating Environment. Hogarth, London.

Winnicott DW (1971) Playing and Reality. Tavistock, London.

Winship G (1999) Group therapy and drug addiction. In: Waller D, Mahony J (eds) Treatment of Addiction. Routledge, London.

Wolf E (1988) Treating the Self. Guilford Press, New York.

Wood BL (1984) The COA therapist: When the family hero turns pro. Paper presented at the meeting of the American Psychological Association, Toronto, Ontario, Canada.

Wood BL (1987) Children of Alcoholism: the struggle for self and intimacy in adult life. New York University Press, New York:.

Woody GE, Luborsky L, McLellan AT, et al. (1983) Psychotherapy for opiate addicts: does it help? Archives of General Psychiatry 40: 639–645.

Woody GE, McLellan AT, Luborsky L, O'Brien CP (1985) Sociopathy and psychotherapy outcome. Archives of General Psychiatry 42: 1081–1086.

Woody GE, McLellan AT, Luborsky L, O'Brien C (1986) Psychotherapy for substance abusers. Psychiatric Clinics of North America 9: 547–562.

Wurmser L (1981) The Mask of Shame. John Hopkins University Press, Baltimore, MD.

Yalom ID (1974) Group psychotherapy and alcoholism. Annals of the New York Academy of Science 233: 85–103.

Yalom ID (1983) In-patient Group Psychotherapy. Basic Books, New York.

Yalom I (1985) Theory and Practice of Group Psychotherapy, 2nd edition. Basic Books, New York.

Yalom I (1989) Love's Executioner and Other Tales of Psychotherapy. Bloomsbury, London.

Yalom ID (1995) The Theory and Practice of Group Psychotherapy, 4th edition. Basic Books, New York.

Yalom I (2002) The Gift of Therapy. Piatkus, London.

Yalom ID, Bloch S, Bond G, Zimmerman E, Qualls B (1978) Alcoholics in interactional group therapy: an outcome study. Archives of General Psychiatry 35: 419–425.

Index

affect regulation, 5, 20–21
Alcoholics Anonymous chapter 3
  passim, 2, 33
ambivalence, 74–76
art therapy, chapter 8 *passim*
ASRO (addressing substance related
  offending), 195–206
attachment theory, chapter 1 *passim*,
  73–74, 102

Balint groups, 218–220
blame, 154–155
borderline personality disorder, 42
boundaries/rules, 133, 139, 169–70,
  172–3, 190, 221

cognitive-analytic therapy, 82–3, 143
cognitive-behavioural relapse
  prevention, 49
commitment, 70
confrontation, 24
containining, 91
coping skills, 89
counter-transference, chapter 10 *passim*
culture of inquiry, 221–2
custodial groups, chapter 13 *passim*

day care, 101–2, 133–4
demanding patients, 50
depression, 51
dialogue, 35–8, 93–8
drop-outs, 52, 68, 135–7

efficacy, 216–7
emotional resilience, 7

empathy, 14, 63 – 64
endings, 57–8, 102
everyday unconscious, 211–2

family dynamics/interventions, chapter
  10 *passim*, chapter 12 *passim*

gay men's groups, chapter 11 *passim*
group analysis, 58
group climates, 37

holding, 99, 217

inventory of drinking situations, 111
i–we–it triangle, 105

leaderless groups, 33–5
leadership, 25

motivational interviewing, chapter 5
  passim, 198–199

object hunger, 14
obstacles, 66
offending, chapter 13 *passim*
oxford movement, 29

PASRO (prison ASRO), 206–7
pre-group preparation, 54, 67 – 68, 86,
  103, 109
professional defences, 216–7, 218,
  222
Project MATCH, 44
proximal development, 92–3
psychodrama, chapter 9 *passim*

relapse precipitants inventory, 112
relapse prevention, chapter 7 *passim*,
    49, 85, 199
relational models, 4, 61
relative groups, 157–159
residential groups, chapter 8 *passim*,
    chapter 6 *passim*
role security, 65

selection, 53–4, 103, 170
self-medication hypothesis, 21
selfobject needs, 13–14
self-regulation, 20
shame, 14, 152–4, 124
short-term dynamic groups, 44–49

slow-open groups, 57
spirituality, 29–30, 33–4, 74, 79, 86
splitting, 155–7
stepped care, 43, 47–48, 216

theme-centred groups, chapter 7 *passim*
therapist roles, 135–137
transitional objects, 14, 121
twelve step groups, chapter 5 *passim*,
    20, 25, 87–8, 185

vulnerability, 106

worker commitment, 70, 212, 215
working/therapeutic alliance, 6, 9–14, 72